DATE DUE

	PRINTED IN U.S.A.

THE LETTERS OF
QUEEN ELIZABETH I

UNIFORM WITH THIS VOLUME

THE LETTERS OF KING HENRY VIII
    edited by M. St. Clare Byrne

THE LETTERS OF KING CHARLES I
    edited by Sir Charles Petrie

THE LETTERS OF KING CHARLES II
    edited by Sir Arthur Bryant

THE LETTERS OF QUEEN ANNE
    edited by Beatrice Curtis Brown

THE LETTERS OF KING GEORGE III
    edited by Bonamy Dobrée

Queen Elizabeth I
By an unknown artist

(National Portrait Gallery)

THE
LETTERS
OF
QUEEN
ELIZABETH I

Edited by

G. B. HARRISON
M.A., Ph.D.

FUNK & WAGNALLS
NEW YORK

First published 1935
This edition © G. B. Harrison 1968
This edition first published 1968

Library of Congress Catalog Card Number : 68-25020
Published by Funk & Wagnalls, A Division of Reader's Digest Books, Inc.,
by arrangement with Cassell & Co. Ltd.
Printed in Great Britain.

CONTENTS

ALTHOUGH a number of the letters of Queen Elizabeth have been reprinted in various anthologies of historical documents, it is at first sight a little surprising that no one has hitherto attempted to compile a complete collection. James Bruce in 1849 edited for the Camden Society a collection (not quite complete) of the letters which passed between the Queen and King James the Sixth of Scotland, Mrs. M. E. Green printed many of the letters written by the Queen before her accession in her *Letters of Royal and Illustrious Ladies*, and some of the more famous have been included in such works as Sir Dudley Digges' *Compleat Ambassador*, Lodge's *Illustrations of British History*, Sir Henry Ellis's *Original Letters Illustrative of English History*, and Agnes Strickland's *Lives of the Queens of England*. A complete collection would, however, require many volumes, and would be a work of many years' labour, for not only are the originals (when they exist) widely scattered, but it is by no means easy to decide what should be included in any collection.

The letters of Queen Elizabeth are mainly of four kinds. The first, smallest and most interesting are those letters written by the Queen herself with her own hand. The most personal are, for the most part, letters of rebuke, condolence or congratulation; but the majority are concerned more with State than personal matters. There are several long sets of these holograph letters, the longest being the letters written to King James the Sixth, the correspondence with the Duke of Anjou, his ministers, and relations during the long and tedious negotiations for the proposed marriage, and a number written to the French Sovereigns, particularly to King Henry the Fourth. There are very few letters to the ministers of her Council at home; which is not surprising, as the members of the Council were Court Officials, in almost daily attendance, so that most State business was discussed and arranged verbally.

The second group are letters written by ministers or secretaries fully instructed by the Queen, who either corrected their drafts herself or else dictated the contents. To these she would often add little postscripts in her own hand at the time of signing.[1]

The third group are the letters signed or passed by the Queen who knew and approved their contents, but was not responsible for the form or phraseology. These are rather State Papers than letters, but they are not less important, for though they do not preserve the Queen's actual words they certainly show her mind and intentions on many matters.

The fourth, largest, and least important group are the documents of administration and routine directed to various officers of State, which, though in form letters from the Queen, in fact were wholly the work of her ministers. They concern every kind of State business from the levying of armies to the appointment of rectors to country livings.

All are 'letters of Queen Elizabeth', and it is not always possible to distinguish between them, especially in the first three categories. Many, even of the first kind, survive only in the copies kept by the minister concerned, where the frequent note 'Copy of Her Majesty's letter' often leaves it doubtful whether the original was written by the Queen or by the minister unless further qualified by the words 'written with her own hand'; and quite a number even of the most famous letters exist only in the copies made by zealous antiquaries of former times. Of the 180 letters now printed, 65 certainly, and another 35 probably, were first written by the Queen herself with her own hand.

The general principle of the present collection is to show Queen Elizabeth as woman and ruler. Between two and three thousand letters of the various kinds were considered. I chose first from the personal letters those which seemed most significant, and from the official letters those which showed her statecraft in the various crises and problems of her reign. In any collection some fifty would always be chosen, but for the rest an editor can rely only on his own instincts and preferences.

Certain general principles were laid down for the guidance of editors of this series of Royal Letters. Accordingly all letters have been modernized in spelling and punctuation. Furthermore, letters in foreign languages have been translated into English.

---

[1] e.g. pp. 32, 115, 125, 291, 294.

For any errors in those translations for which I am responsible, I would plead that the Queen was not an easy correspondent in any language. No one was more expert in writing letters which should convey the widest variety of possible meanings; and when she wrote in French, with a royal disregard for the normal usages of grammar, the translation must at times be speculative. Brief notes have been added at the head of the letters to explain the circumstances of their writing, and a few longer notes on such complex events as the Anjou marriage and Mary, Queen of Scots, have been included; but in a reign so full of incidents and perplexities there was no space for any fuller account.

From occasional comments in the letters of her ministers, and by consideration of the originals, something of the Queen's methods can be deduced. In negotiations with foreign courts, the actual business was normally conducted by her ambassador, either resident, or sent over for a particular purpose. Instructions to ambassadors were drafted by the Secretary, but frequently the Queen would write a personal letter to the Sovereign, commenting in general terms on the matter in hand, and leaving it to the ambassador to declare her mind in detail, according to his private instructions. A number of these letters have been included, as well as the very detailed orders sent to Sir Henry Norris in 1570, giving him explicit directions for the presentation of the Queen's case against Mary, Queen of Scots,[1] at the Court of France, and the instructions sent over to Walsingham in Paris, at the beginning of the negotiations for the French marriage[2] and, particularly, after the massacre of St. Bartholomew's Eve.[3]

So long as Lord Burghley was alive the Queen entrusted most of her public correspondence to him, for the two understood each other well, but it is clear that she gave him detailed instructions in any important matter. A good instance of this is to be found in the letter sent to the Duke of Norfolk,[4] where, as is obvious, the Queen's instruction was for Norfolk to be commanded to come to Court immediately, and if necessary in a litter. Burghley, being placed in considerable difficulty at such a crisis, drafted two letters, the one mild, the other peremptory, and took the

---

[1] p. 68.   [2] pp. 97, 104.   [3] p. 112.   [4] Printed pp. 57-8.

precaution of safeguarding his own interests by sending a private covering letter. It was rare, however, for Burghley to go behind the Queen's back; Walsingham was more frank in his criticisms. Nor did the Queen often write letters which were kept from her Secretary; one instance is to be found in the letter to Sir Henry Sidney.[1] She was, however, usually independent of her ministers and neither sought nor feared their criticism, though occasionally she asked their advice.[2] She was generally content to trust the judgement of her commanders distant from the Court when she was sure of their integrity: but not all, even of the famous Elizabethan commanders, were single hearted in their loyalty, and the Queen usually knew whom to trust, and whom to watch. Those who tried to compromise with her will were sharply reprimanded, as Heneage found in 1586.[3] At times, especially in her later days, she forced her Councillors to write letters which they regretted. By her orders Southampton was put from his place as Master of the Horse to Essex's expedition in Ireland in 1599, and the command was conveyed in a letter from the Council, in which, however, they added a note that they were regretfully obeying a royal fiat. Similarly her last letters to Mountjoy concerning the submission of Tyrone, though drafted by Sir Robert Cecil, included demands which Cecil himself opposed, for he knew that they could not be exacted, and that peace on any terms was essential.[4]

After Burghley's death, in 1598, the Queen seems to have supervised her State letters more closely. As the older statesmen disappeared, she had less opinion of the judgement and capabilities of the younger generation. At all times she scrutinized important drafts and corrected them, but the letters written in the last few years of the reign seem to carry more of her vigorous phrasing that in the earlier years. Moreover with increasing years of experience, and especially after the defeat of the Spaniards in 1588 and 1589, the Queen grew more entirely confident in herself, her own judgement, and the Divine Protection. The letters to Essex in Ireland, especially that of September 14th, 1599,[5] reflect her mind and indignant vocabulary, though, if Sir

[1] See p. 46.   [2] See p. 46.   [3] See p. 175.
[4] pp. 296-300.   [5] p. 270.

xii

INTRODUCTION

Robert Cecil actually wrote it, he must have done so with zest, for he had endured much from Essex.

A few casual sketches of the Queen as a letter writer survive. On 14th August, 1585, Thomas Mills wrote to Wotton in Scotland: 'Her majesty hath written by him [*i.e. Captain Bruce who was being sent as messenger*] to the King, beginning her letter with her own hand in French in most loving and motherly sort. But before she had finished it, your advertisements made her forget her French clean and fall to as plain English as ever she wrote in her life, whereof I doubt not but you shall hear soon enough, and it is thought those letters will work either the greatest good or the greatest evil.'[1]

Several years later Mills by chance left another little picture of the Queen at work. He was now Clerk to the Privy Council and had been accused of some misconduct in the Star Chamber. The Queen decided that the charges were frivolous and signed a letter to various Councillors that the information against Mills should be revoked and made void. He made a copy of this letter, on which he wrote a gleeful memorandum: 'The original letter of this above copy was delivered to me by her Majesty's Self the 29th of January, being Thursday, and who signed it in a chamber of the Gallery at Whitehall, in the evening, and willed me to carry it to Mr. Secretary with these words, that it was now more than time to sign it, because the paper was almost clean worn out. At that time Mr. Secretary Herbert was with her Majesty, who had signed him two bills, but heard not what her Majesty said to me; and two days after, Mr. Secretary gave orders for the direction of it.'[2]

Another instance of the Queen's prowess as a letter writer is given in *Nugæ Antiquæ*[3] in a manuscript entitled 'A precious token of her Highness's great wit and marvellous understanding'. It records the Queen writing one letter, dictating another, and at the same time listening to a tale.

[1] *Hamilton Papers*, ed. by Joseph Bain, 2 vols., 1892, vol. ii, p. 676. The news which so disturbed the Queen was presumably the murder of Lord Russell.
[2] S.P.Dom. 278: 24, dated 1st February, 1601.
[3] Ed. T. Park, 2 vols., 1804, vol. i, p. 115.

The Queen's handwriting in youth was beautiful, but in middle age it degenerated into a scrawl, very difficult to read, especially when she was writing French in a hurry, but a bold, resolute script nevertheless, running straight across the page, very different from the downhill schoolgirl hand of Mary Queen of Scots. The dislike which the Queen often expressed for letter writing was probably genuine, and though her reasons for delay in answering letters (such as sore throat, illness, excessive sorrow, pain in the arm, etc.) may often have been the mere excuses of common humanity pretending to explain or justify delay, she certainly suffered from rheumatism in her right arm in her later days. On the other hand her great signature at the head of State papers and letters is magnificent. In one specimen this royal *ELIZABETH R*, with all its loops and flourishes, measures eight by three and a half inches. As Princess she had ended her letters with a neat and modest little *Elizabeth*.

Though few rulers have on occasion written better letters, she was not a good correspondent, for the famous letter writers are those who record intimate experiences and share secrets and observations; they are seldom men of action. The Queen wrote to command, to exhort, to censure, to persuade, and sometimes to prevaricate : but she had no familiar confidant, man or woman. It was this loneliness which gave her strength but prevented her from opening her heart to anyone. Her successor, King James, who was by nature far weaker, enjoyed writing letters, and could relax after business to comment amusingly to those whom he took for his friends. During the Hampton Court Conference, for instance, when he had spent two days of concentrated disputation with the divines of the Puritan and Anglican parties, he wrote : ' We have kept such a revel with the Puritans here this two days as was never heard the like; where I have peppered them as soundly as ye have done the Papists there. . . . They fled me so from argument to argument, without ever answering me directly, *ut est eorum moris*, as I was forced at last to say unto them, that if any of them had been in a college disputing with their scholars, if any of their disciples had answered them in that sort, they would have fetched him up in a place of reply; and so should the rod have played upon the poor boy's buttocks.'

Nothing of this kind is to be found in the letters of Queen Elizabeth; she leaned on no man's shoulder.

The literary style of her letters was as varied as her character. When she was writing coyly, or for effect, or to hide her thoughts and intentions, she was diffuse and affected, hunting the metaphor tediously, and indulging in sententious conceits and flourishes of wit. For such occasions she had a small stock of quotations and allusions; Prometheus and Epimetheus, Scylla and Charybdis, constantly occur. Most of the earlier letters to the Duke of Anjou are in this strain, and convey, presumably by intent, vague expressions of encouragement but nothing which could be construed as definite or tangible promise. In later years Essex, whilst still in favour, received several of these enigmatical compositions.[1] This affectation of style was developed very early. In a simpler form it is to be found in some of the letters written to her brother, King Edward the Sixth.[2] On the other hand, when she wished, she could be terse and direct in all her moods. The angry letter to Leicester, written on February 10, 1586, and the note to Perrot a few weeks later[3] are admirably clear and to the point, whilst, in another mood, the little letter to Mountjoy, written in August 1602, is a perfect specimen in its own kind.[4] All these letters were of her own writing.

Her sense of humour was not very subtle,[5] but her irony was keen. In her conduct, and in her letters, she showed that she was afraid of no one. Few kings can have received such straight letters as Henry IV of France or King James whom she rated abusively when they angered her, especially by failing to show the same independent spirit as her own. In such letters she revealed one side of her true self. Another side can be seen in those which she wrote to Lord Mountjoy during his Irish campaigns. Though Mountjoy was no longer one of her particular favourites, he alone of her military commanders won her complete confidence as a man who was entirely faithful and competent, and she was not backward in showing her appreciation of such a rarity.

The letters do not reveal her innermost secrets, for she never

[1] e.g. p. 248. [2] See pp. 15, 16. [3] pp. 174, 175.
[4] p. 294. [5] See pp. 125, 159, 207.

surrendered the key of her mystery, but her personal character, her kingly qualities, and her fundamental beliefs are frequently shown. From the very first she was resolute in the face of her enemies, as is shown in the letters which she wrote, at the age of fifteen, in the Seymour affair, and, a few years later, at the time of Wyatt's rebellion.[1] Her knowledge of kingcraft was instinctive but conscious, and is revealed repeatedly in the letters to King James of Scotland, who at times irritated her beyond measure, though she did not make allowance for his difficulties. She had an acute sense of her own responsibilities, and a high standard of what qualities became a king. The loathing for Mary, Queen of Scots, which shows itself in some of her letters, arose partly from her conviction that Mary, by behaving as a fool, was degrading the kingly office.[2] She believed in herself as absolute monarch, and God's Vicegerent on earth,[3] and for this reason would not tolerate any, such as Presbyterians or Jesuits,[4] who held a contrary doctrine. In her letters, as in her life, she was always the Queen of England.

Her character and personality will still fascinate or repel; but those who would, before passing judgement, first understand her difficulties, will find the best evidence in her letters.

————

I wish to thank, with much gratitude, those who have helped in this collection : Mr. J. R. E. Howard, who checked the translations from the French; Miss Molly Chamberlain for transcribing and checking some of the letters; Miss Margaret Dowling for providing (what seemed impossible) a transcript of the original draft of the letter to Catherine de Medici [translated on pp. 162-163]; the officials of the Public Record Office and British Museum; and above all Mr. D. C. Collins, who with great patience partnered me in the work of selection, transcription and collation.

G. B. HARRISON.

28th July, 1935.

[1] See pp. 9-14, 19-21.　　[2] e.g. p. 50.　　[3] p. 256.　　[4] See pp. 203, 182.

CHAPTER I
1533-1558

Elizabeth, daughter of King Henry the Eighth and Queen Anne Boleyn, was born on 7th September, 1533. Her mother was executed in 1536, when the King married Jane Seymour, who died in 1538 in giving birth to a son, afterwards King Edward the Sixth. In January 1540 the King married Anne of Cleves, whom he divorced in the following July. His next wife was Catherine Howard, who was beheaded in 1542. The following year he married Catherine Parr. Elizabeth now passed under the care of her fourth stepmother. When King Henry died in January 1547, Elizabeth was in her fourteenth year, and precociously clever and intelligent.

Henry was succeeded by Edward the Sixth, a boy of nine, and the government was entrusted to Edward Seymour as Lord Protector. Queen Catherine Parr did not long remain a widow; within three months she married Thomas Seymour, Lord Admiral. Princess Elizabeth continued to live with her stepmother, but before long scandalmongers were suggesting that she was over familiar with the Lord Admiral, and in 1548 she left her stepmother and was established in her own household at Cheshunt, with Mistress Kate Ashley, her governess. In September Queen Catherine died, and the Lord Admiral began, with the connivance of Mistress Ashley, to make advances to marry Princess Elizabeth as part of his intrigue to supplant his brother the Protector. He was arrested and imprisoned in the Tower.

Elizabeth was thus in considerable danger, and attempts were made to entrap her into admissions, but with great skill she maintained her innocence. The Lord Admiral was executed on 20th March. For the remaining four years of the reign of Edward the Sixth, she was allowed to continue her education unmolested, and achieved a reputation as one of the most learned and accomplished Princesses in Europe.

Edward the Sixth died in 1553 at the age of fifteen. He was succeeded by his elder sister, Mary, daughter of King Henry's first wife, Catherine of Aragon. Princess Elizabeth thus became the immediate heir to the throne at the age of twenty. She was now in constant danger, for she had been brought up a Protestant, and Queen Mary was fanatically Catholic. Elizabeth quickly declared herself convinced of the truth of Catholicism, but the genuineness of her conversion was

3

doubted. Queen Mary's zeal in restoring Catholicism increased Elizabeth's danger, for she became (as Mary, Queen of Scots, later) the natural focus of all malcontents. Her greatest danger was when, early in 1554, Sir Thomas Wyatt headed a rebellion in Kent. Wyatt had written to Elizabeth, and his letters were taken. Elizabeth was summoned to London, and sent to the Tower. Great efforts were made to find enough evidence for a charge of high treason, but nothing could be discovered to satisfy even a Tudor Court of Law; and she was too popular for Queen Mary to risk the process of a Bill of Attainder. After two months Elizabeth was released from the Tower and sent to live at Woodstock.

In July 1554 Queen Mary married Philip the Second, King of Spain, and Elizabeth's fortunes turned for the better. After herself, the next heir to the throne was Mary of Scotland, who was betrothed to the Dauphin of France; and it would not suit Spanish policy for the thrones of France, England and Scotland to be united in such an alliance. Elizabeth was therefore brought to Court, and her restraints were gradually removed. Queen Mary meanwhile had declared that she was pregnant, and the birth of an heir was expected in April; but months passed and nothing happened.

In October 1554 Elizabeth was sent to Hatfield, and once more her dangers increased. Queen Mary's Spanish marriage and proselytizing zeal had been so bitterly opposed that there was great risk that Elizabeth might again be implicated in a premature rebellion. She survived this danger, and the equally great risk of being forced into a marriage with the Duke of Saxony, until on 17th November, 1558, Queen Mary died, and Princess Elizabeth was joyfully acclaimed as her successor.

1. To Queen Catherine (Parr)

This is apparently the earliest surviving letter; it was written by Elizabeth in her eleventh year, in Italian. It is little more than a school exercise. King Henry had gone over to France and on 9th July Queen Catherine had been appointed General Regent of the Realm.

July 31, 1544.

Inimical fortune, envious of all good and ever revolving human affairs, has deprived me for a whole year of your most illustrious presence, and, not thus content, has yet again robbed me of the same good; which thing would be intolerable to me, did I not hope to enjoy it very soon. And in this my exile, I well know that the clemency of your Highness has had as much care and solicitude for my health as the King's Majesty himself. By which thing I am not only bound to serve you, but also to revere you with filial love, since I understand that your most Illustrious Highness has not forgotten me every time you have written to the King's Majesty, which, indeed, it was my duty to have requested from you. For heretofore I have not dared to write to him. Wherefore I now humbly pray your most Excellent Highness, that, when you write to his Majesty, you will condescend to recommend me to him, praying ever for his sweet benediction, and similarly entreating our Lord God to send him best success, and the obtaining of victory over his enemies, so that your Highness and I may, as soon as possible, rejoice together with him on his happy return. No less pray I God, that He would preserve your most Illustrious Highness; to Whose Grace, humbly kissing your hands, I offer and recommend myself.

From St. James's this 31st of July.

Your most obedient daughter, and most faithful servant,

ELIZABETH.

11. To Queen Catherine (Parr)

Sent with Elizabeth's translation of The Mirror of the Sinful Soul.

December 31, 1544.

To Our most Noble and Virtuous Queen Catherine, Elizabeth, her humble daughter, wisheth perpetual felicity and everlasting joy.

Not only knowing the affectuous will and fervent zeal, the which your Highness hath towards all godly learning, as also my duty towards you (most Gracious and Sovereign Princess), but knowing also, that pusillanimity and idleness are most repugnant unto a reasonable creature, and that (as the philosopher sayeth) even as an instrument of iron or of other metal waxeth soon rusty, unless it be continually occupied; even so shall the wit of a man or a woman wax dull and unapt to do or understand any thing perfectly, unless it be always occupied upon some manner of study. Which things considered, hath moved so small a portion as God hath lent me, to prove what I could do. And, therefore, have I (as for essay or beginning, following the right notable saying of the proverb aforesaid) translated this little book out of French rhyme into English prose, joining the sentences together as well as the capacity of my simple wit and small learning could extend themselves. The which book is entitled or named, *The Mirror, or Glass, of the Sinful Soul,* wherein is contained, how she (beholding and contemplating what she is) doth perceive how, of herself and her own strength, she can do nothing that good is, or prevaileth for her salvation, unless it be through the grace of God, whose mother, daughter, sister, and wife, by the Scriptures, she proveth herself to be. Trusting also that, through His incomprehensible love, grace, and mercy, she (being called from sin to repentance) doth faithfully hope to be saved. And although I know that, as for my part which I have wrought in it (as well spiritual as manual), there is nothing done as it should be, nor else worthy to come in your Grace's hands, but rather all unperfect and uncorrect; yet do I trust also that, howbeit it is like a work which is but new begun and shapen, that the file of your excellent wit and godly learning, in the reading of it (if so it vouchsafe your Highness to do), shall rub out, polish, and mend (or else cause to mend), the words (or rather the order of my writing), the which I know, in many places, to be rude, and nothing done as it should be. But I hope that, after to have been in your Grace's hands, there shall be nothing in it worthy of reprehension, and that in the meanwhile no other (but your Highness only) shall read it or see it, lest my faults be known of many. Then shall they be better excused (as my confidence is in your Grace's accustomed benevolence), than if I should bestow a whole year in writing or inventing ways for to excuse them. Praying God Almighty, the Maker and Creator of all things, to grant unto your Highness the same New Year's day, a lucky and a prosperous year, with prosperous issue, and continuance of many years in good health and continual joy, and all to His honour, praise, and glory.

From Ashridge, the last day of the year of our Lord God, 1544.

III. To the Dowager Queen Catherine (Parr)

Shortly after the death of Henry the Eighth, Queen Catherine married Thomas Seymour, the Lord Admiral, to whom she had been betrothed before the King claimed her. Elizabeth went to live in their household, but the hearty and boisterous familiarities of the Lord Admiral led to scandalous rumours, and Catherine, to prevent further trouble, caused Elizabeth to be sent away from her household. Shortly after Whitsun 1548 Elizabeth, with her governess, Mistress Ashfield, moved to Cheshunt, and later to Hatfield and Ashridge. On leaving her stepmother, Elizabeth wrote a dutiful letter of thanks.

c. June 1548.

Although I could not be plentiful in giving thanks for the manifold kindnesses received at your Highness's hand at my departure, yet I am something to be borne withal, for truly I was replete with sorrow to depart from your Highness, especially seeing you undoubtful of health; and albeit I answered little, I weighed it more deeper when you said you would warn me of all evilnesses that you should hear of me; for if your Grace had not a good opinion of me, you would not have offered friendship to me that way at all, meaning the contrary. But what may I more say, than thank God for providing such friends for me, desiring God to enrich me with their long life, and me grace to be in heart no less thankful to receive it, than I am now made glad in writing to show it. And although I have plenty of matter here, I will stay, for I know you are not quick to read.

From Cheshunt, this present Saturday.

Your Highness's humble daughter,

Elizabeth.

IV. To Thomas Seymour, Lord Admiral

Written soon after Princess Elizabeth left the Lord Admiral's household.

c. July 1548.

My Lord,

You needed not to send an excuse to me, for I could not mistrust the not fulfilling your promise to proceed from want of good will, but only that opportunity served not. Wherefore I shall desire you to think that a greater matter than this could not make me impute any unkindness in you, for I am a friend not won with trifles, nor lost with the like. Thus I commit you and your affairs into God's hand, Who keep you from all evil. I pray you to make my humble commendations to the Queen's Highness.

Your assured friend to my little power,

Elizabeth.

V. To the Dowager Queen Catherine (Parr)

This was written after Princess Elizabeth had been established in her own household, and as the time of Queen Catherine's confinement drew near. The Queen died a few weeks later.

July 31, 1548.

Although your Highness's letters be most joyful to me in absence, yet, considering what pain it is for you to write, your Grace being so sickly, your commendations were enough in my Lord's letter. I much rejoice at your health, with the well liking of the country, with my humble thanks that your Grace wished me with you till I were weary of that country. Your Highness were like to be cumbered, if I should not depart till I were weary of being with you; although it were the worst soil in the world, your presence would make it pleasant. I cannot reprove my Lord for not doing your commendations in his letter, for he did it; and although he had not, yet I will not complain on him; for he shall be diligent to give me knowledge from time to time how his busy child doth; and if I were at his birth, no doubt I would see him beaten, for the trouble he hath put you to. Master Denny and my lady, with humble thanks, prayeth most entirely for your

8

Grace, praying the Almighty God to send you a most lucky deliverance, and my mistress wisheth no less, giving your Highness most humble thanks for her commendations.

Written with very little leisure this last day of July.

Your humble daughter,

ELIZABETH.

VI. To EDWARD SEYMOUR, LORD PROTECTOR

On the death of Queen Catherine Parr, the Lord Admiral began to make advances to Elizabeth. His movements and familiarities were reported at Court, and the Lord Privy Seal, Russell, warned him of the consequences of a marriage with the King's sister. But Thomas Seymour was rash and ambitious, and was intriguing to overthrow the regency and his brother, the Protector. On 16th January, 1549, he was arrested on a charge of high treason and sent to the Tower. His servants and those of Elizabeth were also arrested and closely questioned. Sir Thomas Tyrwhitt was sent to Hatfield to take charge of the household, actually as her jailer, with instructions to break down her resistance and extract the truth. She successfully resisted Tyrwhitt's questions, and wrote a letter to the Lord Protector in which she corroborated the depositions of Mistress Ashley and her cofferer, Thomas Ashley, so closely that it was evident (as Tyrwhitt complained) that they were 'all in a tale'.

January 28, 1549.

MY LORD,

Your great gentleness and goodwill towards me, as well in this thing as in other things, I do understand, for the which, even as I ought, so I do give you most humble thanks. And whereas your Lordship willeth and counselleth me, as an earnest friend, to declare what I know in this matter, and also to write what I have declared to Master Tyrwhitt, I shall most willingly do it. I declared unto him first, that, after that the Cofferer had declared unto me, what my Lord Admiral answered for Allen's[1] matter, and for Durham House[2] (that it was appointed

---

[1] Allen, one of Elizabeth's chaplains.
[2] Durham House, formerly her mother's (Anne Boleyn) before her marriage to Henry VIII and to which Elizabeth considered she had a right as a town house.

to be a Mint), he told me that my Lord Admiral did offer me his house for my time being with the King's Majesty; and further said, and asked me, whether if the Council did consent that I should have my Lord Admiral, whether I would consent to it or no : I answered that I would not tell him what my mind was. And I further inquired of him, what he meant to ask me that question, or who bade him say so. He answered me and said, nobody bade him say so, but that he perceived (as he thought) by my Lord Admiral's inquiring whether my patent were sealed or no, and debating what he spent in his house, and inquiring what was spent in my house, that he was given that way than otherwise. And as concerning Kate Ashley, she never advised me unto it, but said always (when any talked of my marriage) that she would never have me marry, neither in England nor out of England, without the consent of the King's Majesty, your Grace's, and the Council's. And after the Queen was departed,[1] when I asked of her what news she heard from London, she answered merrily, ' They say there that your Grace shall have my Lord Admiral, and that he will come shortly to woo you.' And moreover I said unto him, that the Cofferer sent a letter hither, that my Lord said, that he would come this way as he went down to the country. Then I bade her write as she thought best, and bade her show it me when she had done; so she write that she thought it not best, for fear of suspicion, and so it went forth. And my Lord Admiral, after he had heard that, asked of the Cofferer, why he might not come as well to me as to my sister : And then I desired Kate Ashley to write again (lest my Lord might think that she knew more in it than he) that she knew nothing in it, but suspicion. And also I told Master Tyrwhitt, that to the effect of the matter, I never consented unto any such thing, without the Council's consent thereunto. And as for Kate Ashley or the Cofferer, they never told me that they would practise it. These be the things which I both declared to Master Tyrwhitt, and also whereof my conscience beareth me witness, which I would not for all earthly things offend in anything; for I know I have a soul to save, as well as other folks have, wherefore I will above all

---

[1] i.e. dead. Mistress Ashley wrote a letter of condolence to the Lord Admiral, apparently with Elizabeth's sanction.

things have respect unto the same. If there be any more things which I can remember, I will either write it myself or cause Master Tyrwhitt to write it. Master Tyrwhitt and others have told me that there goeth rumour abroad, which be greatly both against my honour and honesty (which above all other things I esteem) which be these; that I am in the Tower; and with child by my Lord Admiral. My Lord, these are shameful slanders, for the which, besides the great desire I have to see the King's Majesty, I shall most heartily desire your Lordship that I may come to the Court after your first determination; that I may show myself there as I am. Written in haste from Hatfield this 28th January.

Your assured friend to my little power,
ELIZABETH.

VII. To EDWARD SEYMOUR, LORD PROTECTOR

The unsuccessful attempts to extract a confession, or at least sufficient evidence to incriminate Kate Ashley and her husband, continued. On the 7th February Tyrwhitt sent such few particulars as he had discovered, but with the misgiving that ' they all sing one song, and so I think they would not, unless they had set the note before'. This and the letter following are early examples of the art of appearing to say much and actually saying nothing which Elizabeth practised so skilfully in different situations. She was aged fifteen and a half at the time.

February 6, 1549.

MY LORD,

I have received your gentle letter and also your message by Master Tyrwhitt, for the which two things especially (although for many other things) I cannot give your Lordship sufficient thanks, and whereas your Grace doth will me to credit Master Tyrwhitt, I have done so, and will do so as long as he willeth me (as he doth not) to nothing but to that which is for mine honour and honesty. And even as I said to him and did write to your Lordship, so I do write now again, that when there doth any more things happen in my mind which I have forgotten, I assure your Grace I will declare them most willingly, for I would not (as I trust you have not) so evil an opinion of me that I would conceal anything that I knew; for it were to no purpose, and surely forgetfulness may well cause me to hide things, but undoubtedly else I will declare all that I know.   From Hatfield the 6th of February.

Your assured friend to my little power,

ELIZABETH.

VIII. To Edward Seymour, Lord Protector

February 21, 1549.

MY LORD,

Having received your Lordship's letters, I perceive in them your goodwill towards me, because you declare to me plainly your mind in this thing; and again, for that you would not wish that I should do anything that should not seem good unto the Council, for the which thing I give you most hearty thanks.   And whereas, I do understand that you do take in evil part the letters that I did write unto your Lordship,[1] I am very sorry that you should take them so, for my mind was to declare unto you plainly, as I thought, in that thing, which I did also the more willingly because (as I write to you) you desired me to be plain with you in all things.   And as concerning that point that you write that I seem to stand in mine own wit in being so well assured of mine own self, I did assure me of myself no more than I trust the truth shall try; and to say that which I knew of myself I did not think should have displeased the Council or your Grace.   And surely, the cause why that I was sorry that there should be any such about me, was because that I thought the people will say that I deserved through my lewd demeanour to have such a one, and not that I mislike anything that your Lordship or the Council shall think good, for I know that you and the Council are charged with me; or that I take upon me to rule myself, for I know they are most deceived that trusteth most in themselves; wherefore, I trust you shall never find that fault in me, to the which thing I do not see that your Grace has made any direct answer at this time, and seeing they make so evil reports already, shall be but an increasing of their evil tongues.   Howbeit, you did write that if I would bring forth any that had reported it, you and the Council would see it redressed, which thing, though I can easily

---

[1] Cf. her letters of 28th January and 6th February.

12

do it, I would be loath to do it for because it is mine own cause; and, again, that should be but abridging of an evil name of me that am glad to punish them, and so get the evil will of the people which thing I would be loath to have. But if it might so seem good unto your Lordship and the rest of the Council to send forth a proclamation into the counties, that they refrain their tongues, declaring how the tales be but lies, it should make both the people think that you and the Council have great regard that no such rumours should be spread of any of the King's Majesty's sisters, as I am, though unworthy, and also I should think myself to receive such friendship at your hands as you have promised me, although your Lordship hath showed me great already. Howbeit, I am ashamed to ask it any more, because I see you are not so well minded thereunto. And as concerning that you say that I give folks occasion to think in refusing the good to uphold the evil, I am not of so simple understanding, nor I would that your Grace should have so evil an opinion of me that I have so little respect to mine own honesty that I would maintain it if I had sufficient promise of the same; and so your Grace shall prove me when it comes to the point. And thus I bid you farewell, desiring God always to assist you in all your affairs. Written in haste. From Hatfield this 21 of February.

Your assured friend to my little power,

ELIZABETH.

IX. TO EDWARD SEYMOUR, LORD PROTECTOR

Thomas Seymour, Lord Admiral, was attainted on 4th March, and beheaded on the 20th. In spite of the difficulty of her own position, Elizabeth wrote to the Lord Protector on behalf of Mistress Ashley and her husband.

March 7, 1549.

MY LORD,

I have a request to make unto your Grace which fear has made me omit till this time for two causes; the one because I saw my request for the rumours which were spread abroad of me took so little place, which thing, when I considered, I thought I should little profit in any other suit; howbeit, now I understand that there is a proclamation for them (for the which I give your

Grace and the rest of the Council most humble thanks), I am the bolder to speak for another thing; and the other was, because peradventure your Lordship and the rest of the Council will think that I favour her evil doing for whom I shall speak for, which is Katherine Ashley, that it would please your Grace and the rest of the Council to be good unto her. Which thing I do, not to favour her in any evil (for that I would be sorry to do), but for these considerations that follow, the which hope doth teach me in saying, that I ought not to doubt but that your Grace and the rest of the Council will think that I do it for three other considerations. First, because that she hath been with me a long time and many years, and hath taken great labour and pain in bringing me up in learning and honesty; and therefore I ought of very duty speak for her, for Saint Gregory sayeth, ' that we are more bound to them that bringeth us up well than to our parents, for our parents do that which is natural for them that is bringeth us into the world, but our bringers-up are a cause to make us live well in it.' The second is, because I think that whatsoever she hath done in my Lord Admiral's matter, as concerning the marrying of me, she did it because, knowing him to be one of the Council, she thought he would not go about any such thing without he had the Council's consent thereunto; for I have heard her many times say that she would never have me marry in any place without your Grace's and the Council's consent. The third cause is, because that it shall and doth make men think that I am not clear of the deed myself, but that it is pardoned to me because of my youth, because that she I loved so well is in such a place. Thus hope, prevailing more with me than fear, hath won the battle, and I have at this time gone forth with it, which I pray God be taken no otherwise than it is meant. Written in haste. From Hatfield, this 7th day of March. Also, if I may be so bold, not offending, I beseech your Grace and the rest of the Council to be good to Master Ashley, her husband, which, because he is my kinsman, I would be glad he should do well.

Your assured friend to my little power,

ELIZABETH.

x. To King Edward the Sixth

Sent with a present of her portrait.

May 15 [?].

Like as the rich man that daily gathereth riches to riches, and to one bag of money layeth a great sort till it come to infinite, so methinks your Majesty, not being sufficed with many benefits and gentleness showed to me afore this time, doth now increase them in asking and desiring where you may bid and command, requiring a thing not worthy the desiring for itself, but made worthy for your Highness's request. My picture, I mean, in which if the inward good mind toward your Grace might as well be declared as the outward face and countenance shall be seen, I would not have tarried the commandment but prevent it,[1] nor have been the last to grant but the first to offer it. For the face, I grant, I might well blush to offer, but the mind I shall never be ashamed to present. For though from the grace of the picture the colours may fade by time, may give by weather, may be spotted by chance; yet the other nor time with her swift wings shall overtake, nor the misty clouds with their lowerings may darken, nor chance with her slippery foot may overthrow. Of this although yet the proof could not be great because the occasion hath been but small, notwithstanding as a dog hath a day, so may I perchance have time to declare it in deeds where now I do write them in words. And further I shall most humbly beseech your Majesty that when you shall look on my picture, you will vouchsafe to think that as you have but the outward shadow of the body before you, so my inward mind wisheth that the body itself were oftener in your presence; howbeit because both my so being I think could do your Majesty little pleasure, though myself great good; and again because I see as yet not the time agreeing thereunto, I shall learn to follow this saying of Horace, ' *Feras non culpes quod vitari non potest.*' And thus I will (troubling your Majesty I fear) end with my most humble thanks. Beseeching God long to preserve you to His Honour, to your comfort, to the Realm's profit, and to my joy. From Hatfield this 15 day of May.

Your Majesty's most humbly sister and servant,

ELIZABETH.

[1] i.e. forestall.

15

XI. To King Edward the Sixth

On the fall of Edward Seymour, Lord Protector, power passed to John Dudley, Duke of Northumberland, whose policy was to prevent any intercourse between the King and his sister. From the following letter it is evident that Elizabeth made an attempt to visit him in one of his periods of sickness, but was intercepted on her journey and forced to return.

Undated.

Like as a shipman in stormy weather plucks down the sails tarrying for better wind, so did I, most noble King, in my unfortunate chance a' Thursday pluck down the high sails of my joy and comfort and do trust one day that as troublesome waves have repulsed me backward, so a gentle wind will bring me forward to my haven. Two chief occasions moved me much and grieved me greatly, the one for that I doubted your Majesty's health, the other because for all my long tarrying I went without that I came for. Of the first I am relieved in a part, both that I understood of your health, and also that your Majesty's lodging is not far from my Lord Marquess's[1] chamber. Of my other grief I am not eased, but the best is that whatsoever other folks will suspect, I intend not to fear your Grace's good will, which as I know that I never deserved to faint, so I trust will stick by me. For if your Grace's advice that I should return (whose will is a commandment) had not been, I would not have made the half of my way, the end of my journey. And thus, as one desirous to hear of your Majesty's health, though unfortunate to see it, I shall pray God for ever to preserve you. From Hatfield this present Saturday.

Your Majesty's humble sister to commandment,

ELIZABETH.

XII. To Princess Mary

October 27 [?].

Good Sister, as to hear of your sickness is unpleasant to me, so is it nothing fearful; for that I understand it is your old guest

[1] The Marquess of Northampton, brother to the late Queen Catherine Parr.

that is wont oft to visit you, whose coming though it be oft, yet is it never welcome, but notwithstanding it is comfortable for that *iacula præuisa minus feriunt.* And as I do understand your need of Jane Russel's service, so am I sorry that it is by my man's occasion letted, which if I had known afore, I would have caused his will give place to need of her service. For as it is her duty to obey his commandment, so is it his part to attend your pleasure; and, as I confess, it were meeter for him to go to her, since she attends upon you, so indeed he required the same, but for that divers of his fellows had business abroad that made his tarrying at home.

Good Sister, though I have good cause to thank you for your oft sending to me, yet I have more occasion to render you my hearty thanks for your gentle writing, which how painful it is to you, I may well guess by myself; and you may well see by my writing so oft, how pleasant it is to me. And thus I end to trouble you, desiring God to send you as well to do, as you can think and wish, or I desire or pray. From Ashridge, scribbled this 27th of October.

Your loving sister,
ELIZABETH.

XIII. TO THE LORDS OF THE COUNCIL

Elizabeth was always tenacious of what she considered her rights, and in 1553 was in dispute with the Lord Privy Seal, the Earl of Bedford, over certain pasturage at Woburn in Buckinghamshire. Upon this matter she wrote to the Privy Council.

May 31, 1553.

If both apparent points touching mine honour and my necessity also constrained me not, good my Lords, I should soon have served all your expectations touching Woburn, and long sithence have appeased my Lord Bedford's mind therein. But since your wisdoms, informed of that other side, do affirm that it were mine honour and a point of common justice not to intromit[1] therewith, the matter being litigious; so, trusting in your good wills towards me, do for answer resolve with you in this manner, as knowing myself a long time to have great need of pastures for my pro-

---

[1] Meddle with, deal with.

visions, the lack whereof hath been to my great charges. At Shrovetide last, and long time before my Lord Privy Seal to my knowledge did intromit in such sort therewith, I contracted indeed with one Smith for his interest therein, being then (parcel thereof for a few years yet to come only excepted) clearly discharged of all former contracts and other things in his own hands and right. And he, upon such considerations of recompense as I took with him, to discharge the thing clearly at and until Our Lady day last, and myself to bear the charges thenceforward, by force whereof I entered, and am thereof as ye may now well understand, by just order of the laws justly possessed, from the which to be now rejected were to my great dishonour since all the country knoweth it. And for your Lordships' further satisfaction in this matter, since I heard of the controversy between my Lord and Smith, it is not unknown that I sent unto him my whole state and condition herein, with far larger and more benevolent offers than I received answer, or being evil handled can be contented to offer again : and, therefore, this I say, that if it be my right to hold it, I trust that ye will not mislike that I keep it, for I will not, God willing, forego it until I may be better provided. And if my Lord have better right thereunto than I have, then I will give it over with all my heart unto him without contention, and as I utterly deny to Smith any supportation at my hands in any of his misdemeanours against my Lord, and do and shall leave him to suffer that he hath most deserved at my Lord's hands; so do I hope quietly to enjoy that that I thus justly have come by with my Lord's good will, both because I have been such one towards my Lord for the good service he did my father, as if ability served I would not have failed to have given of my own a far better thing. And again because it is not unknown to my Lord, nor to any of you all, but that it is most requisite for me to seek some pastures for myself which had never none out of lease appointed me by others. And thus I commit you all to God, desiring you to make my humble commendations to the King's Majesty, for whose health I pray daily, and daily and evermore shall so do during my life. At Hatfield the last day of May 1553.

Your very loving friend,

ELIZABETH.

XIV. TO LADY CATHERINE KNOLLYS

Lady Catherine Knollys was the daughter of William Carey and Mary Boleyn (elder sister to Anne Boleyn, Elizabeth's mother) and so first cousin to Elizabeth. Sir Francis was a Protestant, and on the accession of Queen Mary, he and his wife fled overseas: this was the occasion of the letter.

1553

Relieve your sorrow for your far journey with joy of your short return, and think this pilgrimage rather a proof of your friends, than a leaving of your country. The length of time, and distance of place, separates not the love of friends, nor deprives not the show of good will. An old saying, when bale is lowest boot is nearest; when your need shall be most you shall find my friendship greatest. Let others promise, and I will do, in words not more, in deeds as much. My power but small, my love as great as them whose gifts may tell their friendship's tale, let will supply all other want, and oft sending take the lieu of often sights. Your messengers shall not return empty, nor yet your desires unaccomplished. Lethe's flood hath here no course, good memory hath greatest stream. And, to conclude, a word that hardly I can say, I am driven by need to write, farewell, it is which in the sense one way I wish, the other way I grieve.

Your loving cousin and ready friend,
COR ROTTO.

XV. TO QUEEN MARY

Written when the order came that she was to be sent to the Tower, on suspicion that she was implicated by Wyatt's rebellion. Wyatt's correspondence with Elizabeth was seized, and amongst the evidence produced was an alleged copy of a letter written by Elizabeth to Henri II; this was apparently a forgery.

March 16, 1554.

If any ever did try this old saying, 'that a king's word was more than another man's oath,'[1] I most humbly beseech your Majesty to verify it to me, and to remember your last promise

---

[1] Said by King John of France when he returned to his captivity in England.

and my last demand, that I be not condemned without answer and due proof, which it seems that I now am; for without cause proved, I am by your Council from you commanded to go to the Tower, a place more wanted for a false traitor than a true subject, which though I know I desire it not, yet in the face of all this realm it appears proved.   I pray to God I may die the shamefullest death that any ever died, if I may mean any such thing; and to this present hour I protest before God (Who shall judge my truth, whatsoever malice shall devise), that I never practised, counselled, nor consented to anything that might be prejudicial to your person anyway, or dangerous to the state by any means. And therefore I humbly beseech your Majesty to let me answer afore yourself, and not suffer me to trust to your Councillors, yea, and that afore I go to the Tower, if it be possible; if not, before I be further condemned.   Howbeit, I trust assuredly your Highness will give me leave to do it afore I go, that thus shamefully I may not be cried out on, as I now shall be; yea, and that without cause.   Let conscience move your Highness to pardon this my boldness, which innocency procures me to do, together with hope of your natural kindness, which I trust will not see me cast away without desert, which what it is I would desire no more of God but that you truly knew, but which thing I think and believe you shall never by report know, unless by yourself you hear.   I have heard of many in my time cast away for want of coming to the presence of their Prince; and in late days I heard my Lord of Somerset say that if his brother had been suffered to speak with him he had never suffered; but persuasions were made to him so great that he was brought in belief that he could not live safely if the Admiral lived, and that made him give consent to his death.   Though these persons are not to be compared to your Majesty, yet I pray God the like evil persuasions persuade not one sister against the other, and all for that they have heard false report, and the truth not known.   Therefore, once again, kneeling with humbleness of heart, because I am not suffered to bow the knees of my body, I humbly crave to speak with your Highness, which I would not be so bold as to desire if I knew not myself most clear, as I know myself most true.   And as for the traitor Wyatt, he might peradventure write me a letter, but on my faith I never received any from him. And as for the copy of the letter sent to the French King, I pray God confound me eternally if ever I sent him word, message, token, or letter, by any means, and to this truth I will stand in till my death.

Your Highness's most faithful subject, that hath been from the beginning, and will be to my end,

ELIZABETH.

I humbly crave but only one word of answer from yourself.

XVI. TO THE MARQUIS OF WINCHESTER

Although released from the Tower Elizabeth still considered herself in danger and wrote to the Marquis of Winchester for assistance.

October 29, 1554.

With my hearty commendations I do most heartily desire you to further the desires of my last letters, that thereby the health of my mind and sickness may be the rather restored; and as you were constrained to come the first unto me in the entry of my troubles,[1] so would I wish yourself to be now the last that should freely end the same. And for this, my Lord, I will most heartily thank you. And as you would I should assure myself of your Lordship's good will and friendship, so do I evermore desire you, that of myself and my own things and doings, mine own words may stand in most credit with you and all my Lords. For in the earth, my Lord, none of my state hath been, and yet is more misused with them of mine own family than myself; as knoweth God, Who judgeth all, and Whom I pray to keep you.

Ashridge, this 29th day of October.

Your assured friend to my little power,

ELIZABETH.

XVII. TO QUEEN MARY

In June, 1556, an impostor named Cleobury landed in Sussex and passed himself off as Edward Courtenay, Earl of Devonshire. In Yaxley Church he proclaimed Elizabeth Queen and himself

---

[1] Winchester and the Earl of Sussex delivered to Elizabeth the first mandate for her committal to the Tower.

King as her husband. An account of the affair was sent to Princess Elizabeth by Queen Mary, to which this dutiful letter was the answer.

August 2, 1556.

When I revolve in mind (most noble Queen) the old love of pagans to their princes, and the reverent fear of the Romans to their senate, I cannot but muse for my part, and blush for theirs, to see the rebellious hearts and devilish intents of Christians in name, but Jews in deed, towards their anointed King, which methinks if they had feared ʼGod (though they could not have loved the state), they should, for the dread of their own plague, have refrained that wickedness, which their bounden duty to your Majesty had not restrained. But when I call to remembrance that the devil, *tanquam leo rugiens circumvenit, quaerens quem devorare potest*, I do the less marvel that he have gotten such novices into his professed house, as vessels (without God's grace) more apt to serve his palace than meet to inhabit English land. I am the bolder to call them his imps, for that Saint Paul saith, *Seditiosi filii sunt diaboli*; and since I have so good a buckler, I fear less to enter into their judgement. Of this I assure your Majesty, it had been my part, above the rest, to bewail such things, though my name hath not been in them; yet it vexeth me too much that the devil oweth me such a hate as to put me in any part of his mischievous instigations, whom, as I profess him my foe, that is all Christians' enemy, so wish I he had some other way invented to spite me. But since it hath pleased God thus to bewray their malice, afore they finish their purpose, I most humbly thank Him, both that He has ever thus preserved your Majesty through His aid, much like a lamb from the horns of this Basan's bull, and also stirred up the hearts of your loving subjects to resist them, and deliver you to his honour and their shame. The intelligence of which, proceeding from your Majesty, deserves more humble thanks than with my pen I can render which as infinite I will leave to number. And among earthly things I chiefly wish this one, that there were as good surgeons for making anatomies of hearts that might show my thoughts to your Majesty, as there are expert physicians of the bodies, able to express the inward griefs of their maladies to their patients. For them I doubt not, but know well, that whatever other should subject by malice, yet your Majesty should be sure by knowledge, that the more such misty clouds offuscate the clear light of my truth, the more my tried thoughts should glisten to the dimming of their hidden malice. But since wishes are vain and desires oft fail, I must crave that my deeds may supply that my thoughts cannot declare, and they be not misdeemed, these as the facts have been so well tried. And like as I have been your faithful subject from the beginning of your reign, so shall no wicked persons cause me to change to the end of my life. And thus I commit your Majesty to God's tuition, whom I beseech long time to preserve, ending with the new remembrance of my old suit, more for that it should not be forgotten, than for that I think it not remembered. From Hatfield, this present Sunday, the 2nd of August.

Your Majesty's obedient subject and humble sister,

ELIZABETH.

CHAPTER II
1558-1570

Elizabeth was twenty-five when she became Queen. In the first months of her reign no events of great importance occurred. Several husbands were offered her, but she rejected them. At home the most pressing problem was the settlement of the Church. As it happened, four bishoprics were vacant at Mary's death, five other bishops died within a year. With one exception, the Marian Bishops refused to accept the new compromise in religion and were deprived of their sees. Their protests called forth the vigorous letter printed on p. 29. A year later the affairs of Mary, Queen of Scots, began to trouble Queen Elizabeth.

Mary, Queen of Scots, was the only daughter of James the Fifth of Scotland and Mary of Guise. She was born in 1542, and on the death of her father in the same year she became nominal Queen. At the age of six she had been sent to France to be educated at the French Court, where in 1558 she married Francis, the Dauphin of France. On the death of Queen Mary of England, she and her husband claimed the throne of England by right of her direct descent from Margaret, daughter of Henry the Seventh. Francis became King of France in 1559, but died in December 1560. He was succeeded by his younger brother, Charles the Ninth, but, as he was still a minor, Catherine de Medici, the Queen Mother, was appointed Regent. In the following August, Mary returned to Scotland as Queen. She had been brought up as a strict Catholic, and from the first there was trouble in Scotland, where the more violent forms of Protestantism were firmly established.

In July 1565 Mary married, in spite of Queen Elizabeth's disapproval, Henry Stuart, Lord Darnley, who, though of Scottish descent, was actually an English subject. The marriage was a failure. Darnley quarrelled with his wife, who refused to allow him to have any share in the government. Instead she took as her confidant David Riccio, an Italian musician. Darnley was so jealous that he plotted with the Protestant Lords, and on 9th March, 1566, they dragged Riccio from the Queen's table and brutally murdered him. On 19th June, Mary gave birth to a son (afterwards James the Sixth of Scotland, and First of England) at whose christening Queen Elizabeth was godmother. Meanwhile Mary had fallen in love with James Hepburn, Earl of Bothwell. In the night of 9th/10th February, 1567, the house at Kirk o' the Field where Darnley was sleeping was blown up by gunpowder and his body was discovered in the garden. The evidence strongly suggested that Bothwell was his murderer. Bothwell was already married, but he divorced his wife on the 7th May and went through a form of marriage with Mary on the 15th.

This was too much for the Scottish Lords. They revolted, and within a month Mary was a captive; Bothwell escaped to the Continent and ultimately to Denmark, where he died insane in 1578. The Queen was imprisoned in Loch Leven, and on the 24th July she abdicated in favour of her infant son. She remained a prisoner until the following May (1568), when she escaped and joined an army of her followers. They were defeated, and Mary fled for safety to England. Henceforward till her death, nearly twenty years later, Mary was a captive in England, and a constant anxiety to Elizabeth. For the first few weeks she remained at Carlisle, but was removed thence to Bolton Castle. Queen Elizabeth endeavoured to mediate between Mary and her subjects, and in October an inquiry into the events leading up to Mary's flight was begun at York, and continued at Westminster, where attempts were made to bring about a settlement in Scottish affairs.

The presence of Mary as a captive, injured and Catholic Queen soon led to trouble. Discontented noblemen, of whom the chief were the Duke of Norfolk, and the Earls of Northumberland and Westmorland, plotted with Mary. It was agreed that she should be proclaimed Queen Elizabeth's successor to the English throne; that she should marry Norfolk; and that all should work for a restoration of Catholicism in England. Norfolk's intentions were discovered and he was imprisoned in the Tower in October 1569. In the north Northumberland and Westmorland were summoned before the Earl of Sussex, Lord President of the Council in the north, to answer charges against them. They protested their loyalty and were dismissed, but as suspicions increased, they were commanded to come to London. They were thus forced either to submit themselves to the Queen, or else to proclaim themselves open rebels. Very unwillingly they chose rebellion, and on the 14th November, 1569, the rebels entered Durham.

Sussex was not in a position to give battle until loyal reinforcements reached him, but by Christmas he had beaten the rebels, and the two Earls fled into Scotland. Another rebel force, led by Leonard Dacres, still kept the field until February, when it was defeated by Lord Hunsdon, and the rebellion in the north brought to an end. Norfolk, having promised loyalty for the future, was released from the Tower in August 1570; Northumberland was sold to Hunsdon by the Scots in 1572 and beheaded at York; the other rebel leaders ultimately took refuge in the Low Countries, where they became pensioners of the Spanish King.

Norfolk, in spite of his promise of loyalty, began again to plot with Mary and was led on by the scheming of a Florentine banker named Ridolphi, who engineered intrigues in Rome, Madrid, the Low Countries and Scotland. Their correspondence was seized by Lord Burghley, and the whole plot was unravelled. Norfolk was condemned to death for high treason on 16th January, 1572. The Queen, however, was very reluctant to allow his execution. It was not until the Parliament, which met in May, showed itself in an ugly mood, demanding the death both of Mary and Norfolk, that she consented. Norfolk was beheaded on 2nd June.

1. TO THE DEPRIVED BISHOPS

On 4th December, 1559, five of the Catholic bishops, who had been deprived of their sees for refusing to accept the new order in the Church of England, wrote to the Queen entreating her not to ' be led astray through the inventions of those evil counsellors, who are persuading your Ladyship to embrace schisms and heresies in lieu of the ancient Catholic faith, which hath been long since planted within this realm by the motherly care of the Church of Rome '. The letter was read in Council, and the Queen, before she rose, returned this answer.

Greenwich, December 6, 1559.

E.R.   SIRS,

As to your entreaty for us to listen to you, we wave it: yet do return you this our answer. Our realm and subjects have been long wanderers, walking astray, whilst they were under the tuition of Romish pastors, who advised them to own a wolf for their head (in lieu of a careful shepherd), whose inventions, heresies, and schisms be so numerous, that the flock of Christ have fed on poisonous shrubs for want of wholesome pastures. And whereas you hit us and our subjects in the teeth, that the Romish Church first planted the Catholic faith within our realms, the records and chronicles of our realms testify the contrary; and your own Romish idolatry maketh you liars : witness the ancient monument of Gildas;[1] unto which both foreign and domestic have gone in pilgrimage there to offer. This author testifieth Joseph of Arimathea to be the first preacher of the word of God within our realms. Long after that, when Austin[2] came from Rome, this our realm had bishops and priests therein, as is well known to the wise and learned of our realm by woeful experience, how your church entered therein by blood; they being martyrs for Christ, and put to death, because they denied Rome's usurped authority.

As for our father being withdrawn from the supremacy of Rome by schismatical and heretical counsels and advisers; who, we pray, advised him more, or flattered him, than you, good Mr. Hethe, when you were bishop of Rochester? And than you, Mr. Boner, when you were archdeacon? And you, Mr. Turberville? Nay further, who was more an adviser of our father, than your great Stephen Gardiner, when he lived? Are not ye then those schismatics and heretics? If so, suspend your evil censures. Recollect, was it our sister's conscience made her so averse to our father's and brother's actions, as to undo what they had perfected? Or was it not you, or such like advisers, that dissuaded her, and stirred her up against us and other of the subjects?

And whereas you would frighten us, by telling how Emperors, Kings, and Princes have owned the Bishop of Rome's authority; it was contrary in the beginning. For our Saviour Christ paid His tribute unto Cæsar, as the chief superior; which shows your Romish supremacy is usurped.

As touching the excommunication of St. Athanasius by Liberius and that Council, and how the Emperor consented thereunto; consider the heresies that at that time had crept into the church of Rome, and how courageously Athanasius withstood them, and how he got the victory. Do ye not acknowledge his creed to this day? Dare any of you say he is a schismatic? Surely ye be not so audacious. Therefore as ye acknowledge his creed, it shows he was no schismatic. If

---

[1] British historian who *c.* 570 wrote an account of the conquest and destruction of Britain, *Liber de Excidio.*
[2] St. Augustine.

Athanasius withstood Rome for her then heresies, then others may safely separate themselves from your church, and not be schismatics.

We give you warning, that for the future we hear no more of this kind, lest you provoke us to execute those penalties enacted for the punishing of our resisters : which out of our clemency we have forborne.

11. To Eric, King of Sweden

Translated from the Latin

Eric, King of Sweden, was a most persistent suitor in the early months of the Queen's reign. In spite of the definite refusal of this letter, and other communications, in the summer follow-ing he set sail for England, but was driven back by storms.

February 25, 1560.

Most Serene Prince, our very dear Cousin,

A letter truly yours both in the writing and sentiment, was given us on 30 December by your very dear brother, the Duke of Finland. And while we perceive therefrom that the zeal and love of your mind towards us is not diminished, yet in part we are grieved that we cannot gratify your Serene Highness with the same kind of affection. And that indeed does not happen because we doubt in any way of your love and honour, but, as often we have testified both in words and in writing, that we have never yet conceived a feeling of that kind of affection towards any one. We therefore beg your Serene Highness again and again that you be pleased to set a limit to your love, that it advance not beyond the laws of friendship for the present nor disregard them in the future. And we in our turn shall take care that, whatever can be required for the holy preservation of friend-ship between Princes, we will always perform towards your Serene Highness. It seems strange for your Serene Highness to write that you understand from your brother and your ambas-sadors that we have entirely determined not to marry an absent husband; and that we will give you no certain reply until we shall have seen your person. What [   ] very true, and we have often given the same answer that we certainly think that if God ever direct our heart to consideration of marriage, we shall never accept or choose any absent husband, how powerful and wealthy a Prince soever. But that we are not to give you an answer until we have seen your person is so far from the thing itself that we never even considered such a thing. But I have always given both to your brother, who is certainly a most excellent Prince and deservedly very dear to us, and also to your ambassador likewise, the same answer with scarcely any variation of the words, that we do not conceive in our heart to take a husband but highly commend this single life, and hope that your Serene Highness will not longer spend time in waiting for us. But we will not greatly reprehend those things in your letter, nor will we blame your brother or your ambassadors, since it can come to pass that either your mind may gladly think these things, or has given ear to one telling the like, so that what the mind greatly wishes, as often happens, it thinks to be true. Your most noble brother in this cause has certainly been always so insistent, and with such ready will and eager zeal has pursued it, that for himself he could not have shown more anxious care. Such indeed was his constancy in labouring and his skill in persuasion, that had your Serene Highness been present, nothing, as we think, would have been added to his zeal or carefulness or counsel or advice. We write thus with our own hand and mind, without summoning any to our counsel, because I understand that such is your Serene Highness' wish. What indeed appertains to all the remaining duties of humanity and kindness, that can be pleasing to your Serene Highness, or convenient and safe for the subjects of us both, we will never omit. God keep your Serene Highness for many years in good health and safety. From our Palace at Westminster, 22 February, 1559 [-60].

Your Serene Highness' sister and cousin,

ELIZABETH.

Concerning your coming, however earnest your desire, yet we dare not approve the plan. Since nothing but expectation can happen to your Serene Highness in this business, and indeed we very greatly fear lest your love, which is now so great, might be turned to another and alien feeling, which would not be so pleasing to your Serene Highness, and to us also would be very grievous.

III. To Sir William Cecil

One of several official letters concerned with the new religious settlement. Cecil was Chancellor of the University of Cambridge.

Westminster, March 26, 1560.

Whereas we be credibly informed that the study of Divinity and the Scriptures is at this present very much decayed within the University of Cambridge, by mean that the towardly scholars for that learning, have in some part lacked the benefit of exhibition, and partly also have withdrawn themselves, by reason of the late altercation of the times past; We have therefore determined for some help in this matter, to provide that both the promotions reserved to our gift, and such prebends also as be within the compass of the grant of the Keeper of Our Great Seal, should be bestowed upon those scholars that by your allowance and commendation shall be fittest to receive the same exhibition and promotions. For the more assured doing whereof, according to this our meaning, we will that you shall from time to time address several schedules containing the names of all such able scholars, whereof the one to remain with you our Principal Secretary, for our better remembrance in the bestowing of the things of our gift, and the other with the said Keeper of our Great Seal, for the semblable to be performed in his behalf not doubting but you will have earnest regard hereunto, according to your good will to learning, and trust committed unto you for advancement of the same.

IV. To Mary, Queen of Scots

In July 1560, a treaty was negotiated at Edinburgh whereby Francis II and Mary, who had hitherto claimed the English throne, were to agree to abandon their claims, to cease using the English coat of arms, and to withdraw French troops from Scotland. The treaty was not ratified. Francis died in December, and the following August Mary set out from Calais for Scotland. The English ships were out in the Channel, but opinions were divided whether they were to give Mary honourable escort, to intercept her, or to capture certain pirates. Mary's

33

ship, however, passed them by in a fog, and on 19th August she landed at Leith.

August 16, 1561.

The Lord of St. Colme brought us your letters dated the 8th of this present at Abbeville, whereby ye signify that although by the answer brought to you by M. Doyzel ye might have had occasion to have entered into some doubt of our amity yet after certain purposes passed betwixt you and our Ambassador, ye would assure us of your good meaning to live with us in amity, and for your purpose therein ye require us to give credit to the said St. Colme. We have therefore thought meet to answer as followeth the said St. Colme hath made like declaration to us in your part for your excuse in not ratifying the treaty as yourself made to our Ambassador. And we have briefly answered to every of your same points as he can show you, and yet, lest in the mean season you might think that your reason had satisfied us, we assure you that to our request your answer cannot be taken for a satisfaction. For we required no other thing of you but to perform your promise whereunto you are bound by your seal and your bond. For the refusal whereof we see no reason alleged can serve, specially considering we covet but that which is in your own power as Queen of Scotland, that which yourself in words and speech doth compass, that which your late husband and our good brother's Ambassadors and yours concluded, that whereto your own nobility and people were made privy, that which indeed made the peace and [amity] betwixt us. Yea, that without which no perfect amity can continue betwixt us, as if it be indifferently weighed we doubt not but ye will perceive, allow and accompt for. As for other parts of the treaty, that concerned your late husband as French King we regard not, only we require to have the treaty ratified by you, and that to be taken of such force as shall concern you. Nevertheless, perceiving by report of the bringer that you mean further upon your coming home to follow herein the advice of your Council in Scotland, and therein to proceed to the ratification, we are content to suspend our conceit of all unkindness . . . by this delay offered unto us and we are resolved upon this being as it ought to be performed, to live in neighbourhood with you as quietly, friendly, yea, as assuredly in the knot of friendship as we be already in the knot of nature and blood, and herein we will so determine with ourself that the world shall see, if the contrary shall follow (which God forbid), the very occasion to be in you and not in us. Finally, where it seemeth that report hath been made unto you that we had sent our Admiral to the seas with a navy to [stay] your passage, both your servants here do well understand how false the report was, considering for a truth that we have not any mo than two or three small barques upon the seas to apprehend certain pirates, being thereto entreated, and in a manner compelled, by the complaint of the Ambassador of our good brother, the King of Spain, made to us of certain your . . . Scottish haunting our seas as pirates under pretence of letters of marque, which matter also we do earnestly require you now at your coming to your Realm to have some good consideration, and the rather for respect of the amity that ought to be betwixt your Realm and the countries of us, of France, of Spain and of the House of Burgundy. And so, Right High [&c.], we recommend us to you with most earnest request not to neglect this our friendly offers of friendship, which before God, if you give no cause to the contrary, we mean and intend to accomplish.

v. To Edward Warner, Lieutenant of the Tower

Edward Seymour, Earl of Hertford, was eldest son of the late Lord Protector Somerset. He secretly married Lady Catherine Grey, sister of Lady Jane Grey, and, by the will of Henry the Eighth, heir to the throne after Queen Elizabeth. The Queen was angry, and tried, unsuccessfully, to question the validity of the marriage. When the marriage was made known, Lady Catherine was sent to the Tower, where she gave birth to two children.

August 17, 1561.

Our pleasure is that ye shall, as by our commandment, examine the Lady Catherine very straightly, how many hath been privy to the love betwixt the Earl of Hertford and her from the beginning; and let her certainly understand that she shall have no manner of favour except she will show the truth, not only what ladies or gentlewomen of this Court were thereto privy, but also what lords and gentlemen : for it doth now appear that sundry personages have dealt therein; and when it shall appear more manifestly, it shall increase our indignation against her, if she will forbear to utter it.

We earnestly require you to show your diligence in this. Ye shall also send to Alderman Lodge secretly for Sentlow, and shall put her in awe of divers matters confessed by the Lady Catherine; and so also deal with her, that she may confess to you all her knowledge in the same matters. It is certain that there hath been great practices and purposes; and since the death of the Lady Jane, she hath been most privy. And as ye shall see occasion, so ye may keep Sentlow two or three nights more or less, and let her be returned to Lodge's or kept still with you, as ye shall think meet. We have signed a licence for your absence, but we would that ye should forbear for a fortnight, and not to depart, until also our pleasure be further signified.

vi. To Philip the Second, King of Spain

Calais was lost to the French in 1558, in the campaign which Queen Mary undertook on behalf of her husband Philip II of Spain. In the following spring Queen Elizabeth made peace with France and by the Treaty of Cateau-Cambrésis it was agreed that the French King should recognize her right to Calais but should hold it for eight years; if at the end of that period it was not restored, then he should pay 500,000 crowns. In 1561, in view of the situation in France, where the Catholic Guises, taking advantage of the minority of the boy King Charles IX, were oppressing the Protestants, the Queen began to strengthen her army and navy. In 1562 she sent 6,000 men into Normandy to aid the French Protestants. In this letter to the Spanish King, she explains and justifies her action.

September 22, 1562.

Although your Ambassador here resident with us hath of late times in your name dealt with us, to understand our disposition touching these troubles in France; and the rather because he perceived that we did put a number of our subjects in order of defence, both for the sea and land; to whom we made such reasonable answer as ought to satisfy him : yet because we have been in mind, now of a long time to impart to you our conceit and judgement hereof; wherein we have been occasioned to forbear, only by the mutability of the proceedings of our neighbours in France (and for that also we have some cause to doubt of the manner of the report of your Ambassador; having found him in his negotiations, divers times, to have more respect towards the weal of 'others, than of us and our country) we have thought, not only to give special charge to our Ambassador there resident with you to declare plainly and sincerely our disposition and meaning, but also by these our own letters to impart what we think of these troubles in France, for our particular; and secondly, what we are advised, upon good considerations; not doubting but both for your sincere and brotherly friendship and for your wisdom, ye will interpret and allow of our actions with such equity as the causes do require.

Surely we have been much troubled and perplexed from the beginning of these divisions in France, and upon divers causes : first, because we had a great compassion to see the young King,[1] our brother, so abused by his subjects, as his authority could not direct them to accord. Next thereto, we feared that hereof might follow an universal trouble to the rest of Christendom; considering the quarrel was discovered and published to be for the matter of religion. Lastly, which toucheth us most nearly and properly, we perceived that the Duke of Guise and his House was the principal head of one part; and that they daily so increased their force, as in the end they became commanders of all things in France; and thereupon such manner of hostile dealing used, in divers sorts, against our subjects and merchants in sundry parts of France, as we were constrained to look about us, what peril might ensue to our own estate and country.

And thereupon could we not forget, how they were the very parties that evicted Calais from this crown; a matter of continual grief to this realm, and of glory to them; and unjustly observed also the first capitulations, for the rendition thereof into their hand. Neither could we forget how hardly by their means we were dealt withal at the conclusion of the peace at Casteau in Cambresy; where (you, the Duke of Savoy and others, having

---

[1] i.e. Charles IX, born 1550.

restitution in possession) our right, notwithstanding your good will to the contrary, was differed to the end of certain years, without restitution of any thing: and then, how, immediately, notwithstanding a show of peace made with us, they privately for their own particular estates, by practices, by counsels, by labours, by writing both public and private, by publishing of arms and such like, and lastly even by force and arms conveyed into Scotland for our offence, they invaded the title of our Crown. And finally, being disappointed of all their purposes, and constrained to come to a peace with us; which was concluded by authority of the French King and the Queen their niece, whom they only had then in governance; by their direction and counsel the confirmation thereof was unjustly and unhonourably denied (and so remaineth until this day) contrary to the several promises and solemn covenants of the said French King and the Queen their niece, remaining with us in writing under the Great Seals both of France and Scotland.

Upon fresh remembrance and good consideration of which things, we, seeing no small peril towards us and our Realm growing by these proceedings for the remedy thereof, and for the procuring of quietness and peace in France by ceasing of this division, did first seek by all manner of good means that we could, to bring them and the parties at controversy with them to some accord. And seeing we find plainly them of the House of Guise who hath both the power and authority of the King at their direction utterly unwilling hereunto, and the only stay thereof; we are constrained, contrary to our own nature and disposition towards quietness, for the surety of us, our Crown and Realm, to put a reasonable number of our subjects in defensible force; and by that means to preserve such ports as be next unto us from their possession, without intent of offence to the King, until we may see these divisions compounded, or at the least them of Guise, whom only we have cause to doubt, out of arms in the parts of Normandy next to us. And so we mean to direct our actions, as without any injury or violence to the French King or any of his subjects, we intend to live in good peace with the said French King, and to save to our Realm in this convenient time our right to Calais with surety: which manifestly we see by their proceedings they mean not to deliver; although in very deed we can prove that they ought presently to restore it to us.

And now, our good brother, seeing this is our disposition and intent, wherein it may appear that we mean to do to no person wrong, but to provide and foresee how apparent dangers to our estate may be diverted; and that we might not remain in this kind of unsurety to have our Calais restored to us (whereof, we be assured, you for diverse good causes will have special regard) we trust you will not only allow of our intent, but also, as ye may conveniently, further us as far forth as our purpose to have Calais and peace with our neighbours doth extend. And in so doing, we assure you that we shall be found most ready to revoke our forces, and to live as we did before these troubles in full and perfect rest : to the recovery whereof we do heartily require you to be such a mean, as may stand with the indifferency of your friendship, and with the opinion that the world hath conceived, how ready you ought to be to procure the restitution of the town of Calais to this our Crown of England.

VII. To Sir Thomas Smith

In this period of strained relations with France, matters were further complicated by a diplomatic incident, details of which are given in the letter. Sir Thomas Smith was fellow ambassador with Sir Nicholas Throckmorton to the French Court.

January 13, 1563.

We think the tarrying of our servant John Sommer somewhat long; not so much for the matter of his charges, although thereof we desire to hear, as for that we be very desirous to understand, how the journey of the Queen Mother to Chartres hath taken place : and yet considering her journey is so far from thence, we do hold this delay of Sommer's dispatch for excused. It is very necessary for us to hear from thence upon all alterations; for thereupon must we also direct our own proceedings.

Of late a matter hath happened here very strange and odible. An Italian hath been hired to kill one other, privately with a dag,[1] being our servant. The act was enterprised at the gate of

---

[1] A large pistol.

Durham House, where the Spanish ambassador lodgeth; who also received the malefactor, and conveyed him away. The author and conductor, as the malefactor confesseth, was one of the hostages, named the Provost of Paris. The party that shot the dag was missing two days, and by diligence was taken beneath Gravesend, stealing into Flanders in a Flemish hoy, having disguised himself to be unknown : and within two days, after some other feigned speeches, he hath frantically uttered that the Provost of Paris hired him thereunto. And thereupon our Council caused the Mayor of London to take into his house the Provost; where he remaineth with good and gentle usage : and one de Ville, his servant, was then also sent to prison; who also hath confessed the matter of delivering of the dag to the murderer by the Provost's commandment.

The next day following the committing of the Provost, the French Ambassador came to our Council, and required to know the cause of the committing of the hostage : and being told particularly of the matter, he seemed to abhor the fact, and judged it worthy death; but he challenged the party, being here a public person and so privileged, to be delivered to him, and to be sent in France, to be there judged. Whereunto our Council did not consent; but maintained by reason that neither the hostage nor the Ambassador himself be free from our laws in criminal causes. And so the Ambassador descended to entreaty, that for his sake and for friendship, he might have the Provost with him, promising to deliver him to justice. Therein he was better allowed and made to understand that after examination of the Provost, he, the Ambassador, should find consideration had of his request.

It appeareth that the Ambassador is more earnest in this cause of the Provost than he would be for the like of another : for the Provost is known to be a sore and extreme adversary to the Prince of Condé and his cause, and wholly devoted to the Guises. And, therefore, the Ambassador concluded with a request that we would cause the King there [to] understand of the matter, and how earnest he had been here for the recovery of the Provost to his custody : and so he was promised. Wherefore we will, that with speed you give knowledge of the matter, as by the copies of certain writings ye shall certainly understand that herewith are sent unto you; out of the which ye shall collect that which for the present may suffice, and in declaration hereof ye shall exaggerate the intent of this crime as ye see cause. And so we end, wishing that ye will impart the whole hereof to Sir Nicholas Throckmorton, if he be not come from thence hitherward, so as with his advice ye may also herein proceed. The Provost is not yet examined, but shall be to-morrow or the next day, who although by likelihood will deny the fact, yet the proofs are too evident to convince[1] him therein.

VIII. To Charles the Ninth, King of France

In this letter the Queen demands to know whether the French have formally declared war on England or not.

Translated from the French

January 26, 1563.

Since it is, that we have understood and had most certain intelligence of a Proclamation made and published in your name and in your city of Paris, the 11th day of December last, containing a publication of war against us and our subjects in these words among others, ' Forasmuch as the Queen of England hath falsified her faith and seized upon places belonging to the King and aided his rebels; the King declares and denounces war against her, her lands and subjects.' We, willing upon this to use all the best and mildest means that we could to understand your intention in this matter, dispatched one of our Secretaries, Mr. Sommer, the present bearer, to you with our letters of credence, and to tell you in sum, that if you intend that the said Proclamation should be in place of a denunciation of war against us, you would avow it openly; or that otherwise if such was not your intention, and that you hold our amity dear to obviate the inconveniences which may arise from [war] you would cause publish some public act, as well to notify to the world that your intention is not such as has been spread abroad and divulged, as to put a stop to the hostile deliberations which have been and still are entertained by our subjects even upon our coasts, grounding their views upon the said Proclamation and to several acts of hostility executed

---

[1] i.e. convict.

upon your subjects in some of your posts by virtue of the same : about which we could not give order, without such a publication to the contrary. Upon which you made answer by our good sister, the Queen, your mother, to our Ambassador resident with you and to our said Secretary, that you had not caused make, nor had knowledge of any such Proclamation; but that, however, you did not think fit to cause publish a public act to disapprove and revoke it. With which answer not finding ourselves any way satisfied, and being fully persuaded and assured of this our opinion we have thought proper to send back to you our said Secretary, to declare to you anew, as well by these our letters as by word of mouth, that it is our desire that you would [either] cause publicly revoke that which has been thus published, or assure us and notify directly by your letters to us, signed by you and under your seal, that you did not cause, make nor know of such a Proclamation and intention : and that you do not intend that any such shall be made; and with letters would quickly send back to us our said Secretary. Upon which we shall found our actions and proceedings according as the case shall require.

IX. To Catherine de Medici, Queen Mother of France

The Queen's answer to the complaint of the Queen Mother of France in the affair of the Provost of Paris (detailed on p. 40).

Translated from the French

February 7, 1563.

By your letters of the 25th of this month, delivered to us by your son, our good brother's Ambassador, we perceive that you take it for a matter extraordinary that the Provost of Paris is here hardly treated and imprisoned, and one of his gentlemen also; whereof although you have heard of the occasion, yet you are abashed and believe that we, having well thought thereof, will agree to such remonstrances as le Sieur de Foix shall thereupon make unto us. Upon the reading of which letter with that which he hath required of us, that he should be sent thither into France or delivered to him, we have found both your letters strangely written and the requests not to be granted by us in manner as they be made and grounded : wherein we have showed our meaning to the said Sieur de Foix, your son's Ambassador. And for that ye find it extraordinary to have imprisoned your Provost of Paris; howsoever your letter hath been conceived in favour of the said Provost, we should have done very extraordinarily, and contrary to the office that we bear by God's goodness in this our realm, if we had in so horrible and extraordinary a fact permitted him to have escaped, as one that had some extraordinary power, not of Almighty God (for it is before Him abominable) but some other ways to procure the death of men; in such a sort, as, being thereto permitted, he might kill more in a day than otherwise he durst do in a whole year. And, for his imprisonment, he was used therein with so much favour, being only in the house of one of the principal merchants and aldermen of our City of London, that we rather looked for thanks than for any reprehension. And when you shall, good sister, have better considered on the indignity of this matter, and remember what charge God hath laid upon us Princes for administration of justice, we doubt not, but ye will use some other speech towards us, both for commending of us in our proceeding and to procure favour towards him, whom we can tell how to use, in order both of justice and also of favour, we need not be taught: and according to the manner of proceeding with us herein, so can we answer thereto in our actions: avowing ourselves for administration of justice upon any fact committed by any person, of what estate soever he be, in our countries and dominions, to acknowledge no superior under God: and yet in demonstrations of amity towards any Prince our neighbour, being thereto friendly provoked, we mean to be inferior to none. For the rest, we remit the declaration of our further doings herein to such report as our own Ambassador shall make unto you.

x. To Ambrose Dudley, Earl of Warwick

The French Protestants under Condé made peace with their King, without consulting the Queen, and joined in the attack on the English garrison at Le Havre (known to Englishmen as New-haven), which was under the command of Ambrose Dudley, Earl of Warwick. The English defended themselves very valiantly, but the pestilence broke out.

May 25, 1563.

Like as we have great cause to thank Almighty God for the special favour showed towards us in the prosperous success of all our actions, both at home and abroad; so have we now presently offered unto us a most evident argument of His goodwill to the maintenance of our just quarrel for the recovery of our right by the late overthrow given to our enemy there at Newhaven, the 22nd of this month, through the good direction of you, and the great courage and manhood of our captains and soldiers there: of which victory, besides the plain and modest declaration made by your letters unto us, we have been very glad to understand at length the particularities by our servant, William Winter. And considering the notable service done by those captains and soldiers, which have so manfully served in the overthrowing of the enemy being in number so many above ours, we cannot contain but require you to call them before you, and in our name expressly give them our hearty thanks: and to assure them, that this their faithful service shall remain with us in memory to be rewarded, as the same doth well deserve. And for the more assured conservation thereof in our mind, we pray you to cause the very names of all the captains and soldiers that did execute that service to be enrolled and sent unto us, with a brief declaration of the very manner and proceeding therein. And we assure you, that hereafter we ourselves will have as good consideration, that your necessities in all things, and specially for victuals, shall be supplied, as though it were in our own household for our own diet and food. And to lay the better foundation, we have presently sent your brother-in-law, Sir Henry Sidney, Knight, in post to Portsmouth, for the execution of certain things thereto belonging, from whom we doubt not but ye shall hear, before these our letters can come to your hands.

XI. To Ambrose Dudley, Earl of Warwick

Owing to the heavy casualties of the siege of Le Havre, the Queen decided that the place was too costly to hold. Sir Hugh Paulet, who had already been in negotiation with the besiegers, was sent over to England to explain the situation to the Queen.

He returned with instructions that Le Havre was to be surrendered.

July 4, 1563.

Right trusty and right well beloved cousin we greet you well. We have at sundry times heard and conferred with Sir Hugh Paulet, Knight, upon such matters as he had in commission to inform or demand of us. And therein we think before this time you are advertised at good length by letters from our Council. And therein we have also particularly debated with the said Sir Hugh Paulet upon all the matters by him to us propounded, not doubting but he will declare unto you our earnest determination to go through with all things that any wise shall concern the defence of that town against all violence and force, that can be devised by the enemy. And considering the substance thereof dependeth upon three principal things, men, money and victual, we are resolved and have already put in execution, that there shall be no lack of any of them. And we pray you to notify unto all our good servants and subjects, the gentlemen and captains there, that we take it no small augmentation to the honour of our Crown and Realm, and specially to our nation, that they have hitherto so manfully and skilfully acquitted themselves against the Rhingrave and his best soldiers. And although the preservation of that town tendeth to the importance of great commodity to our Crown, yet beside that we make no small accompt, that by the straight defence thereof against the whole force of France, this our nation shall recover the ancient fame which heretofore it had, and of late with the loss of Calais lost also. This our opinion we pray you to communicate to our subjects there, in such sort as ye shall think meetest. And for yourself, we assure you the constant good report made by all persons coming from thence, of your honourable and serviceable behaviour in that charge, meriteth such singular favour at our hands as we mean rather to show some argument thereof by our deeds and reward, than by writing. Given under our signet at our manor of Greenwich the 4th of July the fifth year of our reign.

[Postscript added in the Queen's hand]

My dear Warwick, if your honour and my desire could accord with the loss of the needfulest finger I keep, God help me so in my most need as I would gladly lose that one joint for your safe abode with me; but since I cannot that I would, I will do that I may, and will rather drink in an ashen cup than you or yours should not be succoured both by sea and land, yea, and that with all speed possible, and let this my scribbling hand witness it to them all.

Yours as my own, E.R.

Elizabeth R.

XII. To Sir William Cecil

A private note, endorsed by Cecil ' 23 Sept. 1564 at St. James. The Q. wrytyng to me being sick. Scotland.' Thomas Randolf was the English Agent in Scotland at this time.

Translated from the Latin

September 23, 1564.

I am in such a labyrinth that I do not know how to answer the Queen of Scotland after so long delay. Therefore find something good that I may put in Randolf's instructions and indicate your opinion to me.

XIII. To Sir Henry Sidney

In 1565 Sir Henry Sidney was sent over to be Lord Deputy of Ireland where he found Munster in a state of confusion because of the quarrels between the Earls of Desmond and Ormond. The Queen privately wrote him the following enigmatic letter of advice.

1565.

Harry,

If our partial slender managing of the contentious quarrel between the two Irish Earls did not make the way to cause these lines to pass my hand, this Gebourest[1] should hardly have cumbered your eyes. But, warned by my former fault, and dreading worser hap to come, I rede[2] you, take good heed that the good subjects' lost state be so revenged, that I hear not the rest

---

[1] Query ' gibberish '.
[2] Counsel.

be won to a right byway to breed more traitors' strokes, and so the goal is gone. Make some difference twixt tried, just, and false friend. Let the good service of well deservers be never rewarded with loss. Let their thank be such as may encourage mo strivers for the like. Suffer not that Desmond's designing deeds, far wide from promised works, make you trust to other pledge, than either himself or John for gage. He hath so well performed his English vows, that I warn you trust him no longer than you see one of them. Prometheus let me be, Epimetheus[1] hath been mine too long. I pray God your old strange sheep late (as you say) returned into fold, wear not her woolly garment upon her wolfy back. You know a kingdom knows no kindred, *si violandum est ius regandi causa.* A strength to harm is perilous in the hand of an ambitious head. Where might is mixed with wit, there is too good an accord. In a government essays be oft dangerous, specially when the cupbearer hath received such a preservative as, what meet soever betide the drinker's draught, the carrier takes no bane thereby. Believe not though they swear that they can be full sound, whose parents sought the rule that they full fain would have. I warrant you, they will never be accused of bastardy; you were to blame to lay it to their charge, they will trace the steps that others have passed before. If I had not espied, though very late, *leger de main* used in these cases, I had never played my part. No, if I did not see the balances hold awry, I had never myself come into the weigh-house. I hope I shall have so good a customer of you, that all under-officers shall do their duty among you. If aught have been amiss at home, I will patch though I cannot whole it. Let us not, nor no more do you consult so long, as till advice come too late to the givers. Where, then, shall we wish the deeds, while all was spent in words? A fool too late bewares when all the peril is past. If we still advise we shall never do; thus are we ever knitting a knot, never tied. Yea, and if our web be framed with rotten hurdles, when our loom is wellnigh done, our work is new to begin. God send the weaver true prentices again, and let them be denizens, I pray you, if they be not citizens; and such too as your ancientest aldermen that have,

---

[1] Emendation for ' and Prometheus '.

or now dwell in your official place, have had best cause to commend their good behaviour. Let this memorial be only committed to Vulcan's base keeping, without any longer abode than the leisure of the reading thereof: yea, and with no mention made thereof to any other wight. I charge you as I may command you. Seem not to have had but Secretaries' letters from me.

Your loving mistress,

ELIZABETH R.

XIV. TO LADY ELIZABETH HOBY

A letter of condolence to Lady Elizabeth Hoby on the death of her husband, Sir William Hoby, Ambassador in France. This lady was daughter of Sir Anthony Coke, and aunt to Robert Cecil and Francis Bacon. She was one of the most conspicuous and strident ladies of Queen Elizabeth's court.

September, 1566.

MADAM,

Although we hear that since the death of your husband, our late Ambassador, Sir Thomas Hoby, you have received in France great and comfortable courtesies from the French King, the Queen Mother, the Queen of Navarre and sundry others; yet we made account that all these laid together cannot so satisfy you as some testimony and spark of our favour with the application of the late service of your husband, and of your own demeanour there: wherefore though you shall receive it somewhat lately in time, yet we assure you the same proceedeth only of the late knowledge of your return. And, therefore, we let you know that the service of your husband was to us so acceptable, as next yourself and your children, we have not the meanest loss of so able a servant in that calling. And yet, since it hath so pleased God to call him in the entry of this our service, we take it in the better part, seeing it hath appeared to be God's pleasure to call him away, so favourably to the service of Him, especially in the constancy of his duty towards God, wherein, we hear say, he died very commendably.

And for yourself, we cannot but let you know that we hear out of France such singular good reports of your duty well accomplished towards your husband, both living and dead, with other your sober, wise and discreet behaviour in that Court and country, that we think it a part of great contentation to us, and commendation of our country, that such a gentlewoman hath given so manifest a testimony of virtue in such hard times of adversity. And, therefore, though we thought very well of you before, yet shall we hereafter make a more assured account of your virtues and gifts, and wherein soever we may conveniently do you pleasure, you may be thereof assured. And so we would have you to rest yourself in quietness with a firm opinion of our especial favour towards you. Given under our signet at our City of Oxford the . . . of September 1566 : the eight year of our reign.

Your loving friend,
ELIZABETH R.

xv. To Mary, Queen of Scots

Mary's husband, Lord Darnley, was murdered on 9th February, 1567. Under cover of a letter of condolence Queen Elizabeth pointed out, with great frankness and without any of the usual circumlocutions common in her diplomatic correspondence, the dangers of Mary's actions.

Translated from the French

February 24, 1567.

MADAM,

My ears have been so astounded and my heart so frightened to hear of the horrible and abominable murder of your husband and my own cousin that I have scarcely spirit to write : yet I cannot conceal that I grieve more for you than him. I should not do the office of a faithful cousin and friend, if I did not urge you to preserve your honour, rather than look through your fingers at revenge on those who have done you that pleasure as most people say. I counsel you so to take this matter to heart, that you may show the world what a noble Princess and loyal woman you are. I write thus vehemently not that I doubt, but for affection. As for the three matters communicated by Melville, I understand your wish to please me, and that you will grant the request by Lord Bedford in my name to ratify the treaty made six or seven years past. On other things I will not trouble you at length, referring you to the report of this gentleman.

E

XVI. TO MARY, QUEEN OF SCOTS

Written on receipt of the news that the Scots had rebelled after Mary's marriage with Bothwell.

June 23, 1567.

MADAM,

It has been always held for a special principal in friendship that prosperity provideth but adversity proveth friends, whereof at this time finding occasion to verify the same in our actions, we have thought well both for our profession and your comfort in these few words to testify our friendship not only by . . . you of the . . . but to comfort you for the best.

We have understood by your trusty servant, Robert Melville, such things as you gave him in charge to declare on your behalf concerning your estate and specially of as much as could be said for and allowed of your marriage. Madam, to be plain with you, our grief hath not been small that in this your marriage no slender consideration has been had that, as we perceive manifestly no good friend you have in the whole world can like thereof, and, if we should otherwise write or say, we should abuse you. For how could a worse choice be made for your honour than in such haste to marry such a subject who, besides other notorious lacks, public fame has charged with the murder of your late husband, besides the touching of yourself in some part, though we trust in that behalf falsely. And with what peril have you married him, that hath another lawful wife alive, whereby neither by God's law nor man's yourself can be his lawful wife nor any children betwixt you legitimate? Thus you see plainly what we think of the marriage; we are heartily sorry that we can conceive no better, what colourable reasons soever we have heard of your servant to induce us therein. Whereof we wish upon the death of your husband that first care had been to have searched out and punished the murderers of our near cousin, your husband, which having been done effectually, as easily it might have been in a matter so notorious, there might have been many more things tolerated better in your marriage than now can be suffered to be spoken of, and surely we cannot but for friendship to yourself besides the natural instinction that we have of blood to your late husband, profess ourselves earnestly bent to do anything in our power to prevent the due punishment of that murder against any subject you have, how dear soever you should hold him, and next thereto, to be careful how your son, the Prince, may be preserved to the comfort of you and your Realm. Which two things we have from the beginning always taken to heart, and therein do mean to continue, and would be very sorry but you should allow us therein, what dangerous persuasions soever be made to you for the contrary. Now for your comfort in such adversity as we hear you should be whereof we know (?) not well what to think to be . . . having a great part of your nobility, as we hear, separated from you, we assure you that whatsoever we can imagine meet for your honour and surety that shall lie in our power, we will perform the same that it shall and will appear you have a good neighbour, a dear sister and a faithful friend, and so shall you undoubtedly always find and prove us to be indeed . . . you for which purpose we are determined to send with all speed one of our own trusty servants, not only to understand your state but also thereupon so to deal with your nobility and people as they shall find you not to lack our friendship and power for the preservation of your honour in quietness. And upon knowledge had what shall be further right to be done for your comfort and for the tranquillity of your Realm we will omit no time to further the same as you shall and will see, and so we recommend ourselves to you good sister in as effectual a manner as heretofore we were accustomed.

XVII. To Catherine de Medici, Queen Regent of France

Acknowledging an appeal on behalf of Mary, Queen of Scots, now a prisoner in Loch Leven.

Translated from the French

October 16, 1567.

Having learned by your letter, Madame, of which Monsieur Pasquier is the bearer, your honourable intention, and that of the King, my brother, on the part of my desolate cousin the Queen of Scots, I rejoice me very much to see that one Prince takes to heart the wrongs done to another, having a hatred to that meta-morphosis, where the head is removed to the foot, and the heels hold the highest place. I promise you, Madame, that even if my consanguinity did not constrain me to wish her all honour, her example would seem too terrible for neighbours to behold, and for all Princes to hear. These evils often resemble the noxious influence of some baleful planet, which, commencing in one place, without the good power, might well fall in another, not that (God be thanked) I have any doubts on my part, wishing that neither the King my good brother, nor any other Prince, had more cause to chastise their bad subjects than I have to avenge myself on mine, which are always as faithful to me as I could desire; not-withstanding which, I never fail to condole with those Princes who have cause to be angry. Even those troubles that formerly began with the King have vexed me before now. Monsieur Pasquier (as I believe) thinks I have no French, by the passions of laughter into which he throws me by the formal precision with which he speaks and expresses himself.

Beseeching you, Madame, if I can at this time do you any pleasure, you will let me know, that I may acquit myself as a good friend on your part. In the meantime, I cannot cease to pray the Creator to guard the King and yourself from your bad subjects, and to have you always in His holy care.

In haste, at Hampton Court this 16th of October.

Your good sister and cousin,
ELIZABETH.

XVIII. To Mary, Queen of Scots

After her escape from Loch Leven and the defeat of her supporters, Mary fled to England with the Lords Herries and Fleming, and landed at Workington in Cumberland on 17th May. Here she wrote to Queen Elizabeth, giving her account of the rebellion of her subjects and begging to be brought into the Queen's presence. Queen Elizabeth refused. Hereupon Mary wrote again, sending the letter by Lord Herries, begging either that she might see the Queen, or be sent back to Scotland. This letter is the Queen's reply.

Translated from the French

MADAM, Greenwich, June 30, 1568.

I am greatly astonished that you press me so for Lord Fleming's going to France, and will not take my answer by Lord Herries at his first coming. You surely doubt my wisdom, in asking for such a thing as to let the keeper of such a place to go there, being at this moment the only strength where the French can enter, not so much to aid Scotland, as to annoy England, and serve themselves under cover of your distress. I love no dissimulation in another, nor do I practise it myself; that made me give the same reason to the King my good brother's ambassador. Begging you to have some consideration of me, in place of always thinking of yourself, the rather as the King makes no complaint of his stay, knowing from me your object in sending him. As to Middlemore : I swear to you those same persons have written, that if I had not sent him, he might have been taken for your party. Which moved John Wood to contrive such a letter as himself confessed before Lord Herries, without cause given by any of my servants, fearing his arrival would cause too much fear in his master who wishes to help your cause. After reading your letters, Herries came to tell me two things I thought very strange : one, that you would not answer but before myself; the other, that without force you would not stir from your present abode unless licensed to see me. Your innocence being such as I hope, you need not refuse answer to any noble personage I shall send : not to reply judicially (a matter not yet come), but only to assure me by your answers not to your subjects but to tell me your defences for my satisfaction, the thing I most long for. As to the place I have ordained for your safeguard, pray do not give me occasion to think that your promises are but wind. I assure you I will do nothing to hurt you, but rather honour and aid you. Awaiting your reply, I shall keep your trusty Herries with me on a matter touching you, and learn by him if any doubt occurs in our letters which he can explain. I have been bold to do this in your interest. Yet I trust in your honour to send Lord Fleming to Scotland and return to you, as he has begged of me, without going elsewhere. Credit the bearer with my news. Your good sister and cousin, ELIZABETH.

XIX. To Mary, Queen of Scots

The inquiry into Scottish affairs, nominally a charge by Mary against her rebellious subjects, had been begun at York in October 1568, and was continued at Westminster. Amongst other evidences here produced were the ' Casket Letters '—the letters which Mary was said to have sent Bothwell at the time of Darnley's murder. Queen Elizabeth now wrote for some direct answer from Mary on some of the points raised.

Hampton Court, December 21, 1568.

MADAM,

Whilst your cause hath been here treated upon we thought it not needful to write anything thereof unto you, supposing always that your Commissioners would advertise as they saw cause. And now sithence they have broken this conference by refusing to make answer as they say by your commandment, and for that purpose they return to you. Although we think you shall by them perceive the whole proceedings, yet we cannot but let you understand by these our letters, that as we have been very sorry of long time for your mishaps and great troubles, so find we our sorrows now double in beholding such things as are produced to prove yourself cause of all the same; and our grief herein is also increased in that we did not think at any time to have seen or heard such matters of so great appearance and moment to charge and condemn you. Nevertheless both in friendship, nature, and justice, we are moved to cover these matters, and stay our judgement, and not to gather any sense thereof to your prejudice before we may hear of your direct answer thereunto, according as your Commissioners understand our meaning to be : which at their request is delivered to them in writing. And as we trust they will advise you for your honour to agree to make answer as we have motioned them; so surely we cannot but as one Prince and near cousin regarding another, most earnestly as we may in terms of friendship require and charge you not to forbear from answering. And for our part, as we are heartily sorry and dismayed to find such matter of your charge, so shall we be as heartily glad and well content to bear of sufficient matter for your discharge. And although we doubt not, but you are well certified of the diligence and care of your ministers having your commission; yet can we not, beside an allowance generally of them, specially note to you, your good choice of this bearer the Bishop of Ross, who hath not only faithfully and wisely, but also carefully and dutifully for your honour and weal behaved himself and that both privately and publicly, as we cannot but in this sort commend him unto you, as we wish you had many such devoted discreet servants. For in our judgement, we think ye have not any that in loyalty and faithfulness can overmatch him. And this we are the bolder to write, considering we take it the best trial of a good servant to be in adversity, out of which we wish you to be delivered by the justification of your innocency. And so trusting to hear shortly from you, we make an end.

xx. TO MARY, QUEEN OF SCOTS

Mary, being dangerously ill, had bequeathed her rights in the Kingdom of Scotland and her claim to the English succession to the French King and his heirs. On her recovery, the Queen wrote to her.

Translated from the French

May 25, 1569.

MADAM,

To my infinite regret I have learned the great danger in which you have lately been; and I praise God that I heard nothing of it until the worst was past, for in whatever time or place it might have been, such news could have given me little content; but if any such bad accident had befallen you in this country, I believe really I should have deemed my days prolonged too long, if previous to death I had received such a wound. I rely much on His goodness Who has always guarded me against such mal-accidents, that He will not permit me to fall into such a snare, and that He will preserve me in the good report of the world till the end of my career. He has made me know, by your means, the grief I might have felt if anything ill had happened to you, and I assure you that I will offer up to Him infinite thanksgivings.

As to the reply that you wish to receive by my Lord Boyd, regarding my satisfaction in the case touching the Duke of Anjou, I neither doubt your honour nor your faith in writing to me that you never thought of such a thing, but that perhaps some relative, or rather some Ambassador of yours, having the general authority of your signature to order all things for the furtherance of your affairs, had adjusted this promise as if it came from you, and deemed it within the range of his commission. Such a matter would serve as a spur to a courser of high mettle; for, as we often see a little bough serve to save the life of a swimmer, so a light shadow of claim animates the combatants. I know not why they[1] consider not that the bark of your good fortune floats on a dangerous sea, where many contrary winds blow, and has need of all aid to obviate such evils and to conduct you safely into port.

XXI. To Thomas Howard, Duke of Norfolk

On 21st September, Norfolk (being then at Howard House) received a command to present himself at Court. On the next day he wrote to Burghley that he had taken a purgation, ' wherefore I am afraid to go into the air so soon, but within four days, I will not fail (God willing) to come to the Court accordingly '. Two days later he wrote to the Queen from Keninghall that, being so daunted by the sinister rumours which he heard from Court, he had withdrawn himself to be able to win time to make his humble declaration of innocency to the Queen. Hereupon the following was sent:

September 25, 1569.

We have received your letters by delivery of the same to us by our Council, finding by the same that upon pretence of a fear without cause you are gone to Keninghall, contrary to our expectation, which was that as you wrote to certain of our Council from London not past four days, that you would without fail be at our Court within four days. But now we will that as you intend to show yourself a faithful subject, as you write you are, you forthwith without any delay upon the sight of these our letters, and without any manner of excuse whatsoever it be, do speedily repair to us here at our Castle of Windsor, or wheresoever we shall be: And this we command you to do upon your allegiance, and as you mean to have any favour showed you by us, who

---

[1] i.e. the Royal Family of France.

never intended in thought to minister anything to you but as you should in truth deserve.

XXII. To Thomas Howard, Duke of Norfolk

The Queen was so angry at Norfolk's letter and his refusal to return to Court with her messenger that she ordered Burghley to write to command him to come at once, if necessary in a litter. Burghley thereupon prepared two draft letters, the first mild but firm, the second peremptory. At the same time he wrote a private personal letter to the Duke: ' Let it not trouble Your Grace that may be reported of the Queen's Majesty's offence. I trust surely the effects thereof will not exceed words; or for a time such order as here she hath taken with my Lords of Arundel and Pembroke, whom she hath willed to forbear coming into her presence; as Your Grace knoweth she did in the last Parliament upon her offence. They both accept this humbly and very wisely; not doubting, but seeing they are not chargeable with any unloyalty, to recover her favour and presence.'

September 28, 1569.

First draft.

We have by your letters, and by this bringer, our trusty servant, Edward Garrett, understand that the cause of your not coming to us presently, according to our former letters, should be for that you were entered into a fever; but yet that you would very shortly take your journey to us. Whereupon we have thought it meet for sundry respects to return this bringer with all haste, and do charge you, as before we have done, immediately to make your repair hitherward. And for avoiding of the peril you seem to doubt by your ague, that, in that respect, if the same do continue, you may come to us by some shorter journeys than you were accustomed, and rather in a litter than to delay any further time. And so shall you make just demonstration to the world of that loyalty and humbleness that by your letters and speeches you do profess; and in so doing we shall also in like manner persuade ourself of you.

Alternative draft.

Which manner of answer we have not been accustomed to receive from any person; neither would we have you to think us of so mean a consideration as to allow an excuse by a fever, having had so straight a commandment from us; and the case being also made so notorious, as first, by your departure, and now by your delay in coming, that our estimation herein cannot but be in some discredit, except you do immediately repair to us, though the same be in a litter, and so we do expressly command you : in which doing you shall make demonstration by deeds of the humbleness and loyalty that you have by your letters and messages expressed.

XXIII. To Thomas Radcliffe, Earl of Sussex

On 14th November the rebel Earls of Northumberland and Westmorland entered Durham—the first overt act in the Rebellion of the North. Here they caused Bibles and liturgies to be burnt and destroyed. They were preceded by a banner of the Five Wounds of Christ, which was carried by one Richard Norton, a distant relative of Queen Catherine Parr. In the following letter, the Queen asks for further particulars of the rebel army than had been given in Sussex's dispatch of the 15th, and what support they were likely to receive. At the same time she details the plans being made to strengthen Sussex's position.

November 18, 1569.

By your letters of the 15th of this month, which we received yesterday, we do at good length understand, as well what you have discovered of the proceedings and intentions of the Earls of Northumberland and Westmorland and their adherents, as also how you have provided for the meeting with the same; and lastly, what you have by probable reason been induced to think of these men's dealings. And albeit we cannot but very greatly commend your advertisements of the state of things presently there; yet because there be some points of your said letters, which we would for some better satisfaction had been more particularly expressed, and were perhaps for lack of time by you omitted, we have thought convenient both to note the same particularly unto you, to the end you may by your next satisfy us in the same; and also, to answer the other parts of your letters for your better proceeding and direction.

We perceive by your said letters in what outrageous sort the said Earls and their company used themselves at Durham, by tearing the Holy Bible to pieces, overthrowing the Communion Table, and persuading the people there to take their parts; but what the names of the principal persons that accompanied them in this their insolent doings are, or what number of men they had at that time with them, how the townsmen allowed or misliked of their doings, or whether any resistance was made by any person against these their outrageous disorders, is not expressed in your letters. And where also in the discourse of these matters, you note that the Earls have been induced by civil counsel to enter (in the beginning) into the dealing with some matters offensive, but as they were persuaded, not perilous to them, we find not that you make any particular mention, either what these matters that they first attempted to deal in are, or what the names of those that persuaded them thereunto, and were their chief counsellor thereunto, be; of all which points it had been very necessary we had been particularly advertised; and so we require you we may be, as soon as commodity may serve.

You also note, amongst other things touched in your said letters, that these rebels do make religion to be the show of their enterprise, where in very deed, as yourself well knoweth, their intention is grounded upon another device: And therefore we think it necessary, and so do require you, that, as well by your own declaration and speech unto the gentlemen of that County, as by any other means and ways that you can best devise, you do earnestly and effectually publish and notify unto the whole County, how untrue this pretence is: letting them plainly understand, as the truth is indeed, that these rebels have nothing so much to heart, nor seek any other thing so greedily in this traitorous enterprise, as the subduing of this Realm under the yoke of foreign Princes, to make it the spoil of strangers, as by practices long since hath not been unknown, and so breed the destruction of our faithful and loving subjects; and under colour of religion, to bring this and other their seditious and lewd intentions to pass, to the manifest contempt of Almighty God, to the trouble and danger of our Estate and utter desolation, spoil and ruin of our whole Realm, as farforth as in them lieth: Which it is the rather likely they will not spare to do, for that the one of the

Earls themselves hath already so wastefully spoiled his own patrimony, as he will not let to spoil and consume all other men's that he may come by.

We perceive also how diligently you do prepare to assemble a convenient force to suppress the force of the rebels, and that you do intend to be with the same in the field, and within twelve miles of Bransby, the 21st of this present: Your resolution wherein we do very well allow, and require you in any wise to go forwards with the same, which you shall now the easilier and better bring to pass, having our Commission of Lieutenancy, which we doubt not is before this time come to your hands. In the prosecuting of which enterprise, we think it shall be well done that you use all good foresight and circumspection, specially in this point, that if you shall find yourself to be of such strength, which we trust you shall have no cause to doubt, as you may with advantage set upon the rebels without delay of time, that you then give the adventure upon them: But if contrariwise you shall see any disadvantage, or that you do find yourself over weak at this time to meet with them, then we would you used such convenient means to entertain the rebels with talk and other devices, as may best serve for the drawing forth of time, until our Cousin of Hunsdon may be come to the place, where he may back and assist you with such force as he is appointed to provide for that purpose, which, we mistrust not, shall be very shortly: Which matter nevertheless would be used with such good order and circumspection, as the rebels may in no wise gather thereby, that this delay groweth by lack of sufficient power to meet with them, but for other respects tending to their own benefit, for the pacifying of our indignation towards them.

And although we find no mention made in your letters sent at this time of any numbers of horsemen that you have prepared for this service, yet, considering that the use of horsemen is most necessary for any speedy execution, we mistrust not but you have good regard thereto, and have provided thereafter as much as you conveniently may. The doubt that you have conceived of the steadfastness of our subjects of that County, that are to go with you in this service, seemeth somewhat strange unto us; for although we do well enough consider that amongst a great multitude, some may perhaps for private respects forget their duty towards us; yet doubt we not but we have a great number of faithful and trusty subjects, both gentlemen and others in that country; and do not mistrust but you will make choice of those that be by reasonable conjectures most likely to continue in their duty and faithfulness towards our service.

And in case you shall have any probable cause to mistrust any particular person, we know your wisdom and consideration to be such as you both can and will so provide, either by forbearing to use their service, or by some other means, as they shall not be able to do any hurt to our service. And herein good regard would be had to lay diligent wait for the intercepting of all espials or any other seditious person that might privily, or by any colourable means, resort to your side to stir any mutiny amongst those that serve under you; of which sort of people, if any such may be come by, you shall do well by the speedy execution of two or three of them to make an example of terror to others of their nature and quality. And for any foreign attempt or inconvenience that may be offered or doubted of at this time, we will cause such good and substantial order to be taken out of hand (God willing) both by sea and land, as there shall be no cause (by God's grace) to mistrust any hurt that way.

And for the more surety we have determined to send our Commissions for Lieutenancy throughout the several shires of our Realm, and have already sent forth those that shall serve for the shires next adjoining unto you; that is to say, unto our Counties of Lincoln, Nottingham, Derby, Stafford, Lancashire and Cheshire, for your better strength and backing. We find also amongst other points of your letter, in laying open unto us the state of these present troubles, and the consideration that may be had in two degrees, for the dealing in the same, that you put us in remembrance on the one side, what may be hoped for by granting pardon unto the Earls and their partakers; and on the other, what may be doubted of by hazarding of battle against desperate men. And truly as we have been always of our own nature inclined to mercy, and have showed and continued the same from the first beginning of our reign (peradventure in farther degree than might well stand with the surety of our Estate and person); yet in a matter that toucheth us so near, we can in no wise find it convenient to grant pardon or other show of favour unto those that do not humbly and earnestly sue for the same; yea, and though they should so sue for it, yet we doubt not but you can consider that it standeth not with our honour to pardon the Earls and their principal adherents without farther deliberation by us to be had thereof, seeing they have so openly showed themselves rebels, and so grievously and arrogantly offended us and our laws; and for the meaner sort that have not been principal doers in this rebellion, we have already by our special letters, authorized you to grant our pardon, as you shall by your discretion think convenient, which you may do well to publish by Proclamation, according to our former letters, as soon as you shall find necessary. Finally, like as we doubt nothing of your perseverance in the fidelity that we have always found in your service towards us, so do we take in very good part your constant affirmation thereof, used at this time in the end of your letter, and do make no less account thereof than it well deserveth.

XXIV. To Ambrose Dudley, Earl of Warwick

The immediate danger from the rebellion being over, Elizabeth, as always, was concerned to reduce expenses. This letter to the Earl of Warwick recalls him and commands him to reduce his army to garrison strength as speedily as possible.

December 26, 1569.

Forasmuch as we are credibly advertised of the dispersing of this late rebellion by fleeing away of the two Earls, heads of the said rebellion, so as we find no cause to continue our army under the charge of you and our Admiral; and therewith perceiving also that you have been lately troubled with some sickness, whereof you cannot be delivered remaining in those North parts; we are contented and well pleased that you shall, and may, return at your commodity at our presence, or elsewhere, as you shall find best for your recovery, leaving such numbers as shall not be discharged with our Admiral. And for your painful service and great pains taken and sustained divers ways in this service, like as we shall let you understand what good cause we have to allow well thereof, so do we by these presents for the same heartily thank you, and wish to see you here in good health; Trusting that you and our Admiral will have regard that such officers, as have only served to govern, lead and conduct our army under you, shall cess, and no more continue; but such particular captains and their ordinary under officers as shall be meet for ordering of the particular numbers that shall remain for a season in some garrisons there in those North parts. And though this cannot percase be accomplished before your return, yet we doubt not but you will thereof agree with our Admiral, whom we are sure will have like consideration for the diminishing of our charges.

XXV. To MARY, QUEEN OF SCOTS

The Bishop of Ross, who had acted as Mary's Agent at the English Court and had vigorously supported her cause, was put in the custody of the Bishop of London for complicity in the rebellion of the north. In answer to Mary's complaint at this treatment of her Agent, the Queen wrote to justify her action, indignantly recapitulating Mary's dealings with herself. The draft of the letter was damaged in the Cotton Fire.

February 20, 1570.

MADAM,

I have well considered of your earnest long letter to me by the Bishop of Ross, who in the principal matters [of] the said letter was able by reason of his sundry conferences heretofore had with me to have either stayed you before writing, from such unquietness of mind as your letter [pre]senteth, or at the least upon the sending of the same to have satis[fied] you with assurance of more good will and care of you on [our] part than it seemeth by your letter you have by bruits and untrue suggestions conceived of me. Wherein I find myself somewhat wronged; yet for this present I set it as imputing a great part thereof to others, who to [   ] with you outwardly make a game of your favour to br[ing] you in doubt of me that have in your greatest dangers been your only approved friend, and when all ways attempted, must be the chief pillar of your stay. And thus bold am I, at this present, to declare mine ability to do your good, above all others, your friends, [so] it seemeth nobody else of those whom you trust, [   ] you in remembrance thereof.

But considering since the sending of your letter I have had just cause [to] deny to the Bishop of Ross such freedom of access to me or to others as he had had, whereby you may [have] advice from him, I have thought good with this mine own letter to impart somewhat to you, whereby you m[ay] deliver yourself of such vain fears as others [   ] you in, and not be bitten with sharper grieves th[an] your own doing hath or may nourish within your he[art], wishing nevertheless howsoever your conscience may [her   ] trouble you, for your unkindness towards me and my State, yet that God may instruct you to consider your former dealings, and direct you sincerely and unfeignedly either to make me and my Realm amends for things passed, or if that cannot be in your power, yet to make your intentions manifestly appear to me, how I and my States of my Realm, may be hereafter assured, that for my good will both past and to come, no cause may ensue on the part of you and yours, to the just offence of me and my Realm. And in so doing or intending, you may surely quiet your mind and conscience, and be free from all suspicions that other flatterers or evil disposed persons seek to nourish in your [blank in copy]

In your letter I note a heap of confused troubled thoughts, earnestly and curiously uttered, to express your great fear and to require of me comfort, concerning both which many kinds of speeches are diversely expressed and [   ] in your letter, that if I had not consideration the same did proceed from a troubled mind, I might rather take occasion to be offended with you than to relent to your desires, for what can be said more unworthy of my former good will than in [   ] to doubt without cause given by me that any inventions of such whom you call your enemies with the aid of any whom you name your secret evil willers about me (of which sort truly I know none) should be able to induce me to consent to anything that might touch your life, or for what respect of any of my doings passed to you, Madam, or to any other of meaner estate, yea, to any of mine own subjects.

Need you to press me with the remembrance that I should

not violate my vow nor the laws of amity, of hospitality, and parenta[ge] and such like neither recompense your affected and [   ] put in with my cruel conclusion? Or what example is the extent of my actions to move you to remember unto me, that th[ose] to whom favour hath been promised ought not to be treated [as] an enemy, if the same be not first thereof advertised? For as you also write, a mortal enemy will not assail his contrary without defiance before he strike him, and so forth you pass with divers speeches, which because they are through your whole letter so [   ] of passions, I of compassion will leave to represent th[em] to your eyes, and will rather by some short remembrance [of] my former actions full of good will, induce you [to] believe and trust rather to me in all your difficulties than lightly to credit other bruits of the brainless vulgar, or the viperous backbitings of the sowers of discords.

Good Madam, what wrong did I ever [   ] to you or yours in the former part of my reign, whom [   ] know what was sought against me, even to the sp[   ] of my crown from me? Did I invade your country and take or detain any part thereof, as all the w[orld] knoweth I might, and as any King or Queen of m[y] condition being so wronged might with justice and [   ] have done? But therein my natural inclination to yo[u] overcame myself. Did I when I might have [   ] or put to ransom the whole army of the French that were sent into Scotland on your behalf to invade [my] Realm and to oppress my crown? Did I not, I say, friendly send them home into France in my own ships? Yea, did I not victual them and lend them money? Was I not content to accord with your Ambassadors authorized by you and your husband to remit all injuries passed to my great damage and charges? And what moved me thereto but my natural inclination towards you, with whom I desired to live as a neighbour and a good sister? After this how patiently did I bear with many vain delays in not ratifying the Treaty accorded by your own Commission? Whereby I received no small unkindness, besides, that manifest course of suspicion that I might not hereafter trust to any your treaties. Then followed a hard manner of dealing with me to intice my subject and near kinsman, the Lord Darnley, under cover of

65

F

private suits for lands to come into your Realm to proceed in treaty of marriage with him without my knowledge, yea, to conclude the same without my assent or liking? And how many unkind parts accompanied that fact by receiving of my subjects that were base renegates and offenders at home, and enhancing them to places of credit against my will, with many such like I will leave for that the remembrance of them cannot but be noisome unto you. And yet all these did I as it were suppress and overcome with my natural inclination of love towards you, and did afterward gladly as you know, christen your son,[1] the child of my said kinsman, that had before so unloyally offended me both in marriage with you, and in other undutiful usages towards me his sovereign. How friendly dealt I also by messages to reconcile him, being your husband, and you, when others nourished discord betwixt you, who as it seemed had more power to work their purposes, being evil to you both, than I to do you good without respect of the evil I had received.

Well, I will overpass your hard accidents that followed for lack of following of my counsels, and in your most extremity when you were a prisoner in deed, not as you have times noted yourself to be here in my Realm, and then [   ] notoriously by your evil willers to the danger of your life, how f[ar] from my mind was the remembrance of any former unkindness showed to me? Nay, how void was I of respect to the d[eeds] that the world had seen attempted by you to my crown and the security that might have ensued to my State [by] your death, whom I, finding your calamity so great, as you [   ] at the Pit's brink to have miserably lost your li[fe] did not only entreat for your life but so threatened su[ch] as more irritated against you that I only may say it, even I was the principal cause [to] save your life.

And now, Madam, if these my actions were at any time laid before your eyes or in your ears, w[hat] malicious persons incense you with mistrust of me, I [   ] would reject their whispering tales or false writings [   ] messages and deal plainly with me, and not only [   ] thankful for my good deeds, but would discover to me s[uch] pernicious persons as to

---

[1] Queen Elizabeth was godmother to James of Scotland.

advance their own evil, seek to m[ake] you the instrument of inward troubles and rebellions in m[y] Realm, whereof you see how frustrate their purpo[ses] be by the goodness of Almighty God, Who rewardeth my sinc[erity] and good meaning with His blessings of peace, notwithstanding the vehement labours both of foreigners and domestics w[hich] trouble my State with wars.

If I should now enter into the accidents happened since flying for your succour out of Scotland into my Realm, as well of your manner of coming and your usages sithence that time, as of my benefiting towards you, seeing you have been charged with such heinous facts offensive to God and to the world, I should exceed the length [of my] letter and percase overmuch oppress you with remembrance of m[y] goodwill [   ] that I delight not to touch where so little hath been deserved. It m[ay] suffice to remember you how favourably I dealt in the trial of your great cause to stay from any [open] publication of your faults, how I have forborne to fortify your son's title by show not being by the states of your Realm according to the laws of the same a crowned king, otherwise than for the conservation of the mutual peace betwixt the people of both the realms hath been thought very necessary and could not be avoided. But if I should remember to you, your contrary late dealings by your ministers to ingender and nourish troubles in my Realm, to bolden my subjects to become rebels, to instruct and aid them how to continue in the same, and in the end to make invasions into my Realm, I should percase move you to continue in your fear from the which at this time of compassion I seek to deliver you, and indeed do earnestly wish you not only to be free from that fear expressed in your letters but that you will minister to me hereafter a plain probation and a demonstration, how I may be assured by some contrary course both by yourself and your ministers in answering with some like fruits of good will, as mine hath been abundant; for otherwise surely both in honour and reason, not only for myself but for my people and my country's, I must be forced to change my course, and not with such remissness as I have used towards offenders, [who] endanger myself, my State and my Realm. And so for this time I think good, though the matter of your letter might have ministered to me occasion of more writing, to end. And to conclude I have thought good to assure you that the restraining of the Bishop of Ross, your minister at this time, hath proceeded of many reasonable and necessary causes as hereafter you shall understand, and not of any mind particularly to offend you, as the proof shall well follow; Requiring you not to conceive hereby otherwise of me, but that very necessity hath thereto urged me, and although he may not come to me, yet may you use your former manner in writing to me as you shall find meet, to the which you shall receive answers, as the courses shall require, though he be not at the liberty which heretofore he had, otherwise than my favourable usage did grant him. And so, Madam, with my very hearty commendations I wish you continuance of health, quietness of mind, and your heart's desire to the honour of Almighty God, and content of your best friends, amongst whom in good right I may compare with any howsoever.

xxvi. To Sir Henry Norris, Ambassador in France

The French King by his Ambassador had complained that Queen Elizabeth was helping the French rebels; he had also charged her with ill-treating his kinswoman, the Queen of Scots. In this very long letter to her Ambassador in France, the Queen gives her own detailed account of matters between the Queen of Scots and herself, and justifies her actions. It was intended to be read out by the Ambassador. The letter is typical of Elizabeth on the defensive; she makes out an excellent case, which is set forth very plausibly and well seasoned with irony. As for the complaint that Englishmen are aiding the rebels in Rochelle, she disclaims any responsibility.

February 23, 1570.

Elizabeth R.

Trusty and right well-beloved, we greet you well; whereas Monsieur Monluet late with us, did not only bring several letters from the French King our good Brother, and the Queen Mother, by which the said King and she expressly required us to use towards the Queen of Scots all honest and favourable treatment, due to a Queen of her quality, and to set her at liberty, and aid her to be restored to her Realm with Authority due to her; but also according to the credit given by the said letters, he, the said Monluet, did at length with very earnest speech deal with us therein, alleging that in this doing we should much satisfy the King his master, and procure to our self great honour; adding many other allegations to induce us thereunto to the maintenance of the said Monluet's speeches and negotiations.

Thereunto we have made some brief answers, as the time then served, and as we thought meet to satisfy them. But yet finding them to continue in their earnest solicitations, and in the end earnestly requesting our answer to the French King, we told them, that the time did not then conveniently serve us to send such an answer to them (as the case required) to our good Brother, but we would shortly impart our meaning herein more at length by you, being our Ambassador there Resident, in such sort, as we trusted our said good Brother and Queen Mother should find the same reasonable.

And so will we, that you shall with your best opportunity resort to them both, and declare to them, that because of the length and variety of the matters which we have committed unto you to be declared; it may percase be hard for you to express the same so orderly and readily in speech as you gladly would do, you may require license of the King to read it to them in such sort as you have turned it into French, a thing usual to this their Ambassador, and not to be misliked, especially in you that most therein use their language, and not your own natural, as their Ambassador doth here, to his great commodity. And this being granted, when you have read it, our meaning is not, that you shall deliver the same out of your hands to be kept or copied, unless it be earnestly pressed by them. And thus it followeth that you shall declare :—

We have considered of the letters sent unto us by Monluet from them both, with also the further explanation of the contents thereof by him, according to the credit given. The sum whereof, was to require our favour towards the Queen of Scots, in using her with favourable treatment due to a Queen of her quality, and aiding her with our power to be restored to her Realm, and obedience of her subjects: And though we did say suddenly somewhat to Monluet on our own part, to have satisfied him, as we have done the like at sundry other times to their Ambassador here Resident; yet not knowing how they have related or delivered our speeches to the King our good Brother, nor how therewith he is satisfied, which we are desirous to do in all reasonable requests, according to the good amity that is and ought to be betwixt us, we have thought good at some more length, to impart to our good Brother and Queen Mother, both our meanings and doings in this case of the Queen of Scots, nothing doubting but the same being by them considered with their indifferent judgements, it shall appear that we have done nothing hitherto in this case contrary to honour and reason, or otherwise then very necessary and urgent cause hath moved us, or might have moved any other Prince having the like cause; yet in denying the request of our good Brother the King in such sort and condition as it is made, have we given him any occasion of offence towards us. And this to do, we are moved in goodwill, in respect of the mutual amity that is betwixt the King and us, and not of any necessity we have to be accountable to any person for our actions; and so we trust the King will accept the same in friendly manner.

And before he shall hear what is to be said on our part, we do earnestly require them both, as a good Brother, and good Sister, according to the fervent offers of their good amity and perfect love made to us, not only by their letters, but by messages, that they both will give ear hereunto, as Princes and persons standing indifferent in this cause, without declination of their affection, or diverting their judgements to the instigations of any particular persons that are more affectionate of their nature to the person of the said Queen, than to the truth of the matter; and this being granted, as in honour it cannot be denied, specially betwixt friends, as we make account of them both in all our honourable causes, we doubt not but they shall well see, that instead of request or expostulation made to us, we shall be found to have deserved praise and thanks for our doings past, and shall not be disallowed in forbearing hereafter to grant simply to their requests as they are made. And after the King and his Mother shall grant to us this reasonable request, you shall proceed and say : first, we require our good Brother to consider what part of his request hath been already accomplished of our natural disposition; and next, what part have we not as yet yielded unto; and then shall he also see upon what just reasons we forbear to assent to the rest of their requests, as it is made, where we are required to use all honest and gracious treatment due to a Queen of her quality.

The truth is, since her flying into our Realm, where she escaped an evident danger of her life, we manifestly caused her to be always honourably attended upon with persons of nobility, and such as were of the ancient families of our Realm; we have entertained her at our charges with a company of her own, of such Lords and Ladies as she herself made choice of to remain with her, and appointed her houses of such commodity of pleasures and pastimes as the country would yield: And herein being constrained to say somewhat more for ourself, than otherwise we would, but to answer calumniations, we are assuredly informed, that for her own person, her diet and commodity of pastime meet for the conservation of her health, she for the most part when she lived at her own will in Scotland, had no better entertainment or diet, but many times worse and baser, as it is well known to all persons that understand both: So as for the state, and honest and favourable treatment of her own person, we are sure no lack can be found, the truth being known, which we see hath been suppressed, or rather untruly reported of us, wherein we have been much wronged, contrary to our deserts, and the King our good Brother, and his Mother, not a little abused with such untruths.

If fault have been found that she hath not been used according as a Queen of her quality; if therein be meant, that she hath not such honour done in the services of her, as is due to a Queen, she herself is to answer for the same, for by her own servants she hath been, and is continually served. And we think not but that they have therein accomplished their duties according to her desire, at the least, to speak the truth, we are credibly informed, that in Scotland she had commonly less reverence done to her in her services by the selfsame servants, than hath been done by them here. And as to such of ours as have attended upon her, we think they have not forborn to do their duties at all times agreeable to her estate, except percase she herself have of courtesy at some times remitted some part thereof to them. But for our part truly, notwithstanding such great offences as she hath diversely made unto us, we have been always careful of her person to be honourably used, and of her health to be by all possible good means preserved, esteeming it our own honour so to have her treated and used, being brought into calamity, and flying into our Realm as she did.

But now if the rest that be required, be not granted, that is, to have her aided with our power to the restitution of her Realm; we trust to make it manifestly appear, that to consent thereto, as is required, were not only a great folly in us, and dangerous to our Estate, but against all common reason, and such an error, as neither Prince nor private person, having any sense of understanding, would commit, the circumstances being well considered. And though many things be well known commonly to the world, for maintenance of this our judgement, yet the beginning of these things could not be known to the King our good Brother, in respect of his young years, and to the Queen Mother, though they have been well known, yet either her time since being occupied with her own dangerous causes, or the continuance of partial informations for the Scottish Queen, or else some part thereof touching the time of her worthy husband King Henry, and her son also King Francis, may percase have brought the most part of things to oblivion, or at least, have altered her judgement, or else may make her to give the less heed to them, being now remembered : nevertheless, as briefly as we can, with passing over of a great number of accidents and scruples of offences, and especially such as concerned the time of King Henry, or the King Dauphin, which were of no less importance than the assailing of our Crown and Title, as the world knoweth, we will lay before their eyes these things following, to show the acts and dealings of the Scottish Queen towards us have provoked us to deal in another manner with her than hitherto we have.

First, she is the person by whom, and for whom only it is manifestly known, that our Kingdom and Crown was challenged almost as soon as Almighty God called us by right thereunto. And how many ways that challenge was furthered and maintained, prosecuted and published, needeth not to be recited, for all Nations in Christendom understand it. And if we should enter to inform our good Brother the King, of the particularities hereof, howsoever the same should touch the time of his noble Father King Henry, and his Brother King Francis, it may be that though he be Son and Brother of such Kings, yet he would in his judgement inwardly in himself think us not well used. But for avoiding things displeasant, and considering since the same unkindness was shown in his Father's and Brother's times, a reconciliation and amity hath followed, which we resolve firmly to observe: we will omit all other parts, and remember only the things done by the Scottish Queen after the death of her husband King Francis, when she was at her own liberty.

We sent our Ambassador to her, and being in France, we requested her, according to a certain Treaty of Peace concluded in July 1560, by sufficient Commission from King Francis the Second her husband, and the Queen herself, under the several hands and seals, as well of Scotland as of France, to confirm the said Treaty, as was by their Commissioners, having authority, covenanted and concluded.

In which Treaty were concluded articles of good amity betwixt us and her in our countries, and those as beneficial for her as for us. And also a provision and special covenant, that she should forbear from thenceforth to attempt or offer us any like wrongs by challenging of our Crown as she had done before-time. To this our request, delay was used, not with alleging anything to the contrary of our right or maintenance of her former challenges. But that she must now (being a widow, and sole Governor of her Kingdom of Scotland) in these causes have the presence of some of her nobility or Councillors of the Scottish Nation; at whose coming she would not confirm the said Treaty. This was not much misliked by us. Shortly some of her nobility and Councillors came to her from Scotland, and then being since required and in friendly manner, remembered of her promise by the Ambassador, having commission so to do, and offering to deliver her the reciproque of our part under our Great Seal, it was again referred, until she should herself return into Scotland; which she said should shortly be, and then she should not fail to perform it well; though these delays were not convenient to nourish friendship, but rather to engender suspicion, with some other secret practices then discovered, yet in respect of our natural desire to have her come into her own Kingdom, and then to live neighbourly with us, we forbore to show any great offence for these great delays.

And when she returned into Scotland, we eftsoons sent to her, and demanded the same again, with offer of all manner of good friendship, which being again deferred, upon pretence she was not fully settled in her Realm, we forbore also for that time, though not without great cause of misliking; and then in the mean season following, notwithstanding many good offices used on our part, by sending sundry times both messages and Ambassadors to her to visit her, to offer unto her all good offices, it chanced that a young Nobleman, our near kinsman, brought up in our Court, named the Lord Darnley, was secretly enticed to pass into Scotland upon other pretences, of private suits for land and such-like. And there without our knowledge, according to the same former practices, whereof we were not altogether ignorant, though we could not seem so jealous of the same, he was suddenly accepted by that Queen to be affied in contract of marriage with her, as one thought to be a meet person to work troubles in our Realm for her advantage, yea, contrary to the advice of the wiser sort of her Council, and consequently contrary to our will and liking, was married to her in great haste.

And after that it was there devised to make him an instrument to work danger to us and our estate by sundry practices, not only with certain our subjects, but also with foreign persons with intent to renew the first matter of the greatest offence, as far forth as the power of the same Queen and her said husband being our born subject could extend; in which their doings, sundry other practices were discovered to us, and made frustrate : And yet after that nevertheless, when the said Queen had a Son of that marriage, we were of nature moved to set aside all occasions of unkindness, and did send thither an Ambassador, a person of honour, the Earl of Bedford, to assist the christening of her Son, to whom we also were Godmother. At which time, unkindness being known to be betwixt her and her husband, although he had grievously offended us, we having compassion of the unnatural discord betwixt them, and fearing some event thereof, caused our said Ambassador at that time to use all the good means he could with her to repair the same, which he was not able to do, such was become her misliking of her husband, although in him on the other side (as we heard say) was found all manner of lowliness meet for him to recover her favour.

And then also we required her to perform that, which in justice and honour she was bound to do, and had so often delayed; which was, to confirm the Treaty afore concluded, sending unto her at the same time under our hand and seal the reciprocal for our part. But then she began to allege a matter not before heard of; which was, that from some words in a certain part of the Treaty, it was doubted, that she might be prejudiced in such right as she pretended to be due to her next after us, and to the children of our body; whereof we being advertised, caused it to be answered, that if there were any such words, we would be content they should be drawn quite out of the Treaty, and she should not be moved to conform any such Clause. But that answer being not accepted, which was very strange and unreasonable, a new matter of delay was invented, pretending that she would send shortly some of hers into England, to treat with us thereupon, and so finish that which we did demand; whereof indeed nothing ever followed well, although we had these great causes of miscontentation, as very indifferent persons may well perceive, and did now clearly see whereunto these delays did tend very ungrateful and not without danger, if we should not regard ourselves well; yet when a miserable calamity ensued shortly after to her, that the King her husband, with whom she was lately grievously offended, was cruelly strangled, and horribly murthered, the principal murtherer named the Earl Bothwell, having a virtuous lawful wife (of a great house) living, became suddenly her husband being first immediately upon the murther committed, and directly and openly imputed to him advanced by her to high degrees of honour and estates of lands, who nevertheless vilely misused her, to the great grief of all her faithful subjects and friends; we were stricken with inward compassion of this her great extreme miseries and infamy, which was spread upon her, and sent to her special messengers, not then to request her (as we had before done) to confirm the Treaty, but to have regard to her name and honour, and to relinquish such an odible person, being the known murtherer of her husband and an unlawful person to be married to her; and generally so evil a man in all vices, as he had the common name to excel all others in iniquity, wherein no advice of ours could prevail. But in the end being hated of all her estates, and seeking by force to subdue them that intended to prosecute the murtherer was forced to fly the Realm. And leaving her lamentably in field desolate, she was conducted from thence to a place of restraint, where she refused to renounce the said murtherer, whilst she was thereby in present danger to have her life taken away from her by fury of her Nation, as she well knoweth: We, not only by speedy messages, and other kind of earnest means used towards them that were most irritated against her, saved her life, a benefit such as she never received the like of any worldly creature. And full glad we were, that God gave us such power and disposition of mind, to bestow so great a benefit upon her, who nevertheless had offered us the greatest worldly injuries that could be devised.

It followed, that when she had found means to escape to her liberty, whereof we were very glad, she fell again, by God's sufferance, into a second calamity as dangerous as the former; for having attempted, by force, to overcome the party that adhered [to] her son, who was then crowned, and accepted King by the States of the Realm, and that also with her consent, as they affirmed, wherewith her party was overthrown in her own sight (and she thereby forced to escape, by flying), with a very small number. And being hardly pursued, she was driven for safety of her life to enter into a simple vessel, and crossing over an arm of the sea, came into England, unknown in the port where she landed; yea, she herself dissembling her person for a time. But yet shortly after being discovered who she was, and we hearing thereof, within three or four days (for sooner we could not, in respect of the distance of the place) sent forth commandment to have her comfortably and honourably used: And afterwards ordered certain persons of honour and credit to attend and wait upon her (to bring her from the borders of our Realm), where she was in manifest danger of her contrary part of Scotland to be surprised : And granted her to remain further within our Realm, in a Castle of an ancient Nobleman, with all her company that escaped with her, and some others that did follow her; and there she had such entertainment altogether upon our charges as was meet for a Queen, and for a person brought into such calamity, or for one that had notoriously challenged our Crown, and would not perform that which she was bound to do for our satisfaction.

After she had been there some time, and that she had now through her own Realm been newly recharged with the former crimes, as to have been directly the procurer and deviser of the horrible murther of the King her husband, to have married the principal murtherer, to have defended and succoured all the rest of the murtherers, whereof some of the principal were her own servants, with a number of infamous crimes : We caused her to be friendly dealt withal, to understand what she would have us to do for her, that with our honour we might relieve her of these infamies wherein we were nearly touched, even in the inward part of our heart, considering the fresh death of her husband was yet unpunished, he being next kinsman both to her and us living, on the King our Father's side, and on hers also. After many things propounded, at length she agreed, that her cause of crimination should be tried as one that was not guilty of the principal crime, of the murther, and that we should have her allegations for her defence; whereunto we assented, assuring her, that if by any means it might appear that she was not to be duly charged to be a deviser and procurer thereof, as she was charged, her accusers should be with all severity punished, as reason [was]. And she should have our aid to be speedily restored to her state, but what followed hereupon; and what [was] the cause that she did not cause her Commissioners to answer to the matters produced against her, we do omit for this time, having been heartily sorry, that where so many matters were produced, to charge her to be culpable, and she by her Commissioners thereof made privy, did not suffer the same to be further tried of what value they were to have such credit as they did pretend. And in this great matter, being so heinous, it is well to be considered of our good Brother and Sister, to what respect more of her honour, and care of her, than of ourself, we hitherto forbear to notify abroad the multitudes of the arguments produced against her; by which if we had [been by] any ways disposed to have hindered her as percase some of her friends would have thought of us, we could have made, and yet may make no small advantage to abase her estimation in the whole world, and yet publish nothing but the only [rude] and bare arguments and matters as they have been manifestly and orderly produced, leaving to the world to consider of the same as should seem most profitable.

But herein we have esteemed more of honour to her than to our own profit, having an intention to overcome evil, if it might be with good; and the rather, for that Almighty God hath so fortified our estate otherwise with His blessings, and so abased hers with the lack thereof, as, we thank Him, we have no need of such means to abase our enemies, or evil willers.

And thus far did things pass until this last year, in which time, whilst we were occupied and travailing at her request with the States of her Realm, who had accepted and acknowledged her Son as their King, to come to some conformity with her for her return into her Realm, and for a concord to be made between her and her States; she again had, without our knowledge, entered into a secret dealing of marriage with a principal Nobleman of our Realm; and not contented therewith, when we did mislike it, she by her ministers entered into such an intelligence with certain [of] our Noblemen in the North part of our Realm, as they now, since Michaelmas, burst out into an open rebellion, making their outward show of intent to change the state of the Religion contrary to the Laws of our Realm; but in very deed, as manifest as it is to us more known, and truly discovered, their meaning was chiefly to have set up her, not only in her own country, but in this our Realm. And though it pleased God to animate all our subjects in general of all estates so to accord to serve us in the speedy suppression hereof; yet her manner of unkind dealing against us in this dangerous sort is not the less to be weighed in respect of that which was by her intended to our utter subversion; a matter worthy consideration of all such as have States and Government, and that mean to preserve them from subversion by such rebellions, wherein the very Crown of the Prince is sought.

And thus having as shortly as so many matters of so many years continuance could suffer, passed over no small number of unkind and dangerous enterprises against us; and contrariwise, of our manifold kind and abundant benefits towards her in all her necessities, we doubt not but now, if the requests that are made to us to aid her to our power, to restore her forthwith to her Realm, shall be applied to these former things preceding, no indifferent person of any judgement will or can think it in conscience reasonable to move us to commit such a dangerous folly, as to be author ourselves to hazard our own Person, or estate, our honour, our quietness of our Realm and People at one instant, without further consideration how we may preserve the same, as God hath given them to us, and not to be lost (as it were) wilfully and with contemning or neglecting the wisdom that God hath bestowed upon us, to possess and maintain our Crown and Dignity with public peace and quietness amongst our subjects. And therefore, although now lately in this time of rebellion, whereunto we well understand that she hath a party, we did cause her to be removed further into our Realm, from the part where the rebellion was stirred, and there forbade resort to be made unto her, as before was commonly for all persons, both of her own and our realm, we see not why this our dealing in so dangerous a time should not be allowed, being assured that no Prince Christian in like case would have done less. And therein we durst appeal to the judgement of any Prince or Potentate in the world that will profess any indifference in judgement; yea, we do think, that even herself and her most affectionate friends cannot think us herein to have dealt unreasonably.

The like might be thought also, in that we have lately restrained one whom she used as her Ambassador, being a Bishop, whom we used almost as one of our own, for her sake, upon due information that he hath been a principal motioner or nourisher of this late rebellion by divers means : A matter to be as much allowed for us to do, in the stay from the subversion of our Realm, as were to stay and restrain one that would bring more fire to a city which he hath already set on fire. In this sort we have merely presented to the King our good Brother, and the Queen his Mother, some part of such circumstances of the state of the

Queen of Scots cause, as we doubt not but reason, honour and goodwill will move them to conceive of us, as we should be ready to do the like towards them, if they had the like cause with any other Prince as we have with the Queen of Scots, having thought meet to omit a multitude of other circumstances, tending also to this end; because we would not extend this our letter to over-much length for wearying the King with declaration thereof.

But if the King could but imagine, or the Queen Mother for him, how some other Prince might have attempted the like dangers to his estate and Crown, and continued the like offences towards him, where he had showed kindness, we are assured he might think it somewhat strange in us, if we should, after the truth declared, move the King for any particular respect of a third person to consent to that, which should plainly hazard his estate, being our friend; and by some such imagination of a like cause, we think their judgements shall be best directed thereof: Sorry would we be that any like indeed should happen unto him, to inform him how to judge in our case.

When you have thus done, if the King or his Mother shall object any thing hereupon, as it were in excuse of the Queen of Scots, or intreating further for her, you may say you show this our answer: But whatsoever it shall please them to move unto you, you will make great report thereof, and doubt not, howsoever the Queen of Scots' doings have deserved other dealing, yet our natural inclination towards her, is by our doings so manifest, as in any reasonable request, we doubt not, but we shall find reasonable to have regard to the King our good Brother's motions and requests, that they may stand with our honour and safety to accord unto. And so we trust the King meaneth not to propound anything unto us, otherwise than in good terms of friendship, whereby always they that are to make demands or requests to their friends, do regard how the same may stand with the safety of their friends; and so hath Monluet and the French Ambassador signified unto us, that the intention of our good Brother is to no other end. You shall also inform the King, that after we had given order to cause thus much to be written, his Ambassador came to us, and signified unto us the good will of our good Brother, in imparting to us the double of such answers as he had made to the demands of the Queen of Navarre, and Prince of Navarre and Condé and others, for the which his dealing with us in such friendly sort to make us participate of his doings we heartily thank him, and as we answered his Ambassador so we may say also to the King, that except we might understand what the said Queen, and the rest, with other have to say to this offer, we cannot give any resolute judgement thereof. But we do think the King shall do a godly act, and both honourable and profitable to himself and his country, if he shall give them assurance of their lives; So as they may change that common opinion which is in the world, that they have their lives safer whilst they take up arms, then they were in time when the peace was granted to them, such hath been the insolency of evil ministers to break the King's commandment and endanger the credit of his word and promise; And in our opinion nothing is so hard in all this matter, as assurance to them to enjoy that which shall be granted, and if our credit or opinion with them may help them, to accept the King's favour, so as we might see in what sort they might, therefore, be sure notwithstanding the interruption of evil ministers, we would be glad to be the furtherer of so good an act, as thereby the King might have an universal quietness in his countries.

The Ambassador also now moved us that we should take care that no aid of armour or weapon should be by us or our license conveyed to Rochelle, to the maintenance of the King's subjects there, whom he nameth rebels; whereunto our answer was that we did direct no person thither, or licensed any to carry any thing thither that might offend the King. But generally we must permit our subjects as merchants to resort for their trade to all places indifferent in France, wishing they find like trade in other parts for their necessity as they do by likelihood in Rochelle, and that we would not doubt but they would follow their commodity in other places and not at Rochelle; for generally merchants follow where gain is most with surety and friendly usage, and so you may make report to the King.

Lastly, the Ambassador moved us in the King's name to understand whether he might assure the King that we made no levy of soldiers in Almain, as it was commonly reported; whereunto we answered that presently we made none, but yet we have such friendship with sundry Princes of Almain, as if we shall have cause to require any numbers for our service, if any unkindness by force should be offered us by any our neighbours we can speedily thereof be furnished, and for the state of our Realm we are determined indeed to prepare a force both by sea and by land; whereof if the King shall hear, we require him to conceive no jealousy of our evil meaning towards him and his countries, trusting that from him no occasion shall grow to alter our amity. Given under our Signet at our Honour of Hampton Court the 23rd of February, 1570, in the 12th year of our reign.

XXVII. To Henry Carey, Lord Hunsdon

Whilst the Earls of Westmorland and Northumberland had been openly involved in the rebellion, a third member of the conspiracy, Leonard Dacres, had kept out of it and still remained in the North. The inquiries which followed the rebellion showed that he was deeply involved, and Lord Hunsdon was sent North to bring him to London. On 19th February, Hunsdon was surprised by Dacres, and in the battle which followed (the only fight in the field) the rebels were decisively beaten. Dacres fled to Scotland. On receiving the news of the victory the Queen caused a formal letter of thanks to be sent to Hunsdon, adding with her own hand one of her characteristic postscripts.

February 26, 1570.

We are right glad that it hath pleased God to assist you in your late service against that cankered subtle traitor, Leonard Dacres, whose force being far greater in number than yours, you have overthrown, and he thereupon was the first that fled, having a heart readier to show his unloyal falsehood than to abide the fight; though we could have desired to have him taken, yet we thank God that he is overthrown, and forced to fly our Realm to his like company of rebels, whom we doubt not but God will confound with such ends as are meet for them.

We will not now by words express how inwardly glad we are that you have had such success, whereby your courage in such an unequal match, your faithfulness and your wisdom is seen to the world, this being the first fight in field in our time against rebels; but we mean also by just reward to let the world see how much we esteem such a service as this is, and we would have you thank God heartily, and comfort yourself with the assurance of our favour. We have also sent our letter of thanks to Sir John Forster, and would have you thank our faithful soldiers of Berwick, in whose service we repose no small trust.

To the above draft by Burghley the Queen added in her own hand:

I doubt much, my Harry, whether that the victory were given me more joyed me, or that you were by God appointed the instrument of my glory; and I assure you for my country's good, the first might suffice, but for my heart's contentation, the second more pleased me. It likes me not a little that, with a good testimony of your faith, there is seen a stout courage of your mind, that more trusted to the goodness of your quarrel than to the weakness of your number. Well, I can say no more, *beatus est ille seruus quem, cum Dominus uenerit, inuenerit faciendo sua mandata*; and that you may not think that you have done nothing for your profit, though you have done much for honour, I intend to make this journey somewhat to increase your livelihood, that you may not say to yourself, *perditur quod factum est ingrato.*

Your loving kinswoman,
ELIZABETH R.

XXVIII.To Thomas Radcliffe, Earl of Sussex

After the rebels had fled into Scotland, Sussex marched to Edinburgh and joined forces with the Regent's party. This action induced the King of Spain to send aid to the Catholic party, and it seemed likely that troops would be sent also from France. As the Queen was anxious to avoid any suggestion of war with France, she sent a letter of instruction to Sussex to with-draw from Scotland. The letter was damaged in the Cotton Fire.

Hampton Court, May 22, 1570.

Where by your last letters it appeareth that our Marshal of
[   ] is gone from Edinburgh with such of our forces as
he had [with him] to Glasgow, to help the Earl Morton and that

party to the siege which the other party hath longed (?) thereto during the time of your communication with the same party for surcease of arms on both sides; Although we cannot mislike to have the party that dependeth upon us to be aided and maintained from ruin, yet we could [have] wished that our forces should not in such sort have e [   ] so far into the country, for thereby we perceive the French Ambassador who was here with us yesterday, had gotten knowledge hereof, that he thinketh surely that his Master will accelerate his succours into Scotland, that by this our manifest taking part with such as be [   ] the Queen of Scots' enemies, it must needs ensue [that] a kind of war will fall out betwixt the French and us. And although we did as we had r[eason] answer him that our forces did but pursue our own and such as openly maintained them, wherein the French King ought not in honour to be offended, except he would profess to maintain our rebels against us, with ma[ny] other things such as yourself have at sundry times in your letters remembered for justification of our doings : yea, considering we have inclined to comen of the Queen of Scots' cause, and to hear what offers shall be made to us, that with assurance and honour we may take, we would gladly have a surceance of all arms com [   ] like as we perceive you have moved. And though we cannot precisely direct you to revoke our forces f[rom] Glasgow, not knowing how dishonourable or harmful that might be to us : yet we have thought g[ood] presently to let you know that we wish the [   ] no urgent cause of their sending thither, but that if it may be without our dishonour, or notable disadvantage they might be retired to our frontiers. And plainly we give you to understand that we mean not that they should go to Donbritton nor any farther into that Realm as the Lords of our party have required you by their letters. We have an intention this day again to treat with the French Ambassador to devise how he can by sending some thither with some of ours, move a disarming on the one party, so as the like may be done on the other part, and that our rebels may be either delivered or abandoned. Which if he will take upon him (as we think it likely) then shall you thereby have a direct occasion without touch of our honour to retire our forces from Scotland, and thereby avoid that pretence of quarrel which the French make, that we do continue the invasion of the Queen of Scots and her realm.

XXIX. To Thomas Radcliffe, Earl of Sussex

A general letter of thanks for his successful conduct of the incursions into Scotland, and for carrying out the instructions of the letter of 22nd May (p. 83). The letter was damaged in the Cotton Fire.

Hampton Court, June 17, 1570.

By your letters of the 4th of this present we perceive amongst other things how upon our pleasure declared to you in our former letters, you have taken order (for the diminution of some part of our charges) to license the horsemen and footmen that were levied in Yorkshire and the Bishopric, being about 1,500 to retire to their dwelling-places, with charge to continue in readiness and so further as by your letters is expressed. In which matter we like very well your device. And for money to be sent you for that purpose, we have according to your advice sent commandment to Sir William Ingoldby to send to our Treasurer there presently with speed two thousand pounds, which we know he hath in readiness. And we also allow well that the rest of our army, which you take to be 2,500 may be distributed to the Warden of our borders, to be in readiness to serve there as occasion shall require. Which also we would you should put in execution as soon as you may. And thereby diminish the extraordinary charges growing by the officers serving only for the army. Whereof when these numbers remaining [shall] be distributed into sundry places to lie in garrison, there shall be no such use as shall require the continuance of such a charge.

And now, Cousin, although we have not in any express writing to you declared our well liking of your service at this time, yet we would not have you think but we have well considered that therein you have deserved both praise and thanks. For indeed we have not known in our own time nor heard of any former that such entries into Scotland with such acts of avenge have been so attempted and achieved with so small numbers, and so much to our honour. And the small loss or hurt of any our subjects [. . . .] we [. . .] good [cause?] hereby to continue and confirm the opinion we have of your wisdom in gover[nment . . .] of your painfulness in executing the same. And of your faithfulness towards us in your direct proceeding to make all your said actions [. . .] with our honour and contentation. And as we know that in such causes the foresight and order is to be attributed to a General, so we are not ignorant that the concurrency of the wisdom, fidelity and activity of others having principal charge with yours have been the furtherance of our honour, and therefore knowing very well the good desert of our Cousin of Hunsdon, we have written at this time a special letter to him of thanks. And for the Marshal, to whom you committed the charge of the last entry into Scotland, we do now see him by his actions both in fidelity, wisdom and knowledge to be the same that we always did conceive him to be, and do think him worthy of estimation and countenance. And so we pray you to let him understand of our allowance of him. And to give the other that now served with him in our name such thanks as we perceive they have deserved. And special[ly] (beside other their deserts) for that they have so behaved themselves in Scotland as by living in order without spoil of such as be our friends they have given great cause to have our nation commended, and óur friends to rest satisfied.

We would that some certain declaration were made of our charges from the beginning, until you shall diminish the numbers and distribute the bands into garrisons. And also what charges shall continue, [by] whom sums have been received and paid. So as we may consider how to maintain the said charges, as shall be meet for our service.

And where you require to know our pleasure for the continuance of the keeping of the castles of [. . . .] and that called Fast castle: we think it good (except you shall see cause to the contrary) that they be still kept and guarded to be at our commandment. Praying you therefore to have regard [thereto] for the surety of them. Using nevertheless to our friends there such persuasions on our part, as they may not conceive, but that the keeping of them is purposely for their weal as the same shall so prove in the end. And indeed (as lately we wrote unto you), we have discovered and do see [   ] indirect practice and dealing here to our danger by the Queen of [Scots'] ministers, as we are justly moved to take some other course for our surety in the cause of the said Queen, than lately we were disposed. Where [   ] you shall shortly understand more. And in the meantime we cannot in any wise (in respect of our service) assent that you should come [?] from thence, though indeed we are [loath] to move you to stay there, being contrary to your health. And yet if removing from that town of Berwick into any part hitherward within your [lieutenancy] might relieve your health, we do gladly assent thereto, hoping nevertheless that you shall shortly see what way we will take with the said Queen. Wherein we well perceive, that which shall be meet for us, will not nor cannot be well executed without the help and direction of you. And so finding you in this your request to come thence, and in all other, to refer yourself to use of our service, we require you to content yourself herewith for some reasonable time.

xxx. To Thomas Radcliffe, Earl of Sussex

In January 1570 James Stuart, Earl of Murray, the Regent, was assassinated. Leonard Dacres was aiding Mary's followers in raids across the Border. As the rebels still continued troublesome the Queen determined to send another punitive expedition into Scotland, under Sussex. The letter was damaged in the Cotton Fire.

Cheyneys, July 26, 1570.

By your [letters] written the 19 hereof to our Secretary, we have understand in what sort you have written to Grange[1] to decipher his intention, which we like very well. And in like manner we very well allow of your device, even for the good respects contained in your letters to take [   ] of the west borders of Scotland at this present, where Leonard Dacres and other our rebels are openly maintained contrary to that which hath been accorded with us by the Queen of Scots' ministers. And for the manner of the executing [   ] we cannot as we see better prescribe the same to you, than [your]self hath devised, and can hereafter further add thereto. Not doubting

---

[1] Laird of Grange, one of the Regent Morton's party.

but you will also retain the intention to yourself in [as] secretness that may be, until you shall attempt it. And then we would have you so to order it, as at that very instant [it] may be known and notified openly as well to our friends [in] Scotland as to the other party, that your intention is only [to] take avenge for the open maintenance of our rebels in [those?] borders, and new invasions into our Realm, which you ta[ke] to be done in contempt of us, and cannot overpass the [same] without your own dishonour, considering at the request of the Queen of Scots we did withdraw our army out of Scotland, and accorded not to offend any person of that Realm except they should invade our Realm, or maintain our rebels. Both which they have now done since our said agreement. And if at your entry, you shall require of the Lord Herr[ies] the restitution to your hands of Leonard Dacres and [the] rest there, it shall be well so to do, for we think [   ] he will not deliver them. And thereby you shall not only have more justice in deed to maintain your actions, but shall here in the sight of the world suf[ficient] appearance to allow the same. We mean [with] all expedition to send you money, which though it be not so much as presently you would have; yet we require you to order the same to our most benefit, that [   ] your intention may take place.

XXXI. To George Talbot, Earl of Shrewsbury

From 1569 until 1584 Mary, Queen of Scots, was in the care of the Earl of Shrewsbury and his Countess (better known as 'Bess of Hardwick'). A letter of instruction for the relaxation of Mary's captivity.

August 4, 1570.

Where the Bishop of Ross, being yesterday with us, seemeth to lament that the Queen of Scots is not by you permitted to take the air abroad; although we cannot find any fault with you, for a due regard to her being in your charge, yet are we content that in your company she may ride and take the air for her health: Wherein we would also be more ready to satisfy all requests made for more license for her liberty there, but that we have frequent advertisements of attempts devised for to abuse us, and to convey

her away, by colour of her riding abroad in hunting: wherein
beside the dishonour to us, we know you can consider how much
it should touch you, considering the singular trust reposed in you;
and therefore so as such peril be prevented by your circumspection, we are very pleased that she be permitted to have any liberty
to take the air, being convenient for her health.

We are also content that you shall suffer one Thomas
Levinston or George Robinson, whom that the Queen shall name,
to repair with her letters to the Lord Herries or Lord Levinston
by way of the West Borders; for which purpose you may give
one of them your letter to the Lord Scroop, our Warden there,
for his safe passage and return. And you may well say to that
Queen, that the delays that are used in her cause groweth merely
by the sinister arts of her subjects, that make profession to obey
her, who, notwithstanding the appointment made by us with the
Bishop of Ross for the entering to the order of her Cause, have
lately made new invasions into our Realm, and, as we hear, do
maintain openly some of the principal of our rebels upon the
West Borders; which surely we cannot suffer, being done in
contempt of us, and consequently cannot but hinder her cause;
whereof we have largely made mention to the Bishop of Ross
who, we think, will thereof advertise her.

XXXII. To Thomas Radcliffe, Earl of Sussex

August 12, 1570.

We have seen your several letters to our Secretary of the 4th
and 6th of this month and with them the copies of sundry letters
sent from Levinston, Liddington, Randolf and the Regent and
your answer to the same, and your further direction that you have
taken for the aid and relief of the party favoured to us. In all
which we are right well satisfied as therein beholding the continuance of your care and wisdom in our service. And amongst
other things we have taken great pleasure to read your answer to
Liddington wherein besides your other good gifts proper to a
nobleman, and meet for th[at] place that ye hold under us; we
do certainly see such a sufficiency of wi[sdom] mixed with good
learning, as we are glad to think that Liddington [who] is

accompted the flower of the witty in Scotland, shall see himself overmatched. And we surely judge upon the matter much confounded, not only with the truth, but with the sharp and good [   ] of the explaining of the same. Truly (Cousin) we have always judged you wise, and we know you very sufficient for the place you hold, but we have not seen at any [time] a more absolute proof of your wit and learning, than in this your late an[swer] to Liddington, and we find all others that do read the same to be of like opinion.

For one matter whereof you desire answer, which is, what assuran[ce] you shall require of the Duke and his party, for performance of the Art[icles] whereof we accorded to the Bishop of Ross. Upon consideration of your own writing doubting that they will not give hostages, we think it suffic[ient] at this time to have their writings with their hands and seals, as Liddington seemeth to offer. But if there shall follow hereafter any argument for the Queen of Scots, we must of necessity then have hostages of good persons and some castles, within our own possession, or the possession of [some] as shall be thought will always depend upon us, and upon the young King. And so we see yourself doth always by your writing to Liddington press; that the sureties to be made for us, must be of that nature, that they may be in our possession to command, and not defend at the pleasure of them from whom they shall proceed. We are sorry that you could not have attempted the enterprise upon the West Border without money, whereof some portion is already upon the way. And we wish ye could devise how to borrow any further sum there, to be repaid here at London, because that the carriage is so tedious and dilatory. And upon your letters and the Treasurer's bills, the same shall be paid.

XXXIII. To Thomas Radcliffe, Earl of Sussex

Sussex again entered Scotland, and in a series of punitive raids so harassed the Duke of Chastellerault (who was in command of French troops), Huntly and Argyle that they signed a treaty to forbear war and to forsake the English rebels. · At the same time Queen Elizabeth, being troubled by the Pope's Bull of Excommunication and the conspiracy of the Duke of Norfolk, decided to restore Mary to Scotland. She notified Sussex of her intention, that he might inform the Regent and others of the young King's party and reassure them of her intentions.

September 19, 1570.

Although [we] have at sundry times in secret sort caused knowledge to be given to th[e] principals of those that obey the young King of Scotland, in [what] sort we have been of long time pressed both by the French King, the King of Spain and other potentates to restore the Qu[een] of Scots to her liberty upon good and honourable assurance to be made unto us for any controversy betwixt us, and being offered the like continually from her since her coming unto [our] Realm. We could not devise how in honour continually to refuse the same; and yet we ever did determine no otherwise [to] proceed with her for ourself, but that we would have [had] like respect as far forth as honour and justice would [be] to the safety of the party of the young King and of all nobility and others that do acknowledge his authority. Of all which we doubt not but the King's party there ha[ve] had consideration, although we have not heard anything [from] them of long time concerning their minds herein. Wher[efore] now at this present we have thought good that both the Reg[ent], the Earl Morton and others being principals of the King's side, should consider how long we have forborne to enter in[to] any treaty or communication with the said Queen of Scots notwithstanding the continual solicitations made to us [on] her behalf, with diverse kinds of threatenings to aid her cause by force, and how we cannot with our honour yield any answer for any further forbearing at the least to treat with [her] and to hear what overtures she can make for our satisfaction. And yet minding to join the safety of the young King and theirs with our own cause, we are desirous to have knowledge presently with speed and secrecy from them of th[eir] opinions, meaning to employ our whole credit and power in providing for their interest, as we shall do for our own. Wherefore we require you to impart unto them secretly by s[ome] discreet person, or by writing, this our intention, as abo[ve] is expressed, and move them to choose such means as they shall think meetest by trusty messengers or by writing to give us information what they shall think requisite for us to deal in on the behalf of the King and them. And you may let them know also that having been importunately thereto pressed by other Princes, we have at length assented to send two of our Privy Council to the said Queen to understand of her what manner of assurances they be that she will make to us for our own causes, who shall have also commission to deal with her in such matters as they may be advertised, may tend to bring quietness betwixt her and her son, and assurance for such as do obey him; so as if they shall be disposed to send any persons instructed with such matters, you may help to address them to the place where our ministers shall be with the Scottish Queen. Of whose going thither you shall hear from us by our next letters, which cannot be now prolonged any long time. And therefore we pray you to use all the speed herein that you possibly can, and yet so use the matter as hitherto you have wisely done, that by this dealing the King's part enter not into any jealousy of our proceeding. But that we will make no end with the Scottish Queen except good provision may be made both for the person of the young King, and all that do adhere unto him, and indeed we are resolutely determined both for our honour and for our own commodity hereafter to continue.

When we had ordered this much to be written we received your letters of the 15th hereof to us with the copies of the bond sent you from the Duke of Chastellerault, the Earls of Huntly and Argyle agreeable to your former demands, and your answer very circumspectly made thereto with other writings mentioned in your letters. All which we allow and require you hereupon the rather to solicit the King's part to conform themselves to the like, considering otherwise the time may be expended. And so meaning to hasten this letter we forbear to enlarge our letter any further. Giving you to understand that we have ordered certain treasure to be presently sent away with all speed possible, praying you that in the meantime you prepare to discharge some of the numbers, as by the next you shall understand how many we will have the same to be.

CHAPTER III
1570-1585

The proposal that the Queen should marry had often been made; so far eleven bridegrooms had been suggested. They were: the Lord Admiral Seymour; Edward Courtenay, Earl of Devon; the Duke of Savoy; Philip the Second, King of Spain; Eric, King of Sweden; the Archduke Ferdinand; the Archduke Charles; Henry, Earl of Arundel; Sir William Pickering; Robert Dudley, Earl of Leicester; James Hamilton, Earl of Arran. Of these the most likely to succeed had been the Earl of Leicester. The last candidates came from the French Court, with which negotiations were carried on for nearly fourteen years.

In 1570, Queen Elizabeth being then in her thirty-seventh year, it was proposed that she should marry Henry, Duke of Anjou, younger brother of the French King, Charles IX. Anjou was at this time aged twenty. After much negotiation the proposal was abandoned in January 1572 because Anjou, who was a zealous Catholic, refused to be content with anything less than the full and open practice of his religion with all its ceremonial.

The Queen Mother now suggested that her youngest son, Francis of Valois, Duke of Alençon, should take his brother's place. The Queen was now in her thirty-ninth year, and the proposed bridegroom was sixteen. All thoughts of such a marriage were, however, abandoned when the news came over of the horrible massacre of Protestants on St. Bartholomew's Eve (23rd/24th August) 1572. Conversations were resumed in 1573. On 30th May, 1574, Charles IX died and was succeeded by his brother, Henry III. Alençon now became heir to the French throne, and there was bitter rivalry between the two brothers which almost led to civil war. Peace, however, was, for a time, made between them, and Alençon, who had hitherto shown Huguenot sympathies, became devoutly Catholic. The hatred between the brothers persisted. Meanwhile in Flanders, the cruelties of the Spaniards, especially in 1576, had united the Flemings. The Queen was helping the Protestant Hollanders; the Catholic Flemings appealed to Alençon for help. On 7th July, 1578, he crossed the frontier.

The Queen was alarmed, mistakenly supposing that Alençon would be aided by Henry III, for at all costs she was opposed to the French becoming powerful in Flanders. A very different Alençon now began to renew the old proposal for marriage, and when the Queen realized that he was not favoured by the French

King she reopened negotiations with zest. After the death of Charles IX Alençon was known as ' Monsieur, Frère du Roi '. In 1578 he became Duke of Anjou, by which title he was known henceforth.

In January 1579, Anjou sent Jehan de Simier, his Master of the Wardrobe, an expert courtier, to the English Court, with lavish gifts. Simier, as representing his master, made love to the Queen with great success. In the following months the Queen wrote many letters to her absent lover, and he more than twice as many to her. But practical details had to be discussed, and hard bargaining continued during the spring and summer. At last in August, Anjou came to England for the first time to visit his intended bride, who was now approaching her forty-sixth birthday. Though Anjou was dark and pockmarked, he was attractive, and the Queen was certainly flattered by his gallantries, if not, for the time, actually in love with him. After her custom with her familiars she gave him a nickname, calling him her ' Frog ', because he had little fingers, unlike her own, which were very long. After ten days' stay Anjou returned to France and landed at Boulogne on 30th August. On that day he wrote her three letters.

Though the intended marriage was vastly unpopular in England, and evoked written protests from such different persons as Sir Philip Sidney and the Puritan John Stubbs, the negotiations went on, the chief difficulty being Anjou's religion, the unpopularity of a Foreign Prince, and the Queen's hesitations. No progress was made in 1580 as Elizabeth could not be persuaded to make a final decision. In August Anjou was invited to become King of the United Provinces and in November a peace was made at Fleix. Simier was now in disgrace with his master, but was keeping up a correspondence with the Queen, and giving her useful information, as that, Anjou was to be put in possession of Catholic Flanders. Hereupon the Queen resumed her love letters and said that she would welcome French commissioners to conclude the business.

In February 1581 Anjou sent Count Clausse de Marchaumont and one of his secretaries, named de Bex, to prepare for the commission. The commission consisted of nearly five hundred persons and included some of the most distinguished French noblemen. They reached London on 21st April and were received with great ceremony. Meetings were held, but nothing was concluded. The Queen expressed a wish that Anjou should himself come over. He arrived secretly in June, stayed for two

days only, and returned with promises of aid. The commis-
sioners departed on 11th June. In the autumn Walsingham was
sent over to Paris and the tedious arguments were resumed, no
one knowing what the Queen wanted or intended. On 1st
November Anjou himself reappeared in London. The Queen
greeted him very affectionately and love-making was resumed.
Matters reached a crisis on 21st November when the Queen
publicly exchanged rings with Anjou and kissed him. Next
day, to Anjou's indignation, she began to change her mind.
Anjou, however, still lingered at the Court hoping for the best
until February 1582, when an urgent deputation from the States
came to seek his return. The Queen accompanied him on his
way as far as Canterbury, and they parted. In spite of all, the
proposal was half-heartedly continued until Anjou died on
11th June, 1584.

1. To Sir Francis Walsingham, Ambassador in France

Walsingham had been sent over to France in August 1570 in
connection with the negotiations which led to the Treaty of St.
Germain between Charles IX and his Huguenot subjects. It was
now suggested that Henry, Duke of Anjou, younger brother of
Charles IX, and a strong supporter of the Catholic Guises, might
be a suitable husband for Queen Elizabeth. The Queen Mother
sent her agent, Guido Cavalcanti, to England to discuss the
matter, and negotiations, apparently serious, were begun between
the two Courts. Cavalcanti came over again in April, and
definite proposals were put forward. At the beginning of June
the Queen sent over her own proposals, with the following cover-
ing letter to Walsingham.

Osterley, June 8, 1571.

Although we did heretofore think it reasonable to forbear
the sending of any Articles to contain the demands on our part,
until we might have a resolute answer from the King to our
former answers made to his first Articles, sent thither by Cavalcanti; and namely, to the Article touching Religion: Yet finding
by your letters, and by the continual solicitation of the French
Ambassador here Resident, how earnestly the King desireth to
see our demands; which when he shall have, he will make answer
to the former, we are, contrary to our own disposition, induced
by these means to send the same at this time, as you shall receive

the same in Articles; whereof you shall advertise the King and Queen Mother, and let them understand, that were it not for the earnest solicitation of their Ambassador, we would have forborne so to have done; for that we take it, it may be interpreted in some manner to touch us in honour, that not having knowledge how the King will satisfy us in the matter of Religion, which is the principal, we should pass further into the Treaty of all the rest, altogether upon uncertainty what to hope in the principal. But to their satisfaction herein, you shall say, that we not only caused the Earl of Leicester and Lord Burghley, whom only of our Council we have used herein, according to our former agreement, to impart our demands in certain Articles to the French Ambassador; but have also sent them now in writing, to be by you showed unto them, having therein followed for the most part the form of things granted to our late Sister, of noble memory, Queen Mary, as by the Treaty of Marriage betwixt King Philip and her may appear. And further, you shall say, that these Articles are but briefly and summarily conceived by our foresaid Councillors, who have not the knowledge of the forms of Law requisite in such case; so as we reserve to ourselves power, if the substance of them shall be granted, to cause the same to be for form of Law enlarged, by such others of our Council, as by learning can better do the same. Besides, we do deliver these demands to be jointly considered with the Articles of our first answer to the demands on the King's part brought by Cavalcanti.

We perceive by the French Ambassador that certain clauses which we agreed should be added to some of the first Articles, were not contained in the writing by you there showed: And not knowing whether in the writing of them there, the same clauses were omitted, for more surety we send you a new copy hereof, to be showed as you shall have occasion: And if indeed those clauses shall appear to have been omitted in the former, the same was omitted but by the writer.

If the King or any other shall press you to understand of our proceedings with the Queen of Scots, as in misliking the restraint of the Bishop of Ross, or in not determining her cause; you shall for the first say, that the evil parts done by the Bishop of Ross are such, and so dangerous to us and our State, as no Prince could suffer, as we think, the like, without some sharp revenge; For wherein the late rebellion in the North, we understood that he had given the heads of that rebellion comfort to enter into the same, which he could not deny, being charged therewith, but that they secretly had sent to him for aid and comfort afore their rebellion, although he did not yield the same unto them, nor thought it meet to utter the same, and so we were content to pass over the same, with hope that he would attend his causes only according to the place he held, to be as an agent or minister for her, and not to intermeddle as he had done with our affairs and to trouble our State. Nevertheless, within a few months after he did eftsoons secretly by night, which was the last summer, enter into such intelligences and practices with some of our nobility, as we could not endure the same, but for a time restrained him of his liberty, until he promised never to be found in the like to offend us. Contrary whereunto he hath now of new entered into practices by his letters and ministers to stir up secretly some new rebellion in our Realm; and hath for that purpose dealt by his ministers with certain our fugitives and rebels in the King of Spain's Low Countries: As also with the Duke of Alva, and further prosecuted his intentions to that purpose, by sending both to the Pope and to the King of Spain; of all which his doings we have full proof, and in certain part to prove the same his own confessions do manifestly argue his guiltiness.

Now therefore you shall require the King or his Mother, if they shall deal with you herein, to interpret well of our doings, for that we may not endure such kind of dealing as may so endanger, or at the least trouble our Estate. And for this purpose, if you shall be so required, why we do refuse to grant to the Bishop of Glasgow passport, you shall say, it is upon the self-same ground; for we do well know his conditions, and specially how unmeet a man he is to come hither to do any good office betwixt the Queen his mistress and us, who we know hath rather been a maintainer than a pacifier of discord betwixt us in times past. And as for our intentions towards the King of Scots, although her Minister the Bishop of Ross hath otherwise deserved;

yet we do continue in mind to proceed to the hearing and order-ing of her cause, upon the coming of certain noblemen out of Scotland, both for her and the King her Son, the delay whereof hath lately grown by the renewing of arms on both sides, whereof being by an express messenger of ours now very lately sent out of Scotland to both parties earnestly charged by us; either of the parties do charge the other and excuse themselves: and yet at length they are now content to re-enter again into treaty, offer-ing to send hither their Commissioners. For which purpose we have even this day returned answer to them of our contentation to hear them, and have required both parties to lay down their arms, which we doubt not but they will; and so doing, we trust, shortly some good end will follow; for so is our desire and full purpose, and so shall it appear by actions.

Of all this we thought good to inform you, to the end you may the better answer thereto, if speech be moved thereof, or else not.

11. To Sir Francis Walsingham, Ambassador in France

In August 1571, Paul de Foix, who had previously been a popular Ambassador in London, was sent to the Queen to discuss the details of the proposed marriage. In this letter the Queen reports the present state of the negotiations to her Ambassador in France.

September 2, 1571.

Although we think you had some great desire to hear how Monsieur de Foix hath here proceeded with us in his charge; and the rather, because we understand, that within a few days after the first speech with us, and conference with our Council, he dispatched letters or message thither; yet surely, until this present time we could not ascertain you of anything certainly concluded with him, by reason that he being not satisfied with our answers, doth still persist in seeking to induce us to reform our answer more towards his satisfaction. But now you shall understand, that he and the Ambassador Resident having had sundry con-ferences, both with us, and apart with our Council, at all times the weight of the matter hath chiefly depended upon the cause of

Religion. For they requiring a toleration, and we denying, they offering to have it tempered and moderated, as our Council shall devise, to avoid offence of our conscience, and of the Duke's, the same was found always impossible, or so hard, as by no device such a mean in plain terms, by words or writing, could be found to satisfy them or ourselves: So as in the end they desire as we would be content to agree secretly, that he should not be impeached in the secret use of his Religion, if we would not consent to a toleration; and so you shall see by a writing, which you shall receive herewith, what hath been said by our Council thereto; and with the same writing also two answers to two other matters by them only propounded, because to the same there was no answer satisfactory given in our former writing to their first demands.

In this writing now delivered to them, we perceived them most troubled with a phrase added of great necessity for our purpose, and specially for satisfying of our conscience, that the Duke shall not be molested for using of any rites not repugnant ' unto the word of God,' which words being in a writing delivered unto them first the 24th of this month, was afterwards now in the last of August by their importunity, as now ye see, altered from the words ' *Verbo Dei* ' to ' *Ecclesiæ Dei*,' which in our judgement is all one; and yet finding themselves better content therewith than with the other, we yielded to have it so altered.

Besides this writing, because we know not how our answer in the Article of Religion shall be there imparted, we have also by express speech declared to Monsieur de Foix, that we shall be well content that our answer may satisfy Monsieur d'Anjou for his honour, for that we have in some sort yielded for him to use other ceremonies than ours; so that as they be not repugnant to the Church of God, and with such other cautions as in our writing are further contained; so our meaning is to be declared plainly to Monsieur de Anjou, that we cannot permit him at his coming to have the use of any private Mass, which speech we have plainly uttered unto him because there should be no misconceiving gathered of our answer, whereby the Duke might hope of a sufferance; for that we cannot find it, without peril to our Estate, and quietness to yield thereunto. And thus having imparted unto you how we have answered him, we will that you also after the consideration of the same, and of the answer given unto him in writing (which we herewith send) shall resort to the King, and affirm the same to be our mind. And if you shall find them doubtful how to interpret our answer, that is, whether we, having our mind satisfied in the cause of Religion, can be content to proceed in the marriage, you shall assure the King, that the rest of the things being by him assented unto, and ordered to be performed; we mean sincerely to proceed in further treaty of the marriage, according to our former answer. And if they shall so move it unto you, we can be contented that special Commissioners may be sent from thence hither, to treat and conclude with us and our Council, as reason shall require. And for that we have causes to think, that sundry there, and some being of credit, will seek to provoke the King to a misliking of [our] answers and to conceive that we have not had a sincere intention in this matter from the beginning, you shall do your best, and so we warrant you, to assure the King of the contrary, whatsoever malice shall devise against us : And where we had some occasion by some of your letters to some here, to think that now at Monsieur de Foix coming hither, though the matter of the marriage should not take effect, yet that same motion of a further league of Amity might be made betwixt us and the King. You shall understand, that not only no motion hath been made thereof unto us, but upon indirect speeches used by some of our trusty Ministers to de Foix in that purpose : he hath earnestly declared, that without prosecution of the marriage, he had no Commission to deal in any other matter at all; but said, that he trusted that the King his Master would continue Amity with us, except contrary cause should be offered [by] us.

Now therefore considering you may see that we have not made any great difficulty but in the matter of Religion, which we cannot see how it may be yielded unto Monsieur and his domestiques, though the number shall be never so small without peril, without discontentation of our best subjects, and comfort to the worse, it shall be your part to insist earnestly to let it be well understood how sincerely we have dealt therein, and how free we ought to be from the calumniation of certain persons that will never be content to say well of us, how well soever we do. The occasion of the long abode here of Monsieur de Foix shall appear to you, we doubt not, by the letters of my Lord of Burghley. As for satisfaction of your desire to have some to assist you in service now this month, whilst you shall attend the recovery of your health; upon the next answer to be made us of these our letters, you shall also have order for some to be assistant to supply your place.

III. To Mary, Queen of Scots

After the discovery of the Ridolphi plot Mary was placed under close restraint. She wrote to the Queen a series of letters culminating in one of 27th January, tending ' to uncomely, passionate, ireful and vindictive speeches'. Elizabeth had hitherto refrained from replying, but her patience was tried too highly and she answered Mary's charges point by point, at the same time sending to the Earl of Shrewsbury a letter of instructions to be read to Mary in which the points were elaborated.

Westminster, February 1, 1572.

Madame,

Of late time I have received divers letters from you, to the which you may well guess by the accidents of the time why I have not made any answer, but especially because I saw no matter in them that required any such answer as could have contented you; and to have discontented you had been but an increase of your impatience, which I thought time would have mitigated as it commonly does when the cause thereof is not truly grounded, and that it be so understood. But now finding by your last letter of the 27th of the last an increase of your impatience, tending also to uncomely, passionate, ireful and vindictive speeches, I thought to change my former opinion, and by patient and advised words to move you to stay or qualify your passions, and to consider that it is not the manner to obtain good things with evil speeches, nor benefits with injurious challenges, nor to conclude, all in one word, good to yourself, with doing evil to myself. Yet to avoid the fault which I note that you have committed in filling a long letter with multitude of sharp and injurious words, I will not by way of letter write any more of the matter, but have rather chosen to commit to my cousin, the Earl of Shrewsbury, the things which I have thought meet, upon the reading of your letter, to be imparted to you, as he hath in a memorial in writing to show to you; wherewith, I think, if reason may be admitted to be with you at the reading, you will follow hereafter the course of the last part of your letter rather than the first (the latter being written in a calm, and the former in a storm), wishing to you the same grace of God that we wish to ourself, and that He may direct you to desire and attain to that is meet for you as well in honour as in all other quietness.

IV. To William Cecil, Lord Burghley

A personal note to Burghley to save the life of the Duke of Norfolk. The original is endorsed in Burghley's hand: 'The Q. Majy, with her own hand for staying of the execution of the D.N. R. at 2 in the morning.' Four warrants for the execution were revoked. Norfolk was at last beheaded on 2nd June.

April 11, 1572.

My Lord,

Methinks that I am more beholden to the hinder part of my head, than well dare trust the forwards side of the same, and therefore sent the Lieutenant and the S., as you know best, the order to defer this execution till they hear farther. And that this may be done I doubt nothing without curiosity of my further warrant, for that their rash determination, upon a very unfit day, was countermanded by your considerate admonition. The causes that move me to this are not now to be expressed, lest an irrevocable deed be in meanwhile committed. If they will needs a warrant, let this suffice, all written with my own hand.

Your most loving sovereign,

Elizabeth R.

V. To Sir Francis Walsingham, Ambassador in France

On receipt of the formal proposal that the Duke of Alençon should take the place of his elder brother, the Duke of Anjou, as the Queen's prospective husband, she wrote this letter to Walsingham, declining the offer on the grounds that the difference between their ages was too great, and that since Alençon was reported to be marked with small-pox she was not likely to be attracted by his person.

Theobalds, July 23, 1572.

Where at the being here with us of the Duke of Montmorency, he and de Foix, after their other ordinary matter of ratification of the Treaty passed over, did many times very earnestly deal with us, and in like manner with sundry of our Council, to move us to incline to an offer of marriage; which the French King and Queen Mother willed them to make to us for the Duke of Alençon, and that we found the matter somewhat strange, considering some things passed not in good order, as you know in the matter of like offer for Monsieur d'Anjou, wherein the said Montmorency and his colleagues laboured much to satisfy us, but especially considering the youngness of the years of the Duke of Alençon being compared to ours; so for those respects, although we could give them no answer of comfort to content them, yet such was their importunacy in reciting of many reasons and arguments to move us not to mislike thereof, in respect as well of the strength of the amity which this amity should give to the continuance of this last league and confederation, as also of the worthiness of the said Duke of Alençon for his excellent virtues and good conditions which they allege to be in him, with sundry other arguments tending to remove the difficulties, and to gain our contentation and liking of the said Duke.

And in them, after their many conferences had both with us and with our Council, when we perceived them very much perplexed to see our strangeness from assenting to their desires, and how loath they were to have any flat denial; we were advised to forbear from making of a plain refusal, and to expect the return of the Lord Admiral, by whom, and by others of his company, we might understand what might be further conceived of the personage and conditions of the said Duke. And so our answer to them at their departure was this : that we found such difficulties in this matter, specially for the difference of his age, as presently we could not digest the same; yet such was the importunacy of our own subjects of all estates to have us to marry, as we would forbear to give any such resolute answer as might miscontent the said Ambassador, and as we know would much grieve our people at this time, and as we would take some further time to be advertised upon the matter. And after one month's space we would make a direct answer to the French King, which also we would first communicate to the said Duke of Montmorency, to be by him, if he so would, delivered over to the said King.

And so with this answer they departed; whereupon after the return of the Lord Admiral, we have considered with him, and with some others that were there; by whom we find that indeed the conditions and the qualities of the said Duke as far forth as they could by their observation gather, or by report of others understand, were nothing inferior to Monsieur de Anjou, but rather better to be liked; but as to his visage and favour, everybody doth declare the same to be far inferior, and that specially for the blemishes that the small-pox hath wrought therein, so as his young years considered, the doubtfulness of the liking of his favour[1] joined therewith, wherein nobody that hath seen him can otherwise report, although otherwise to all purposes he is commended before his brother, we cannot indeed bring our mind to like of this offer, specially finding no other greater commodity offered to us with him, whereby the absurdity that in the general opinion of the world might grow to commend this our choice, after so many refusals of others of great worthiness might be counterpoised, or in some manner recompensed.

Wherefore according to our answer made to the said Ambassador, we have determination that you shall in our name say as followeth to Montmorency. Or, if he shall desire that you yourself (considering the answer is not plausible) shall make it to the King, then you shall so do, requiring him to be present, and to move the King and his Mother to interpret the same to the best, as indeed we mean it plainly and friendly; and then you shall say that we have considered of the matter of the King's offer unto us of Monsieur de Alençon in marriage. And for the same we do most earnestly thank the King and the Queen Mother, knowing manifestly that the same proceedeth of very great good will, to make a very perfect continuance of the amity lately contracted between us by this last Treaty.[2] And considering we

---

[1] Favour, i.e. face.　　　　　[2] Treaty of Blois, April 1572.

have as great desire to have the same amity continued and strengthened, we are very sorry to find so great difficulties in this matter that should be a principal band[1] thereof, as we cannot digest the inconveniences of the same, by reason of the difference of our ages to assent thereunto, praying the King and his Mother to assure themselves that there is no lack of desire in us to continue, yea, if it might be to increase this amity that maketh us think of the difficulties in this offer, otherwise than we think all others that doth consider thereof, and most conceive, which proceedeth almost only of the difference of the age of Monsieur de Alençon, and ours, a matter that cannot be remedied, either by the King his brother that desireth the match, or by us, so as the lack of not perfecting this bond of amity after this manner cannot be justly imputed to either of us, nor to the party himself, of whose conditions and virtues, truly you may say we hear so well, as we cannot but esteem him very much, and think him very well worthy to have as good fortune by marriage as he or any other might have by us. And you may say, if you so see cause, that although we might have known thus much as concerning his age when the Ambassadors were here, and therefore might at that time have given them answer, and not thus to have deferred it until this time; yet to satisfy the King therein, you shall say that, true it is, that although we ourselves were of this mind from the beginning, to think the match inconvenient for his age; yet at the being here of the Ambassadors, we were continually laboured by our Council, and also by our Estates then assembled in Parliament, in laying open before us the necessity of our marriage, both for our own comfort, and also for the weal of the Realm. And some of them alleging unto us that there would be no such difficulty in this matter of his years, but the evil opinion that might be conceived thereof in the world to our lack, might percase be recompensed with some other matter of advantage to us in our Realm, in the sight also of the world, as being overcome with the importunacy of their reasons, we did yield to take some further consideration of the matter; and to prove whether in some time we could work our mind in the mean season to some other purpose, or whether

[1] Band=bond.

any such further matter might be offered with this match, as might counterpoise in the judgement of the world, the inconvenience of the difference of the age. But so it is, that in all this time, we neither can find our mind altered, nor yet hear of any other thing that might countervail the inconvenience; but so for observing of our promise, and especially because we mean to deal plainly with our good Brother and the Queen his mother, we do make them this answer; that surely we cannot find ourself void of doubt and misliking to accept this offer, which is principally for the difference of years, allowing nevertheless of his worthiness for his virtuous and honourable conditions, as much as we can require in any Prince to be our husband. And so we pray the King and his Mother, that the Duke himself may understand our judgement to be of his worthiness. And for the great goodwill we understand that he hath borne to us, we do assure him that we shall for the same esteem him at all times hereafter as well as any other Prince of his estate, reserving only the band of love that ought to accompany marriage.

vi. To Sir Francis Walsingham, Ambassador in France

Two days after writing the previous letter the Queen's interest in Alençon began to increase. She wrote again to Walsingham to say that she wished to have a sight of the proposed bridegroom: meanwhile the difficult question of difference in religion could be held over, for it would be a convenient excuse for either party to break off the match if they did not like each other.

Gorhambury, July 25, 1572.

After we finished our other letters, and determined to have sent them away in such sort as you might have had them in convenient time, to have delivered our answer according to our promise made to the Duke of Montmorency, the French Ambassador here gave knowledge that he had received letters from thence; whereupon he required to have audience before we should send to you, which we did accord; and thereby our former letters were stayed contrary to our determinations, and so we would give out should it be known where you shall find it requisite for answering to their expectation for the time limited for our answer.

And, therefore, at the delivery of our former letters of credit, both to the King and to Montmorency, you shall say that you are to show them our answer as we did conceive it to be given when those letters were written. And upon the Ambassador's access after that time, and the delivery of letters from the King, Queen Mother, and from Monsieur de Alençon, all full of purposes to further the matter of marriage, besides the private earnest dealing also with us of the French Ambassador to the same end; we were occasioned thereby to do some further matter to our former answer : not being any ways so different as it doth alter our said answer. But in respect of our earnestness of the desire we see to be in the King and Queen Mother, and especially in the Duke of Alençon himself, not only by their letters to ourselves, but by the Duke's letters to the French Ambassador, we have thought convenient to enlarge our answer, in some part to lay open before the King our conceit in the matter; which you shall say we do of very sincerity of good will to be answerable to their earnest dealing with us, to be, nevertheless, considered and ordered by them as they shall think best.

After you have used this kind of speech to them, you shall say, that when we think of this matter, we find no other principal impediment, but in the difference of the ages, and the cause of religion. And as to this latter, which is the difficulty about religion, we do not think that such, but the form and substance of our religion being well made known to the Duke, there is no such cause to doubt, but by God's goodness the same may be removed to the satisfaction of us both.

But, as to the other, which concerneth the person of the Duke, of his age and otherwise, for as much as the difficulties thereof may seem to consist rather in opinion than in matter indeed, we do thereto thus yield to think, that in marriage, when the persons are to think one of the other, nothing doth so much rule both parties, as to have their own opinions satisfied. And seeing that in respect thereof nothing can make so full a satisfaction to us for our opinion, nor percase in him of us, in respect of the opinion he may conceive of the excess of our years above his; as that either of us might by some convenient means with our own eyes falsify our own conceits, a matter we know somewhat difficult, but such as in like cases hath been yielded to us, though by other impediments not perfected. And, nevertheless, how this may be granted or allowed by the King and the Queen Mother to be done without offence, we do leave it to them in whom we perceive by our Ambassador's speech the stay hath consisted, when the Duke himself, both by his letters to the Ambassador, as otherwise, hath showed himself thereto disposed, that is, to come hither in person, for the which we cannot but greatly esteem his love and affection that he beareth to us.

This, you may say, is as much as we can conceive of the matter; and if it were not for the desire we have to deal plainly in this matter, being so much provoked by the great good will we find in them there, we would not in that sort propound such a matter, neither do we otherwise propound it, but that it may be friendly interpreted, and not to conceive that thereby we mean any abuse to the disgrace of the Duke, whom we have great cause to love and esteem, but that surely in this sort our opinion by sight may be satisfied, which otherwise we perceive cannot be by report of any others, for that none of our own dare adventure to deliver their advice for our own liking of him as the case is, we plainly affirm that so as the difficulty of the matter of religion be provided for, and that all other points concerning the marriage may be performed as was communed upon in the person of Monsieur de Anjou, we find no cause of doubt, but that the King and Queen Mother shall obtain their desires. And after that you have declared thus much, because it is likely they will object that either this purpose of his coming over to us cannot be granted in respect of the honour of the King, in that heretofore no like usage hath been in the marriages of the children of France with any strange Prince, or that they shall doubt that this is by us in such sort propounded, as thereby to increase our own reputation without any intent to marry him, though his person might not mislike us.

To such objections you may answer thus. To the first you may say as of yourself, that you are not so acquainted with their own stories, and with the marriage of the children of France; yet you dare affirm that you know there can be no example showed of the like of this, that is, that either the elder son of France or any younger was at any time to be matched in marriage with such a Prince, having such kingdoms as we have, by whom such an advancement might have grown as may by marriage with us, both to the Duke himself, and to the King and Crown of France : and, therefore, this special cause can have no former example answerable to rule this, but this all ought to be followed with all manner of means, and all respect set aside.

And as to the second part that may be objected, you shall affirm certainly in our name, that we have no meaning hereby to gain any particular estimation to ourself, but do plainly and simply seek hereby to procure the satisfaction of our own mind in this difficulty, as touching his person, wherein no other of our own dare deal with us, nor we can otherwise be satisfied.   And for the preservation of the Duke's estimation and honour, we shall be as careful as his own brother, the King, shall be.   And, therefore, you shall conclude, that howsoever we have thus propounded our own conceit in the matter, we desire not that the King or the Queen Mother should do or consent to anything that might any wise seem for them dishonourable to the Duke.

Finally, if you shall perceive that they shall stick only upon the reputation of his honour, that is, to come and not be allowed for his person, you may as of yourself, propound it as you see cause, that the matter of religion may utterly be so left in suspense, as the breaking off, if any so should follow, either on his part, or on ours, may to the world be thereunto imputed.   And besides that his coming may be secretly and privately, without any outward pomp or show, whereof we leave the consideration to themselves.

VII. To Sir Francis Walsingham

The massacre of French Protestants begun at Paris on St. Bartholomew's Eve (23rd August), and continued in other cities of France, caused the greatest horror and alarm in England, not only because of its cruelty but because it appeared that this was the first incident in a general Catholic movement to extirpate all Protestants. It was nearly a month before the Queen could bring herself to give audience to the French Ambassador, de la Mothe Fenelon. At this difficult crisis the

Queen now instructed Walsingham to gather further and direct information from the French Court.

Reading, September 28, 1572.

De la Mothe, the French Ambassador, on Monday the 22th of this month having asked audience came to the Court at Reading, and there had large communication with us; the which seemed to us at that time the more strange, because we had heard before of the daily murdering of those of the Religion there in France, at Paris and at Orleans, as also at Lyons and Rouen, and divers other places and cities of that Realm, all the which was said to be done by the King's appointment and command- ment. Whereupon, when we had heard what he could say unto us, he heard us so reply at the time, as we did think he found himself unable to satisfy us, and nevertheless we told him, that we would be further advised for our answer, which he[1] should have within three or four days, whereupon communicating this negotiation, with our Council, upon their French tongue an answer as appeareth by this here enclosed, which is the copy of that which we delivered to Mirasius to interpret in French to the said de la Mothe as our full answer and resolution at the time, with the which, as Mirasius reporteth, de la Mothe seemed very well content and satisfied, in the which yet you may perceive that divers things are left to be further ascertained unto us by you.

Wherefore you shall do well with convenient speed to demand audience of the King, and there to declare, both to him and to the Queen Mother, what hath passed betwixt his Ambassador and us, and upon that point we did at that time stand. And you may say, as touching any worthy punishment executed upon his own subjects, we have not to deal therein, but if they have worthily suffered, we are sorry for their evil doings. But yet the King to destroy and utterly root out of his Realm all those of that Religion that we profess, and to desire us in marriage for his brother, must needs seem unto us at the first a thing very repugnant, and contrary to itself, specially having confirmed that liberty in them of the Religion by an Edict of his, perpetual and irrevocable; of the which to whom the liberty was granted, if any

---

[1] The MS. copy reads ' we ', and appears at this point to be inaccurate.

were partakers of any evil conspiracies against him, surely a great part of them must needs be ignorant, and ignorant of any evil fact or thought against him, especially women and innocent children, who, we do understand, are not yet spared. And therefore if that Religion of itself be so odious unto him that he thinks he must root out all the professors of it, how should we think his brother a fit husband for us, or how should we think that the love may grow, continue and increase betwixt his brother and us, which ought to be betwixt the husband and the wife.

You had in our former letters unto you things that we required you to decipher by all means that you could, especially, whether the King himself is inclined and bent to all these cruelties and the rooting out of true Religion, or whether he be but [   ] and overruled, to the which article hitherto you have not answered, and yet these things might give great light unto us, how to direct our action in the conferences and talks with his Ambassador.

And we would have you to be earnest in that matter of Strozzi, praying him frankly and roundly to declare unto us, what he meaneth, with that great army of ships and men of war, which hath been kept of long time close and undiscovered, to which intent or to what place it should be bent. You may say we have the more occasion to desire to know his meaning and dealing herein because of late they of Strozzi's company there hath spoiled divers of our merchants, some of their artillery and victual, and other of their goods and merchandises, as was accustomed betwixt the two Realms in times past, the which kind of dealing is very much contrary to the amity and to such things as by his Ambassador is propounded unto us; wherefore as we do go roundly and plainly to work with him to show flatly that which we do think or doubt upon, so do we pray him, with the same flatness and roundness to deal with us, for it is the way and means to make the continuance of amity and also the increase, and may induce us the sooner to come for a further resolution of such things as be required of us.

The Vidame of Chartres of whom we have great compassion is come into this Realm, at whose humble and lamentable suit, we have been content to write this letter to my brother the French

I

King, in his favour, which you shall deliver, with as good words as you may to the French King, and require his answer.

If this our letter do chance to come to you in Paris or in the way coming from Paris towards England, after you have obtained licence of the King to come away by favour of our letters, which we wrote unto him, yet, if you be not too far on the way, or very near the sea coast, we would you should return in post otherwise to the Court to hear a direct answer of the King to these our letters, except that great and unfeigned danger of yourself do move you to keep on journey. In which case you shall commit the doing of this passage and receiving of answer to your secretary, whom you shall leave behind, so that he be a man able to do this charge.

VIII. To George Talbot, Earl of Shrewsbury

Camden notes that in this year the Queen, ' who had hitherto enjoyed her health very perfectly (for she never did eat meat but when her appetite served her, nor drink wine without some allaying), fell sick of the small-pox at Hampton Court; but she recovered again before it was known abroad that she was sick.' To Shrewsbury's inquiries the following letter was sent, to which the Queen added a characteristic postscript.

October 21, 1572.

Right trusty and right well-beloved Cousin and Councillor, we greet you well. By your letters sent to us we perceive that you have heard of some late sickness wherewith we were visited; whereof as you had cause to be greatly grieved, so, though you heard of our amendment, and was thereby recomforted, yet, for a satisfaction of your mind, you are desirous to have the state of our amendment certified by some few words in a letter from ourself. True it is that we were about thirteen days past distempered as commonly happeneth in the beginning of a fever, but after two or three days, without any great inward sickness, there began to appear certain red spots in some part of our face, likely to prove the small-pox; but, thanked be God, contrary to the expectation of our physicians, and all others about us, the same so vanished away as within four or five days passed no token almost appeared; and at this day, we thank God, we are so free from any token or mark of any such disease that none can conjecture any such thing. So as by this you may perceive what was our sickness, and in what good estate we be; thanking you, good Cousin, for the care you had of the one, and of the comfort you take of the other, wherein we do assure ourself of as much fidelity, duty and love, you bear us as of any, of any degree within our realm. Given at our Castle of Windsor, the 22nd of October, 1572, the 14th year of our Reign.

[*To which the Queen herself added*]

MY FAITHFUL SHREWSBURY,

Let no grief touch your heart for fear of my disease; for I assure you, if my credit were not greater than my show, there is no beholder would believe that ever I had been touched with such a malady.

Your faithful, loving Sovereign,
ELIZABETH R.

IX. TO SIR FRANCIS WALSINGHAM, AMBASSADOR IN FRANCE

The first horror at the French massacre having subsided, the French King wished to resume negotiations with the Queen. In November he sent over as Ambassador Extraordinary Castelnau de Mauvissière to smooth over difficulties; to invite the Queen to be godmother to the King's infant daughter; to persuade her to refrain from actively helping the Huguenots besieged in Rochelle; and to continue the negotiations for the marriage.

c. December 1572.

There hath been with us Monsieur de Mauvissière, with the letters from the King and Queen Mother, and the Duke of Alençon. His credence was in three points: the continuance of the amity; that we should be godmother to the infant; and to pursue still to the request of marriage with the Duke of Alençon. To whom we answered: first, that as for amity, having it of late by league so straitly made betwixt us on our behalf we never attempted nor minded to attempt anything that should impair it, but rather do study and wish to increase the same if we could. And, therefore, you may say it is that, and the goodwill appertaining to that amity, that made us by you before, and now by de Mauvissière, to declare what we have heard of our good Brother we are sorry to hear.

First, the great slaughter made in France of Noblemen and Gentlemen, unconvicted and untried, so suddenly (as it is said at his commandment) did seem with us so much to touch the honour of our good Brother, as we could not but with lamentation and with tears of our heart, hear it of a Prince so near allied unto us and in a chain of undissoluble love knit unto us by league and oath. That being after excused by a conspiracy and treason wrought against our good Brother's own person, which whether it was true or false, in another Prince's kingdom and jurisdiction where we have nothing to do we minded not to be curious. Yet that they were not brought to answer by law and to judgement, before they were executed, those who were found guilty, we do hear it marvellously ill-taken as a thing of a terrible and dangerous example, and are sorry that our good Brother was so ready to condescend to any such counsel, whose nature we took to be more humane and noble, but when more was added unto it, that women, children, maids, young infants and sucking babes, were at the same time murthered and cast into the river; and that liberty of execution was given to the vilest and basest sort of the popular, without punishment or revenge of such cruelty done afterwards by law, upon those cruel murderers of such innocents: this increased our grief and sorrow in our good Brother's behalf that he should suffer himself to be led by such inhuman Councillors.

And now, sithence, it doth appear by all doings, both by the Edicts and otherwise, that the vigour is used only against them of the Religion Reformed whether they were of any conspiracy or no, and that contrary to the Edict of Pacification so oftentimes repeated, they of the Reformed Religion are either driven to fly, to die, or to recant or lose their offices; whereby it doth appear by all actions now used by our good Brother that his scope and intent doth tend only to subvert that Religion that we do profess, and to root it out of his Realm. At the least all the strangers of all nations and religions so doth interpret it, as may appear by the triumphs and rejoicings set out, as well in the

Realm of France as others, which maketh that it must needs seem very strange, both to us and to all other, that our good Brother should require us to be Godmother to his dear child, we being of that Religion which he doth now persecute and cannot abide within his Realm. And if we should believe the persuasion of others, and the opinion of all strangers our friends, who be not our subjects, we should not in no case condescend to any association in that or any other matter.

But as we have always hitherto had a special love to our good Brother in his younger age and a desire to the consideration of his good estate and quietness which we have indeed manifestly showed, never seeking any advantage of time against him as peradventure other Princes would have done, but ever sought to preserve his estate and his subjects, of what quality or condition in religion whatsoever they were, exhorting them to unity and concord and with loyal heart to live together in quiet under our good Brother, without offering injury the one to the other, glad of their agreement, and sorry of their division and discord. So the late league of straighter amity made betwixt our good Brother and us, to the which he did so frankly and lovingly condescend, or rather procure it at our hands, is so fresh in our memory that we cannot suffer that in any jot it should be diminished, but rather increased daily so long as our good Brother doth show the like unto us, and that maketh us to interpret all things in better part than otherwise by any means they can appear, such is our love to our good Brother, and so can we be content to persuade ourselves for the love that we do bear unto him and for the hope of his continuance in our begun amity, without faintness or dissimulation. And this for the matter of amity, we said to Mauvissière we would not be slack in any good office doing at the request of our good Brother. And so notwithstanding the doubts and impediments beforementioned, we intend to send a worthy personage, a nobleman of our Realm to repair to his Court, and to visit the King our good Brother, the Queen, and the Queen Mother, and the rest that hath written in our behalf, and to do that office which is required, as appertaineth, wishing that these spiritual alliances may be to our comforts and conservation of the amity begun betwixt us.

To the motion of the marriage with the Duke of Alençon, wherein de Mauvissière seemed somewhat earnest, after declaration of inconveniences that might come in that marriage, by the diversity of age and religion, which we termed in our talk extreme and true impediments, we made this final resolution and answer; that forasmuch as we had given to our Ambassador resident there charge to demand and make relation of certain things touching that matter to the King and Queen Mother, to the which you have had no answer, but of the Queen Mother in a certain generality; before that we shall have a special answer to them, we cannot well resolve; the which once being done, we shall the better understand what to answer for any other proceeding in that request.

x. To Sir William Fitzwilliams, the Lord Deputy, and the Council of Ireland

There was considerable trouble in Ireland in the early 1570's, caused partly by an ill-timed attempt at the plantation of Ulster, partly by the jealousies of the Lord Deputy. In the summer of 1572, Brian McPhelim, an Irish chieftain, murdered Henry Savage, one of the new colonists; the crime was not too displeasing to the Lord Deputy, who pardoned the murderer.

Greenwich, June 29, 1573.

We have received your letter of the 12th of June, in the which, for the matter of pardon granted, and also touching Sir Edward Fitton, having read and considered the whole that you have written, and likewise that he hath written, of that matter unto us, we cannot but mislike that you the Deputy should be so hasty to give such and so general a pardon upon the slaying of a gentleman: for, where the corrupt jury of the coroner's quest did find it but *se defendendo*, it may easily appear that was no true verdict, and that it was a murther; or else you would not in that case have made out a general pardon, but a particular pardon upon the indictment, and, of course, as in like cases are wont. But this pardon is so general, that all treasons, murders, and other enormities, and transgressions of laws be pardoned, and from the friend of the man murdered all prosecution of law taken away, such a one as we ourself (for we have seen the copy of it) would be afraid to grant, nor have not granted (to our knowledge) at any time since the first day of our reign : for it is not unknown to our Council here, and to all that have any doings with us, how seldom, and with what difficulty and conscience, we be brought to pardon any man where suspicion of murther and malice pretensed is; and how curious we be to be informed of the matter when any of our subjects be slain, before we will condescend to discharge any man of it. That discretion we looked for in you our Deputy, and therefore we put you in that place, lest the blood of the man slain should cry vengeance upon us and our Realm not doing justice for it, and that the punishment of the murder should be a terror to others to adventure upon the like. But if you our Deputy should overslip yourself in this, either by hastiness or temerity, yet, as it appeareth, you the rest of our Council there have done as little your duties to God and us, in that you would put your hands unto it; as, whatsoever the Deputy therein for the time should do and allow, you would straight run into the same rashness, and affirm it with subscription of your hands as applauders of our Deputy.

You be put there to be grave and sage advisers, to temper such sudden affections either the one way or the other, of love or of hatred, as may chance to our Deputy, being but a man made of flesh and blood, who cannot lightly be without them; and to have regard to God first, and then to our honour and the surety and good government of our Realm. Sir Edward Fitton seemeth to us a true and a good Councillor, who, seeing so unreasonable a pardon so unadvisedly granted, made stay of it to bring it unto you our Deputy to be better advised of it, not resisting, but discreetly requiring more mature consultation; and for this you will agree to put him to that shame as to commit him for a contemner of your doings, imputing rashness unto him in that behalf, where, in truth, he honoured us, in requiring more deliberation and regard than was had, to be had in justice, the which is clean taken away by that rash and unjust pardon. He refused to sit with you, and he had cause so to do, for it appeareth you are all rather followers of the Deputy's affections, than careful ministers of justice or of our honour. If you had done well, you should have done as he did, requiring the Deputy to stay to take better advisement: so should you have showed more care of justice, of our honour, and of the good government of that our realm, than of following the hasty affections of our Deputy. You are adjoined to him from us as Councillors, and in one commission, not to follow one head, or whatsoever the Deputy willeth; but to consider what is just and reason to be done, and so agree with him and set to your hands, and not otherwise; and therefore be you more than one, that, if need be, one may temper the other. Nicholas White, as appeareth by your letter, not daring to dissent against so running a consent, yet showed his conscience not to consent to affection, and would prescribe no punishment to that fact, which in his conscience he thought to be the duty of a good Councillor to do.

If this had been in our father's time, who removed a Deputy thence for calling of one of the Council dissenting from his opinion ' churl ', you may soon conceive how it would have been taken. Our moderate reign and government can be contented to bear this, so you will take this for a warning, and hereafter have before your eyes, not the will or pleasure of our Deputy or any other Councillor, but first God's honour, and then justice and our service, which is always joined to the good government of the realm, not following in any respect any private quarrels or affections. And as to you our Deputy, we shall hereafter write our mind more at large: so will we not forget to give thanks to our good cousin, the Earl of Kildare, for his good service. And we could be content that the Earl of Ormonde were at home. We have written to Sir Edward Fitton, willing him to join with you in Council, and take his place again; and do wish that, all sinister affections laid apart, you do join all in one to do that which may be to the honour of God and of our service, to the execution of justice, and to the good government of that Realm.

XI. To Dr. Richard Cox, Bishop of Ely

Sir Christopher Hatton, now one of the Queen's favourites, coveted Ely Place with its gardens in Holborn. Dr. Cox, the Bishop of Ely, refused to part with the property of his See. The Queen was angry.

PROUD PRELATE,

You know what you were before I made you what you are now. If you do not immediately comply with my request, I will unfrock you, by God.

ELIZABETH.

XII. TO DR. VALENTINE DALE, AMBASSADOR IN FRANCE

When Walsingham returned to England in 1573, he was succeeded as Ambassador in France by Dr. Valentine Dale. The Queen Mother of France was anxious that Alençon should come over to England to advance his suit with Queen Elizabeth, who affected to see difficulties in the suggestion.

Hampton Court, February 3, 1574

Whereas the French Ambassador, since the return of our servant Randolf, hath sundry times had access unto us, requiring our answer whether we could allow of the coming over of the Duke of Alençon upon the view of his portraiture brought over by our said servant: you shall therefore, at the time of your audience with the King and his Mother, show them that the cause of our stay in answering them hath proceeded upon two respects. The one, for that we have had sundry conferences with our Council to know their opinions what inconvenience might follow, if upon a public and open interview there should not grow satisfaction of our persons; for that we would be loath that the King our good Brother, seeking to enter into straighter amity with us by this offer of marriage, there should fall out such discontentment by this occasion through not satisfaction, as might impair the good amity already between us, and therefore we thought it a matter worthy of good deliberation. The other, for that as well upon the discovery of a late enterprise intended against those of Rochelle, as other advertisements from that country, there is conceived in the hearts of our good subjects a new jealousy and misliking of this match, and, therefore, we, desiring nothing more than the conversation and continuance of their good devotion towards us, know not what to resolve. Notwithstanding, being pressed by their Ambassador to yield our answer, he received the same from us as followeth. We showed him that whereas he used divers reasons to persuade us to give our consent to an open and public interview, we could in no case be led to yield thereto: for that we can be put in no comfort by those that desire most our marriage and are well affected to that Crown, who have also seen the young gentleman, that there will grow any satisfaction of our persons. And, therefore, you may say that if it were not more to satisfy the earnest request of our good Brother the King and the Queen his Mother (whose honourable dealings towards us as well in seeking us himself, as in offering unto us both his brethren,[1] we cannot but esteem as an infallible argument of their great good wills towards us) we could in no case be induced to allow of his coming neither publicly nor privately, for that we fear (notwithstanding the great protestations that he and his Mother make to the contrary) that if upon the interview satisfaction follow not, there is like to ensue thereby instead of straighter amity, disdain, unkindness, and a gall and wound of that good friendship that is already between us. The doubt whereof maketh us very much perplexed to yield to a thing that we in our conceit greatly fear will not have that good success and issue that of either party is desired. Notwithstanding, if you shall see that the doubts that we lay before them shall not stay them, but that Monsieur le Duke will needs come over in some disguised sort: that then you shall tell the King from us, that we desire that the gentleman in whose company he shall come over (as one of his followers) may be one not of so great quality as the Duke of Montmorency, nor accompanied with any great train, to avoid the suspicion that otherwise will be of his coming. For that if there follow no liking between us after a view taken the one of the other, the more secretly it be handled, the less touch will it be to both our honours.

We are of late earnestly requested by a daughter of the Duke of Montpensier, who is presently in house with the Elector Palatine in Germany, to recommend her reasonable request unto the King, our good Brother, and to Queen Mother, which is that she may enjoy the benefit of the Edict, such her living as she

---

[1] i.e. first Henri, Duke of Anjou and now King of Poland; and second, the Duke of Alençon.

hath in France, during the time of her absence, being withdrawn from thence in respect of the liberty of her conscience. You shall, therefore, say unto Queen Mother from us, that we desire her to join with you in the furtherance of this suit unto the King her son, our good Brother, who, we hope, as well for our sakes as that the gentlewoman is so near of blood unto her children, and that it is a natural virtue incident to our sex to be pitiful of those that are afflicted, will so tender her case as by her good means the gentlewoman shall be relieved and we gratified, which we shall be ready to requite as occasion shall serve us.

XIII. To John Harington

John Harington was the Queen's godson, and at this time a boy of fourteen. The letter was sent with a copy of the Queen's speech to Parliament delivered on 15th March.

March 1575.

Boy Jack, I have made a clerk write fair my poor words for thine use, as it cannot be such striplings have entrance into Parliament assembly as yet. Ponder them in thy hours of leisure, and play with them till they enter thine understanding; so shalt thou hereafter, perchance, find some good fruits hereof when thy Godmother is out of remembrance; and I do this because thy father was ready to serve and love us in trouble and thrall.

XIV. To Walter Devereux, Earl of Essex

In 1573 Essex went out to Ireland to be Governor of Ulster to pacify and colonize the Province. He met with great difficulties. The Lord Deputy (Fitzwilliams) was jealous of him and hampered his efforts; whilst at home divided counsels and the jealousy of Leicester (who was in love with the Countess of Essex) made it impossible for Essex to carry out any policy. He was ordered to resign his command to the Lord Deputy. Then he was ordered to resume it, and to continue the pacification of Ulster. Hardly had he gathered his forces again when he received instructions to cease the campaign and make as honourable a peace as he could. The Queen endeavoured to justify the vacillations of her policy in the following letter.

St. James's, May 22, 1575.

Whereas it may seem somewhat strange unto you, considering our late commandment given unto you to resume the government of Ulster lately given over by you, as also to proceed in your former enterprise, that we should now be of another opinion; we thought good for your better satisfaction in this behalf, to discover unto you that in very deed, notwithstanding our said commandment, we had no meaning that you should proceed in this service, otherwise than we thought it necessary for a time, in respect of the danger you laid before us of a general revolt, to will you to resume the said government, and to proceed in the said enterprise; which thing we would not have concealed from you, but that we doubted that the knowledge thereof might have quite discouraged you from proceeding therein; whereof there might have followed presently some dangerous issue, if, by a new resumption of the government of that Province, the same should not have been prevented. But now having more just occasion of late to look more inwardly into our estate at home, and finding great cause for us to forbear the prosecution of your enterprise; not for that we have any cause at all to mislike the same, or to doubt of the likelihood of the good success thereof, either for that the matter was not well digested, or should not be by you well executed, if other respects did not most necessarily draw us from the proceeding therein; we thought it very convenient to dispatch this bearer secretly unto you, to give you notice thereof, to the end you may, upon knowledge of the same, direct the course of your proceedings in such sort, as the enterprise may yet be so given over as our honour may best be salved; the safety of such as depend upon us in some good sort provided for: and that Province left in that state, so far forth as shall lie in you, as there may follow no such alteration as may disquiet the rest of that our Realm. And for that upon conference with certain of our Council we find it hard for us here, not seeing the true state of things there, to prescribe unto you any certain form how the same may best be done, we thought it most expedient to refer it to your own good consideration, and when you shall have so yourself thoroughly resolved on the course that in your opinion you think best to be taken, as also conferred therein with our Deputy, then would we have you with all convenient speed advertise us of the same, and yet in the meantime knowing our disposition in this behalf, to direct your proceedings accordingly. And so for some other points, referring you to such instructions as shall be delivered to this bearer, to be communicated unto you, signed by certain of our Privy Council, we end.

xv. To Walter Devereux, Earl of Essex

In the summer of 1575, Essex had achieved some successes in Ulster, but ' in the midst of his course of victory, he was again, beyond his expectation, commanded to resign his authority, and as an ordinary Captain had the command of three hundred men given him, and through Leicester's cunning dealing nothing was omitted whereby to break his wild spirit with continual crosses, one in the neck of another' (Camden). To an official letter thanking him for his services, the Queen added in her own hand:

August 6, 1575.

If lines could value life, or thanks could answer praise, I should esteem my pen's labour the best employed time that many years hath lent me. But to supply the want that both these carrieth, a right judgement of upright dealing shall lengthen the scarcity that either of the other wanted. Deem, therefore, Cousin mine, that the search of your honour, with the danger of your breath, hath not been bestowed on so ungrateful a Prince that will not both consider the one and reward the other.

Your most loving cousin and Sovereign,

E.R.

xvi. To George Talbot, Earl of Shrewsbury, and his Countess

The Earl of Leicester was entertained by the Earl and Countess of Shrewsbury whilst taking the cure at Buxton baths. The Queen wrote a frolicsome letter to his hosts, thanking them for their hospitality and prescribing a suitable diet for Leicester, who was indeed a hearty feeder.

June 4, 1577.

Right Trusty,

Being given to understand from our cousin, the Earl of Leicester, how honourably he was lately received and used by you, our cousin the Countess at Chatsworth, and how his diet is by you both discharged at Buxton, we should do him great wrong holding him in that place in our favour in which we do, in case we should not let you understand in how thankful sort we accept the same at both your hands, which we do not acknowledge to be done unto him but to our self; and therefore do mean to take upon us the debt and to acknowledge you both creditors so you can be content to accept us for debtor, wherein is the danger unless you cut off some part of the large allowance of diet you give him, lest otherwise the debt thereby may grow to be so great as we shall not be able to discharge the same, and so become bankrupt. And therefore we think it for the saving of our credit meet to prescribe unto you a proportion of diet which we mean in no case you shall exceed, and that is, to allow him by the day for his meat two ounces of flesh, referring the quality to yourselves, so as you exceed not the quantity, and for his drink the twentieth part of a pint of wine to comfort his stomach, and as much of St. Anne's sacred water as he listeth to drink. On festival days, as is meet for a man of his quality, we can be content you shall enlarge his diet by allowing unto him for his dinner the shoulder of a wren, and for his supper a leg of the same, besides his ordinary ounces. The like proportion we mean you shall allow to our brother of Warwick, saving that we think it meet that in respect that his body is more replete than his brother's, that the wren's leg allowed at supper on festival days be abated, for that light supper agreeth best with rules of physic. This order our meaning is you shall inviolably observe, and so may you right well assure yourselves of a most thankful debtor to so well deserving a creditor.

XVII. To William Davison

The Queen was utterly opposed to the proposal that Alençon should help the States against the Spanish King, for she thought at this time that Alençon was supported by his brother, the French King, and it was contrary to her interests to have the French predominant in Flanders. She therefore wrote to Davison, who was resident English Agent at Antwerp, to exert pressure on the States to reject Alençon's offer of assistance.

Greenwich, May 22, 1578.

We perceive by your letters of the 17th of this present directed to our Principal Secretaries that the Prince and States are so fully determined to conclude with Monsieur, that the matter is not to be called back, wherein we cannot but think ourself dishonourably dealt withal contrary to the promises of the States made unto us and signified by you in your letters to our said Secretaries bearing date the 5th and 28th of the last month, affirming unto you, as you have delivered it unto us, that whatsoever passed in conference there, nothing should be concluded without our knowledge and consent: the like whereof had been beforetime confirmed unto us under the hands and seals of the said States; which we could not persuade ourself could have been gone from by them, seeing our offices continued as friendly towards them ever since as before. Whereinto if they will thoroughly and thankfully look, they cannot but condemn themselves of ingratitude, considering we have not only yielded to furnish them with great sums of money from time to time, and procured them aid out of Germany, under the conduct of Duke Casimir, and never refused to yield assistance when it should appear unto us that they should stand in need thereof; but also hazarded to cast ourselves into enmity and war with the King of Spain for their sake.

And on the contrary side if they do well look into the course which they are entered into, they shall find that this French aid is more like to turn them to hurt than help, which kind of dealing we see to be of so ill consequence; that were it not for the love we bear to those countries and the care we have of their safety, we should not only be discouraged from further dealing with them, but also be driven to join with Don John. But because we do not yet rest fully informed touching their said proceedings with the French: you shall press both the Prince and Marquis and such other of the State as you shall think meet, to send us a copy of the true capitulation that passed between them and the Deputies for Monsieur with protestations under their hands that they have proceeded no further with Monsieur than is contained in the said capitulation.

And in case they have not further proceeded herein; then (as you write unto our said Secretaries) the Prince assured you of, to wit that the said Monsieur should serve them with ten thousand footmen, and two thousand horse for two months at his own charges; that he was content to employ himself where and in what place they would; that he was content to be commanded of them, or of the Count Bossu or any other they would appoint (the Archduke only except) that he would not give over the action until he had expulsed the enemy, requiring nothing of them, but to be received as their Governor, if after three months time after their deliverance wrought by his means; they should advise and determine to alter the Government and change their masters; that then we receiving assurance under the Prince's hand and the States', that in case they may receive assistance from us besides the aid procured unto them at our charges under Casimir; he and they will proceed to no further dealing with Monsieur : we will be content to send them the said assistance with all convenient speed. In which case if you shall receive answer to our contentment, then we mean to send over with all expedition the Lord Cobham, Warden of the Cinque Ports, Sir Francis Walsingham, Knight, one of our Principal Secretaries, to confer with them touching such aid, as shall be necessary for their defence, and divers other things tending to their benefit.

But in case you shall find the Prince and other of the States to make difficulty in this behalf, whereby it shall appear, that they are altogether given over to the French : then you shall let them understand, that our meaning is, that the money lately sent shall be stayed, and Duke Casimir required to forbear to come to their assistance. And, in the meantime, you shall send with all speed to Duke Casimir to inform him of the States' proceedings with Monsieur, and also of the answer which you shall now receive from the Prince and the States, and of our purpose to send over the Lord Cobham and our Secretary Sir Francis Walsingham, and therefore to advise him for his own safety to make stay in repairing to the place of his general muster until it may be discovered what this conclusion with Monsieur tendeth unto : which being once deciphered, the money shall be sent with all speed, being already (as you may write) in Antwerp; as we hope the same is before the arrival of this letter; from whence it may be conveyed in four or five days space to Cologne, where he desired the same to be delivered.

XVIII. To Francis, Duke of Anjou

The proposed marriage was causing much discontent in England.

Translated from the French

Westminster, February 14, 1579.

If the urgent request of this bearer did not constrain me, I should not have annoyed your eyes with another letter so soon after my last, although my courage was doubled by the good acceptance which the others had; whereby you put me under obligation, as on other occasions of more consequence. Of which your return to France in consequence of your wish to come to me has not been the least. It was not a thing I should have wished, fearing how it might end; but my desire would be quite other if I am to understand by it that you have set aside most of the advice in order to follow the desire which proceeds from yourself. I assure you I am much displeased that that ungrateful multitude, a true mob, should so misuse such a Prince; and I think that God, if not men, will be revenged on them for it, and am glad that you have safely escaped their iniquitous hands. Nor do I doubt that having passed Scylla you will beware of entering Charybdis, as I beg M. Simier to set out to you at more length, as also in respect of the advice which you have asked of me; protesting that though I recognize by lack of wit to instruct you, you may accept it as from one who will never have a thought not dedicated to your honour and will never betray you by her advice, but will give it as if my soul depended thereon.

XIX. To William, Prince of Orange

An example of the everyday correspondence on State matters, showing how Elizabeth could contrive to keep the peace and yet be firm enough in obtaining satisfaction for the wrongs of her subjects.

K

Translated from the French

April 27, 1579.

You will remember how about two years ago some of our subjects, merchants of Ipswich, were captured by the fleet of Holland and Zealand on its way back from Spain and taken to Flushing, contrary to all law, divine and human. Now, though we might justly have taken vengeance for this as for a manifest wrong done to us, yet, remaining constant in our ancient desire for the good and safety of those Provinces, we were content for the time to wink at the fault, and postpone our just wrath to the advancement of their affairs, which would have suffered to no small extent if we had taken up the case of our subjects in good earnest, consenting to the agreement by which the Provinces were to pay them in four years the sum you wot of as compensation, though it was not very advantageous for them. Yet our subjects complain to us that though by their agents they have made demand in Zealand for the payment of the fourth part, due in October last, they have not profited one little bit, but rather have received rude enough answers and no hope of satisfaction. This seems to us so strange, and shows so openly the small respect which those of Holland and Zealand have for us (seeing that instead of being the more prompt to give satisfaction for having been thereto invited by our kindness they have become overproud and insolent), that for the sake of our honour and the care we have for our subjects we can no longer put off taking steps which may chance to be a little rough upon them, if they do not prevent us betimes by taking order for the due satisfaction of our subjects. We beg you to set your hand to this with all your might, that we may be able to continue our good affection to the Provinces, and refrain from attempting aught to their prejudice, which we should be very sorry to be compelled to do. We have thought good to apprise you first, as one who we think would not wish to give an opening to the inconveniences that may ensue.

xx. To Sir Amyas Paulet

Sir Amyas Paulet was Ambassador in France from 1576-1579. In this letter the Queen instructs him to express her

annoyance that Simier, by his instructions, had proposed un-
acceptable conditions for the marriage, whereby her own gifts of
body and mind are slighted.

May 9, 1579.

Trusty &c., Finding de Simier at a certain late conference
between him and some of our Council about the treaty of
marriage between the Duke his master and us, to insist very
peremptorily upon certain articles that have always heretofore
been denied to such Princes as in former time have sought us in
way of marriage, as also to the King, the said Duke his brother (a
thing falling out far contrary to our expectation), considering that
before his repair hither we caused one of our secretaries to advertise him (upon view of certain letters of his directed to the King's
Ambassador here, by which he signified unto him, that he was
to repair hither about the interview and the concluding of the
articles) that our meaning was not to enter into any treaty of
articles, being resolved not to yield to any other than were before
agreed on between us and other Princes that have sought[1] . . .
like case, and therefore advised him to forbear to [come hither]
if he were sent to any such end; only thus . . . that in case any
of the said articles were doubtful or obscure, to explain and make
them more clear. We have therefore thought meet, for that we
know not what to judge of such a strainable kind of proceeding,
even at that time when to our seeming we were growing to a
conclusion touching the interview, to acquaint you therewith, to
the end that you may let both the King and Monsieur know
what we conceive thereof.

And for that you may the more substantially and fully deal
therein, you shall understand that the articles, upon which he did
at the said conference with certain of our Council insist, were
three. The first, that the said Duke might jointly have authority
with us to dispose of all things donative within this our Realm,
and other our dominions. The second, that he might be after
marriage crowned King, offering certain cautions that nothing
should be done thereby to the prejudice of our Realm. And
lastly, that he might have threescore thousand pounds' pension
during his life. Touching the first, the inconveniencies were

[1] The manuscript is damaged in the bottom outer corners.

laid before him by our said Council, who declared unto him that it was a matter that greatly toucheth our Regality, insomuch as Monsieur mought have thereby *vocem negativam*; and also, that, in the marriage between the King of Spain and our late sister, the contents of that demand was by an especial article prohibited in the treaty between them, which afterwards was ratified by Parliament: yet was he not without great difficulty drawn to desist from urging us to yield our consent therein, notwithstanding he was plainly given to understand that our consenting thereto could not but breed a dangerous alienation of our subjects' goodwill from us. And, for the other two articles, it was showed unto him, that the consideration of the said articles being committed to our whole Council, it was by them, after long deliberation had thereon, resolved, that they were not presently to be granted or considered of, but by the Council of the whole Realm in Parliament, without whose consent they could no wise be accorded unto, and therefore thought meet to be held in suspense until the Duke's coming over; with which answers he not resting satisfied, did still peremptorily insist in pressing the granting of the same, plainly protesting as well to ourself as to our Council, that though he had very ample and large authority to treat and deal in the cause, yet durst he not take upon him (considering what curious eyes there were bent to behold his actions and doings in this cause) to qualify the said articles. And th . . . would no otherwise be satisfied unless he might have our private allowance and assurance that the said . . . articles should be both pro . . . ed by consent . . . ; wherein, though it was very [evident] unto him [how]dishonourable it would be for us to give any such private assurance in a matter that rested in the allowance and consent of others, and how much the same would mislike our subjects that any such thing should be yielded unto before such time as it were seen what contentment of our persons might grow by the interview, yet did he not forbear still to press us therein.

Whereupon, we finding that by no persuasion that could be used, either by us or by our Council, he could be induced to allow of our answers, both we and certain of our Council did plainly let him know that such a kind of insisting upon such articles as had been denied to other Princes (specially having before his repair hither let him understand that our meaning was not to alter former articles, but only to clear such as were obscure and doubtful) did minister unto us just cause of suspicion, either to think that they had no mind of further proceeding (by standing upon such hard points as in reason we could not yield unto), or else that they sought this match to some other end than hitherto hath been by them pretended, having always heretofore, as well by letters as by most earnest speeches and protestations, given out that not our fortune but our person was the only thing that was sought : which, upon the conclusion seeming to fall out otherwise, as manifestly appeareth by their insisting upon points chiefly incident, and depending upon our fortune, giveth us just cause to suspect that the mark that is shot at, is our fortune and not our person; for if the affection were so great as is pretended, neither would the Duke have directed him, his minister, to have stood upon so hard conditions, nor himself made so great difficulty to have come over and seen us without standing upon so many ceremonies being persuaded that a Duke of Anjou could receive no dishonour by taking a journey to see a Queen of England, whatsoever success the end of his coming took; when as, at the least there could not but grow thereby increase of friendship. For we are well assured that his repair unto us could not be accompanied with harder success (we will not say with so great dishonour) than his late voyage into the Low Countries; and therefore we saw no cause why the one might not be performed with as little difficulty as the other if they were both sought with like goodwill and devotion. It was also declared unto him, that if they had to deal with a Princess that had either some def[ect] of body or some other notable defect of nature, or l[acking gif]ts of the mind fit for one of our place and quality . . . such a kind of strainable proceeding (carrying a greater show of profit than of goodwill) might in some sort have been tolerated. But, considering how otherwise our fortune laid aside, it hath pleased God to bestow His gifts upon us in good measure, which we do ascribe to the Giver, and not glory in them as proceeding from ourselves (being no fit trumpet to set out our own praises), we may in true course of modesty think ourself worthy of as great a Prince as Monsieur is, without yielding to such hard conditions as by persons of greater quality than himself (being denied your just cause) hath not been stood upon.

And so we concluded with him that seeing we saw apparently by their course of proceeding that we were not sought either with that affection or to that end we looked for, that we had just cause to think ourselves in this action not so well dealt with as appertained to one of our place and quality; having not without great difficulty won in ourself a disposition to yield to the match, in case upon the interview there should grow a liking of our persons. Wherein we showed him that if the Duke his master knew what advertisements were received from foreign parts, what effectual persuasions were used towards us at home, to dissuade us from the same, and how carefully we travailed to win our subjects to allow thereof (who are not the best affected to a foreign match) he should then see what wrong he has done us (we will not say unto himself) to stand so much upon terms of profit and reputation. Assuring him therefore, that seeing we saw we had just cause to doubt that there was not that account made of our plain and friendly dealing in this action towards him that we looked for, and as we conceived that we have deserved, that the Duke his master should perhaps hereafter hardly draw us to yield so far forth as we have already done, unless we should find him, and that by effects, to be otherwise affected towards us than as yet we can perceive he is; wishing him therefore, and rather advising him, to proceed in the other matches that by some of his nearest friends are (as we be not ignorant of) embraced, whereof it should seem by the manner of dealing, both he and they have better liking.

And as for the gentleman himself, de Simier, whom we found greatly grieved for that he saw we could not allow of his insisting upon the said articles as a matter very offensive unto us, we did assure him that we had [no cause] to mislike of him, who [has borne himself] in no other sort than either his was directed; . . . otherwise (though his authority were large) he could not without peril to himself, in respect of such as are not the best affected towards him, follow his own discretion and affection to the cause; having found in him otherwise so great fidelity towards his master, so rare a sufficiency and discretion in one of his years in the handling of the cause, and so great devotion towards the match itself, as we had both great reason to like of him, as also to wish that we had a subject so well able to serve us. And, therefore, we would have you let both the King and the Duke his master understand how well we conceive of the gentleman, and how happy his master may think himself to have so rare a servant. Having thus at large laid before you the whole course of our late proceeding with de Simier, and the effect of such speech as both by ourself and our Council have been delivered unto him, we nothing doubt but that you will report the same both to the King and to the Duke in that good sort as both they may be induced to see their error, and we discharged of such calumniations as perhaps by such as are maliciously affected towards us in that Court may be given out against us.

YOUR SOVEREIGN.

XXI. TO FRANCIS, DUKE OF ANJOU

Written apparently when Anjou was refusing to consider the terms brought back by Simier, especially the clauses concerning his practice of the Catholic religion.

Translated from the French

December-January, 1579-80.

MONSIEUR,

When I remember that there is no debt more lawful than the word of a just man nor anything which binds our actions more than a promise, I should be too forgetful of your behalf and my honour, if I were to overslip the term appointed for my answer to the matter which for so long we have treated. You are not ignorant, my dearest, that the greatest impediments lie in making our people rejoice and applaud. To which effect I have taken time which ordinarily would be more than reasonable, and having tried them all, have not forborne to declare unto you roundly what I know and what you will always find true. I see well that many repent of making rash judgements at the first cast without having weighed in the best balance the depth of their opinions. I assure myself that some, with the hazard of their own lives, wish not to be so foolishly guided. Notwithstanding,

I promise you on my faith, that has never yet received spot, that the public exercise of the Roman Religion sticks so in their hearts that I would never consent for you to come among such a company of malcontents until you be pleased to consider that the commissioners relax the strait terms that Monsieur Simier offered us because I would not wish you to send them without the cause being thereby concluded. I beg you to consider deeply of this, as of a matter which is so hard for Englishmen to bear that you could imagine without knowing it. For my part, I confess that there is no Prince in the world to whom I would more willingly give myself than to yourself, nor to whom I think myself more bound, nor with whom I would pass the years of my life, both for your rare virtues and sweet nature, accompanied with such honourable parts as I cannot recount for number, nor would be so bold to mention for the time that it would needs take. In such wise if you be pleased to consider how that sincerity goes with me in this negotiation, from the beginning until now, I doubt not that I shall appear before the seat of your true judgement to quit me of all subtlety and dissimulation. I doubt of your particular consent, being myself uncertain as much whether I should refuse to comply since I was not assured as, that I should consent, seeing the great questioning which was being made respecting the nation to which you belong, then respecting the form of government, and several other things which must not be written down. In the which having used so many means to make these things agreeable, I do not believe that I have done hard work, but rather mighty labour, for a whole week. And at this hour, I would not deceive you by not laying before your eyes openly how I find the case, and what I think of it, in which I have had so much regard to your ease and content, as if for my own life or the consideration of my estate, which would otherwise have moved me to make different answer. And, to conclude, I cannot and I will not have this negotiation trouble us further, but rather that we may rest faithful friends, and assured in all our actions; unless it please you to make some resolution other than the open exercise of the Religion, and it seems good to you to write to me on that point, or to send some good answer, for I desire nothing but what contents you. There are still several things to be said regarding your allowance, which I have charged this bearer to declare to you much better, as the other matters, whom it will please you of your wonted goodness to hear, and to trust yourself to him as faithful, as you know him to be and as I have well proved; for which I owe you a million thanks for the honour, favour and liberality which you have used in his behalf, wherewith you have greatly obliged me before. I received eight days since a letter which you please to have sent me, wherein I see that your affection is not lessened by absence, nor grows cold by persuasions, for which I can only return a sincere and irremovable goodwill, quick to serve you on all contrary and evil occasions, and such that I will never desert your fortune, but take my share in it. I have never heard from you any news either of France or of the Low Countries, or of any other quarter since the coming of Simier, and believe that you have too much distrust in a woman's silence, or else I should learn less by other means and more by you. For of another place I learn more than you are pleased to communicate, as God knows, Whom I pray keep you in good life and long; with my commendations to my dearest Frog.

XXII. To Francis, Duke of Anjou

The previous letter did not please Anjou, who complained that the Queen (according to general belief) was using the difference in religion as a pretext to break off the negotiations. The Queen now raised further difficulties.

Translated from the French

January 17, 1580.

My excessive delay, my dearest, in not acknowledging the infinite ways in which my obligations on your behalf increase may render me rightly unworthy of treatment so honourable. But the extreme pain in my throat continually this past fortnight will have force, I hope, to blot out such a thought. And at this hour, finding myself a little better, I present my humblest thanks for having shown us a shining rock, against which neither the tempests of false persuasion nor the storm of evil tongues have ever had power to move the constancy of your affection, whereof I confess myself very unworthy for any perfection that I possess, and for that matter, which seems to me so much the more notable as the occasion is simpler. For one thing I rejoice, that you are so well furnished with good advice that you will not be ignorant of some of my defects so that I am assured of not being found worse than they already make me. And besides, being so well advised, you will be well resolved or you will not hazard it. And I pray to God to give you the gift of clear sight to penetrate the abysm of their subtleties and that I live not to be the means of your dis-content. It is so difficult at this time to recognize the difference between seeming and being, so that I wish that the wisdom of Solomon dwelt in your spirit to discern the counterfeit from the true, and such as look further instead of setting you up as the aim for their shafts. Those must be most highly thought of who respect us, but not with a mixture of their greatness and govern-ment. But at this moment I muse as old women are wont in their dreams, not having slept well. I have received news from the King that the commissioners make themselves ready, but do not yet know that they are. I did not think before that France was so ill-furnished of Princes and persons of great rank that they would be constrained to send me a child or man of low birth. I believe that they do it to lessen the greatness of my honour, or to cause impediments not to send at all. I have notwithstanding used roundness with the King, sending to tell him by his Ambas-sador that I would not suffer a matter of so great weight to take any disgrace from the hate which is borne me. I have no mind to allow the chronicles to say that there will be an ill opinion of the makers of so great a feast, promising, I believe, that the King will hold in honourable consideration both the place which you bear and the spirit with which I bear myself. As for your com-missioners I take it for certain that you will chose without change the instrument to complete what he has so well begun. I speak of Simier, of whom having heard all that is laid against him, and seeing no reason to believe it, nor proof to condemn him, I swear to you, my dearest, that if he should go out of my life, I see no occasion for his exile. It is true that I know too much indignity used against your person by those who make the people believe that you are so arrogant and so inconstant that they can easily make us withdraw our favour from our dearest when they have us to themselves. And at convenient time I shall not fail to show you to their disgrace who were the authors of it. See where the love that I bear you carries me to make me act contrary to my nature (quite awry from those who fish in troubled waters) to thrust myself in another man's actions. Notwithstanding I cannot refrain from begging you, with hands clasped, to remember that we other Princes, holding ourselves in high places, are sought by the testimonies of several heads, amongst whom the greater part accuse us, as our favours are bound by slender threads which make them fear for their favour, amongst whom I wish you to be exempt. Behold, Monsieur, the foolishness of my understanding, who write to you of this matter in hope of a good answer, weighing the place in which you hold us with the company which is there. We poor inhabitants of a barbarous island are not willing to appear for judgement where such subtle judges of our comprehension hold so high a place in the seat of our favour. But appealing to Monsieur alone and not divided, I shall not cease from my suit, even if you should condemn me to the strapado. I shall not add gloss to this text, assuring myself that you understand it only too well. And finally I ask you to pardon this troublesome letter, and receive my humblest thanks for the offer that you make me to determine Simier's case as shall seem best to me, assuring you that I have never cared to give you advice which will betray your honour; I will die sooner. I am not partial to him that I forget you, and if there was any infidelity to you of which for my part I have any proof, he is but a stranger to me with whom I have nothing to do, as the Creator knows, Whom I pray grant you a hundred years of life, with my most affectionate commendations.

Postscript.—I beg you send your good pleasure by this bearer who will return in haste.

XXIII. To Sir Edward Stafford

Sir Edward Stafford was sent over in June 1580 to negotiate with Anjou concerning the Embassy which was to be sent to discuss the marriage. On 12th August a deputation of the States formally offered the sovereignty of the Netherlands to Anjou. On hearing the news the Queen, in considerable agitation, wrote to Stafford.

c. August 1580.

STAFFORD,

As I greatly regard your poor man's diligence, so I will not leave him unrewarded. For the charge, I have written to Monsieur[1] what I have given unto you, this it is: First, for the Commissioners' authorities, I have good reason to require that they may be as I desired, both for present mislikes as well as for after mishaps. It happened in Queen Mary her day, that when a solemn ambassade of five or six at the least, were sent from the Emperor and King of Spain, even after the articles were signed, sealed and the matter divulged, the danger was so near the Queen's chamber-door that it was high time for those messengers to depart without leave-taking; and bequeathed themselves to the speed of the river-stream, by water passed with all possible haste to Gravesend, and so away. I speak not this that I fear the like; but when I make collection of sundry kinds of discontentments, all tied in a bundle, I suppose the faggot will be harder altogether to be broken.

There is even now another accident fallen out, of no small consequence to this realm. I am sure the States have accorded to the demands of Monsieur, and do present him the sovereignty of all the Low Countries. Suppose, now, how this may make our people think well of him and of me, to bring them to the possession of such neighbours? Oh, Stafford, I think not myself well used, and so tell Monsieur that I am made a stranger to myself; who he must be, if this matter take place? In my name, show him how impertinent it is for this season to bring to the ears of our people so untimely news. God forbid that the banns of our nuptial feast should be savoured with the sauce of our subjects' wealth! Oh, what may they think of me, that for any glory of mine own would procure the ruin of my land? Hitherto they have thought me no fool; let me not live the longer the worse. The end crowneth the work.

I am sorry that common posts of London can afford me surer

---

[1] i.e. the Duke of Anjou.

news than the inhabitants of Tours will yield me. ·Let it please Monsieur to suspend his answer unto them till he send some unto me of quality and of trust to communicate and concur with that I may think good for both our honours; for I assure him, it shall too much blot his fame if he deal otherwise, not only in my sight, to whom it hath pleased him to promise more than that, but especially to all the world, that be overseers of his actions. Let him never procure her harm whose love he seeks to win. My mortal [foe can] wish me no greater loss than England's hate; neither should death be less welcome unto me, than such a mishap betide me. You see how nearly this matter wringeth me; use it accordingly: if it please him, the deputies may have the charge of this matter joined with the other [   ] that were afore-mentioned. I dare not assure Monsieur how this greater matter[1] will end, until I be assured what way he will take with the Low Countries; for rather will I never meddle with marriage, than have such a bad covenant added to my part. Shall it be ever found true, that Queen Elizabeth hath solemnized the perpetual harm of England under the glorious title of marriage with Francis, heir of France? No, no; it shall never be. Monsieur may fortune ask you why should not the Low Countries be governed by the in-dwellers of that country as they were wont, and yet under my superiority as that of the King of Spain? I answer, The case is too far different, since the one is far off by seas' distance, and the other near upon the continent. We, willingly, will not repose our whole trust so far on the French nation as we will give them in pawn all our fortune, and after-wards stand to their discretion. I hope I shall not live to that hour.

Farewell, with my assurance that you will serve with faith and diligence. In haste,

Your sovereign,

ELIZABETH.

---

[1] The marriage.

XXIV. To Jehan Simier

Written apparently in the summer of 1580 when the State formally invited Anjou to be their King. The Queen treated Simier with great familiarity, nicknaming him her Ape.

Translated from the French

August (?), 1580.

What a strange accident has befallen me that I was made to seem to bear displeasure for any honour which would come to Monsieur. I mean, my Ape, that the cause of the Low Countries will transform me in any other form, if you others treat it in such wise that it would not be possible for me to endure, except with good heart I made myself hated by my subjects and mocked by all the world, who regard the affairs of Princes the more because they are set in so high a place that each one is a spectator of our actions, and makes judgement of them according to the issue of our fortune. There is no pain that I would not endure rather than to give just cause to Monsieur (to whom I confess myself so greatly obliged) to doubt my sincerity in his affairs; but I assure myself he is of such ripe judgement, that being himself a Prince, he will measure me by the same, and will believe that I do not less esteem honour than my own advantage. For if it please him to withhold the reply resolved upon, until by some of his servants he understands what can conveniently be done for us both, I doubt not that you will make good order to content Monsieur, satisfy the States, and delight my subjects, of which the least, I assure myself, he has not the least care to content, considering the time, with what appertains to it. Also that Monsieur do not send the Commissioner with only one commission, but with the other, adding authority for Flanders, upon which will depend all the rest. You are so wise as to know without any other instruction how near it touches me that our people do not perceive in their Prince a negligence or a lukewarmness for their well-being and safety; we were not born only for ourselves. Ask in my name, I pray you, pardon of Monsieur for my hardihood in writing so roundly to him. When he remembers from what reason it arises, he will hold me excused; apart from the fact that young folk owe some reverence for the old, which will plead my cause. God knows from what heart my words proceed, and how it is it that directs my actions. And I conjure you, hold me for such for ever. And, Simier, meanwhile I will pray God to guide your counsels, that they be best for your master. With the best wishes for the Ape that he can desire. Adieu.

xxv. To Francis, Duke of Anjou

In the autumn of 1580, Simier (who had returned to France) was in such disgrace with his master that he was obliged to flee for his life. In November Edward Stafford, who had been sent to Anjou the previous year, was again sent over. On his return the Queen wrote to Anjou, pleading for Simier.

Translated from the French

December 19, 1580.

My dearest, if the thing long awaited had been good when it arrived, I had been better satisfied with the long wait which it has pleased Stafford to afford me. But seeing that the peace seems to be but half made, I do not see too much reason for him to make his sojourn unless he makes me believe that it was by your command, which I have every wish for him to obey : and having for his turn received letters from France that the King prolongs this peace under certain difficulties, which will not be capable of being too soon concluded, I would be well content that they ceased to wonder at his long stay, assuring myself that divers are making a game of him. And for the cause of the King of Navarre and his party, I will take the hardiness to tell you that it will touch you very near in reputation that they should be left in worse estate than they were at the beginning of these new troubles. For if their greatest sureties were snatched from them, how could they have any trust of the King; furthermore that the King himself sent to tell me by his ambassador that he would not deny them the first pacification and would not ask except for those towns and places newly taken. You will pardon me the curiosity which holds me in your actions, to which I wish all the honour and commendation which can accrue to the perpetual renown of a Prince.

I assure myself that the desire of greatness after this peace will not blind your eyes to make you omit that which will be for the safety of those who rely on your goodwill. As for the commissioners, I believe that they will resemble words, which too often repeated make the tongue trip disorderly. I see that the time slips away, and I it, to make me unapt to content you as I wish, and I am almost in accord with the opinion of those who cease not to remind you of my faults. But God, I hope, will govern all to your good. Let it not displease you, Monsieur, that I ask for some reply from Simier, for whom I wish some end of his misfortune; or that he may be justly condemned, and that you may be purged of a charge often laid upon Princes, whose favours are said to be held by very slender threads; or else that he may be employed in your service to stop the mouths of slanderers, who cease not to spend their time in matters and make their own interpretation of them. My dearest, I give you now a fair mirror wherein you may see clearly the foolishness of my judgement, who have found a time so fit to hope for a good conclusion, weighing the place where you dwell with the company which is there. We poor inhabitants of a barbarous isle must be on our guard against appearing for judgement where such wise judges of your knowledge hold their seat in so high a place of your favour. But making my appeal to Monsieur himself, not divided, I would not let fall my suit. And if you will award me the strappado, I would not add gloss to this text, assuring myself that you have understood it only too well. In fine my sole request consists in this that you always hold me for the same that you have obliged me to dedicate to you; and that I cannot but be she who has set you in the first rank of that which is most dear to me, as God can best testify, to Whom I will not cease my supplications that He may grant you a hundred years of life, with my humblest wishes to be commended to my dearest. From Westminster, this 19th of December.

Your very assured as she is bounden,
ELIZABETH R.

XXVI. To Francis, Duke of Anjou

*Written after the arrival of Marchaumont in February 1581
whilst the Queen was still waiting for the Commissioners from
France.*

Translated from the French

March 17, 1581.

My dearest, the honour which you do me is very great, sending me often your letters, but the pleasure I conceive from them
greatly exceeds it, wishing nothing so much as the continuance
of your good opinion towards me, thanking you most humbly
for the sweet flowers plucked by the hand with the little fingers,
which I bless a million times, and promise you that there was
never present better carried, for the verdure remained on them as
if they had been plucked this very instant, and showing me a
lively representation of your verdant affection towards me, and
hope that there shall never be given any just cause that it wither
through me. Monsieur, I have taken care not to lose a leaf or
a flower for all the other joys that I have. I beg you believe that
I cannot express the contentment that the bearer brings me, and
pardon me if he did not return sooner whilst awaiting my courier,
by whom I have received a letter from you, in which you oblige
me infinitely, not least by so many honourable offers quite full of
affection, that although I cannot satisfy them at all, certain it is
I shall not fail to recognize them by all the means in my power.
I am content, Monsieur, that you are assured of me as the most
faithful friend that ever Prince had, and if you . . .[1] all the
tempests of the sea cannot remove, nor any storm by land will
turn it aside from honouring and loving you. There has [not]
been any word written to separate me from your affection, but in
order that you should not be ignorant of all that was done here.
But what I ought to think, I know not, unless that you render
me obliged to you for ever, and I shall never think otherwise of
you than as the same honour and . . .[2] full of all virtues. As
the Creator knows, Whom, with my most cordial commendations,
I pray grant you all honour and contentment in the world, beg-

---

[1] Untranslatable. The original reads, '*espuiras a tel Vochir*'.
[2] '*Monieau.*'

L

ging you always to keep me in your good graces. From Westminster, this 17 of March.

Your most obliged for ever,
ELIZABETH R.

XXVII. TO FRANCIS, DUKE OF ANJOU

Written whilst the French commissioners were deliberating in London.

Translated from the French

May 1581.

Monsieur, I see well that conjurations are both spiritual and diabolic, first of all because they accomplish much in the eyes of the credulous. I doubt not that you will remember how in your last letter it pleased you to charge me by all the affection that you avowed of old that I would give you a final answer for the direction of the commissioners, and that if the time seemed not convenient, then I should defer it. But to this hour I feel myself so bound by the charm which you lay on me that I cannot persuade myself other than that the Holy Spirit this Pentecost has inspired me to obey your desires, having shown me a rare constancy and affection so signal, which gives me hope that all good fortune will follow so noble a beginning; and for that, if it please you to give order, your deputies can hold themselves ready to come at the time which you think most convenient, considering the time of the year, which seems to me very hot, for an assembly so great as our Parliament requires. But I refer all to your good judgement, postponing all impeachments, and stopping my ears to the Sirens that by fair persuasions of my own advantage have somewhat retarded the marriage, considering my age, which could easily make me believe, if there were no other reason, that this conclusion would be very convenient for me. But persuading myself that your denying spirit and understanding, so settled, assures me that you would not willingly buy repentance so dearly, without (not having had so long a time to think of it) well weighing your inclination to perpetuate so good an affection as you have to this present continued, putting entirely on one side my fault; nevertheless, in the name of God, I am resolved to end my days with this sole desire, that you think of me always as I plan to be, drawing no other aim but to be pleasing to you. If the argument of this writing be worthy to plead my excuse, I beg you to hear it, and not to impute it to a lack of goodwill, but rather to some other occasion appertaining to your present knowledge, but very proper for me to know. For the rest, it will please you to incline your ear a little to this bearer, who will tell you from my part certain other matters, from which you will have no need to doubt that you have been negligent in this affair. You know that I am dedicated to your service as you have put me in your obligation. It is time to finish these uneven lines which keep you from your affairs, praying the Creator to keep you in His holy keeping, having trusted myself very cordially in your hands.

Your very assured as well as obliged,
Elizabeth R.

XXVIII.To Francis, Duke of Anjou

Translated from the French

c. June 1581.

I cannot express, Monsieur, the contentment which I feel that the nets are broken and you so happily escaped from such bonds, if I did not greatly regret your discontent and appear to be inhuman in adding to your ills. I should not cease to condemn you as the source of such inconveniences, being very worthy to pluck such a vintage from so ill a harvest. Remove, I beg you, such evil counsels from the favour of your ears and believe that whatever evil deserts, that others bear you, a Prince must always be true to himself. I have communicated to you by Sommer as much as my ignorance can impart. Consider the true foundation of all my writings, which tend to no other aim but to keep you in all safety and honour. God is my witness that I never use subtleties nor shifts to do good to myself at your expense. as perchance more crafty and less faithful men do often. Prove by their fruits the variety and uncertainty of such spirits, and thereupon settle your judgement and treat accordingly those who seek nothing for good, if it be not all for you, in such manner that their souls cast not out sighs for lack of better reward, and that you do not wish them ill when their spirits are dulled instead of wishing to please you.   I do not doubt that the rock will be at this time assailed by various storms and winds, which flow from divers climates.   I wish that you were so good an astronomer that you could judge of the future, and know clearly where they tend, for fear that in avoiding Scylla you fall not upon Charybdis. Monsieur, my dearest, grant pardon to the poor old woman who honours you (I dare say it) as much as any young wench that you will ever find.   I thank you a million times for what you write to me from the borders of your country, where the ruler desires to have the grace to be able to serve you in some place, assuring ourselves that England possesses nothing good but what will be dedicated to your use, provided that you treat for it. Hearing that Dunkirk yields you not too good an air, I wish you some place more healthy, doubting greatly the continuance of your good health, which I hear by de Bex is better than that of various of your following, for which messenger I thank you very humbly, being the first since Baqueville, who remained more than the half year with me, and believe that I shall not be annoyed if every hour I received a letter from him; they are so comforting to me that you need have no scruple in sending them to me, for otherwise I should think myself dead in your opinion which I deserve to be kept sure and unspotted for me: as God knows, Whom I pray keep you from all evil, and give you a hundred years of good life, commending myself a thousand times to the little fingers.

XXIX. To ' The Monk '

Written in the same draft as the preceding letter.   Amongst the followers of Anjou who took part in the negotiations there was one always designated as ' The Monk '.   He has not been certainly identified, but he was intimate with the secrets of both parties.

Translated from the French

1581.

Master Monk, you are so good a divine that you cannot be ignorant how that, when Pilate and Caiaphas were good friends, the Innocent died.   God keep the innocent from enduring the

evil that ill-founded agreements merit.   Friendship is better kept
between like natures; from reconciled enemies *conservat Deus
dominum tuum.*   I hear of strange projects and good commenders,
but those who listen, that have not their part to remember, are
more freed from passion, and more clear-sighted in action.   We
say, *bel fin touta la vita honora.*   Brass shines as fair to the ignorant as gold to the goldsmith.   I will pray for the eyes of your
master that no mask obscure his good judgement from not
discerning the person.   Give him good advice, and be bold, preferring his good to the desire of pleasing him.   Farewell, Monk.

xxx. To Sir Francis Walsingham

*Written in answer to a very straight letter from Walsingham
in France, in which he boldly criticized her for refusing to make
up her mind or to spend money.   As for her marriage, he com-
mented, ' If you mean it, remember that by the delay your Highness useth therein, you lose the benefit of time, which (if years
considered) is not the least thing to be weighed.   If you mean it
not, then assure yourself, it is one of the worst remedies you can
use, howsoever your Majesty may conceive that it serveth your
turn.'   As for her niggardliness, ' Sometimes when your Majesty
doth behold in what doubtful terms you stand with foreign
Princes, then do you wish with great affection that opportunities
offered had not been overshipped; but when they are offered to
you, if they be accompanied with charges, they are altogether
neglected.'   His final observation was ' that if this sparing and
unprovident course be held on still, the mischiefs approaching
being so apparent as they are, that no one that serveth in place
of a Councillor—that either weigheth his own credit or carrieth
that sound affection to your Majesty that he ought to do—that
would not wish himself rather in the farthest part of Ethiopia
than the fairest palace in England.'*

September 1581.

Can you wittingly do me so much wrong as to suppose I am
readier to make strangers acquainted with my mind and let you
run another course?   The goodwill that Monsieur oweth me
might with some hope of their own good move the minister of
the King here and his servants there to let[1] the treaty, for fear

---

[1] Let=hinder.

it should be obstacle to the marriage. You may tell the King that the superiority that Monsieur hath taken upon him must now be maintained, for of retreat I can make no mention, both for his honour and both our goods, since England and France shall feel else the weight of his wrath. Therefore, since the States' ability alone cannot do it, nor Monsieur's apanage, and the King minds it not, how doth it follow but I must bear that yoke. And therefore, he seeth the cause of let for the league that shall be no impeachment to the marriage. But rather than you shall linger thus in vain, crave your return, which I wish not least to see. Over many tragedies that our foreign King hath made us, it is too much that all our charge, care and expense is so far neglected, and we are said to have done but beguile, and even that is done, is demanded, why all this was prepared, who bare it; and why did he not appoint both the Captains and made the provision; and so he is not bound to aught that they have done.

Your loving Sovereign,

E.R.

Forget not to let the King know how strange an action it was to permit a sword to the enemy of his brother, even when he was in person near him. I could wish that half he bestoweth on his favourites were employed on his needy brother.

XXXI. To William Cecil, Lord Burghley

An urgent private note, written apparently to Burghley, concerning the arrival (in theory incognito) *of Anjou.*

c. November 1, 1581.

Do me not such wrong as to think that I have said a single word to Sta[fford] except, shortly, that I am thinking of sending him to M[onsieur]. He said to me: 'Madam, I believe that when he comes, you will treat me like the other time.' I answered that he had other business, that he should approach him. True, I swear to you, that is all I said to him. As for the messenger, it is true that he came this morning to Wals[ingham] and told him that he saw M[onsieur] at Dieppe, and that he knows him as well as his own hand: and declared to him how he put to sea in the Channel and had a very bad time in a great storm, and then returned in perfect safety, and put to sea a second time, and came straight to Rye. He commanded him not to speak of it to anyone, on pain of his head, and that he might assure himself he had not seen him at all, and he was to hold his tongue. As for the merchants they are not yet arrived, but when they get near London they will come straight here, and receive orders to keep from spreading such reports being so false. I have told Wal[singham] not to give a sign to any creature in the world that he has heard, and I am sure he will not. The searcher at Rye knew from the messenger that he thought M[onsieur] was coming under his charge, and he said he wanted to know from Walsingham what he would direct him to do about that Prince. Wals[ingham] laughed at it, and said nothing more. He would have written to him to supply him with horses and necessaries without seeming to recognize him, and also to follow him with seven or eight men for fear of any nocturnal brigands; but I would not consent, saying he would be a great fool who believed it.

When the merchants are come, you shall ascertain whether they recognized him or not; for they would suspect it, I am sure.

XXXII. To Henry III, King of France

Written on the departure of Anjou from England.

Translated from the French

February 1582.

Although it does not well become one who is coming out of an ecstasy to write to a Prince like you, my dear brother, yet the constraint put upon me by your last dispatches makes it suitable for me. I seem astonished to find no answer declared therein, as if paper and ink had been employed with no object, like ciphers signifying nothing; from which I learnt a lesson before I die, namely that a negative was not given to me, and an affirmative was not agreeable to you. I will say no more on this, except that I hope that even if the marriage is broken off you will retain some consideration for your loyal and affectionate brother, for I promise you I think that you ought to be proud of him, and glorify yourself for having so rare a Prince from whom you have experienced so much affection expressed in so many good service and who has risked his life and employed his diligence and so well effected his plans in the conclusion of a good peace, a matter of no small consequence in a country which long has needed it. Of my sincerity in this great affair so long treated of between us, M. Pinart will, I hope, discourse to you fully, how I have discharged my part from the beginning till now with all sincerity, using no precaution or subtlety, things unbecoming to great Princes; and your brother when present will testify how it was necessity compelled these delays in order the better to settle the business, and no indecision on my part. It would be too unjust to impute the faults of others to me; but it happens often to kings to do good and receive no recompense. Wherefore interpret my text as my deserts require, and keep me in the rank of your most genuine friends.

XXXIII. To Francis, Duke of Anjou

Translated from the French

May 4, 1582.

Although, my dearest, the happy arrival of Monsieur de Baqueville has raised my spirit, so that I deem myself to have had the disease of melancholy, which often makes some believe themselves headless, others that they are spoiled of one, others that they are dead entirely, I cannot hide from you the evident reasons which lead me to think that I am not of this world. For assuring myself that for my part, since your sad departure, I have not omitted to the least syllable what I promised, but rather to accomplish it I have made myself shameless in sending and sending again so many times to the King to make clear to him some little difficulty that this matter was stayed by him, begging him to consider it better as a thing which would not too greatly inconvenience him if he had any desire to bring it to a conclusion. To which he answered me, indeed this last week, by assuring me that he could not longer carry out what he promised in the letter sent by Pinart.

Judge, therefore, my dearest, what I can do further, having taken from you such estate as you have; for otherwise, according to your very honourable offer, you could abandon your war and the Low Countries and conclude your pact, notwithstanding the difficulties of agreement, as one having no need for such assurance. But at this present, what shall we do? It is for you to think of it. I beg you not to think that you have made so perilous a journey to have from her, who how she confesses that she is not worthy of a part of such a risk . . . I dare justify myself before the world, that it has never lain with me not to conclude it, since my last promise which I made you on such conditions as you alone know, which for myself I confess are very difficult, notwithstanding, to your contentment I accorded very willingly; and God is my witness that I have never removed from it since. And I swear to you that I never wished to show myself unworthy of the favour of such a Prince, having never need to be reminded of the least grace that I have received from your kindness. And do not doubt that my merits are not always very good advocates of my affection and constancy in your behalf. Consider, my dearest, if I dare say it, if the whole universe was not amazed that the Queen of England has so greatly forgotten England as to bring in new neighbours on the continent near her country. Your good judgement, not blinded by others, will judge what depends upon this opinion, and then see, if for my part I have not hazarded something for you, having the love of my nation dearer than my life, Kings being but of short enduring when that is taken away from them.

To conclude, all that you wish me to do, which will not touch my honour too greatly, I will do, rendering you very humble thanks for your last message, with the letter which has awakened me from a deep sleep, having never heard mention of this cause since the separation of our bodies, not of our souls, whereat I was astonished in a strange fashion. I rejoice to hear that you are so greatly honoured by that people, which seems to me to have very just cause for it. But I doubt not that you hold always in your memory the nature of the vulgar in all countries, and will trust it as the opportunity presents itself, desiring nothing more than the continuation of our contentments, and cursing (my charity in

such a case being very cold) all who overset our designs. You
understand in few words to make an end of this. I pray you
believe that if the King again demand of my Ambassador what
is my intention, I will charge him to sing the same song as before,
blushing to recite so often that which profits so little.

XXXIV. To Francis, Duke of Anjou

*Anjou, having heard from the French King that he had
granted all the Queen's demands, thought that at last the wedding
was to take place. He wrote to the Queen that all he has now
to do is to order his clothes; but added that now he was to be her
husband she would not wish him to perish for want of the assistance so solemnly promised, especially as his troops would need
pay if he was to leave them safely. The Queen's next letter,
however, cooled his hopes, for she was casting doubt on the King's
surety. Anjou wrote again pathetically asking why he could
draw no resolution from her. To this she replied:*

Translated from the French

May 24, 1582.

My dearest, you make me know, that notwithstanding the
great affairs and the importance of your negotiations, you do not
fail to console me with the coming of your long letters, confessing
that I am therefore infinitely obliged to return you a million
thanks. And in reading them I see a mass of affection, containing humours of several qualities. And albeit I am not too wise
in natural philosophy nor too good a physician to make a right
distinction of them, yet I shall take the rashness to enlighten you
on the true property of certain parts which I set in the keeping
of my memory. It seems to me in commemorating the history of
the matters treated between us, it pleases you to put me in mind
of hazards, the losses and plots you have endured for my sake,
which I cannot forget, having them engraved on my soul that till
it be separated from my body, I will not cease to recognize them
and shall be conscious of them always. Only I beg you not to
forget that all these prolongations have not been caused by me,
my considerations not having been devoid of respect for your
happier stay in this country, seeing that not only was my honour,
but your safety at stake. Drive away however, Monsieur, my

dearest, any thought that I was to blame in my passion of anger, which offends you, because your constancy should be in doubt. I clear myself of such a doubt, having never said nor thought it, whatever opinion others may have had of it. I have no care to offer you such an insult; only by the prayer that I might purge myself of the calumnies that they lay on me in France and elsewhere, that I have used subtlety or variableness in what I promised you, and so far was it wrong to say that I was worthy of blame that I ceased not to impute it to the person to whom it most appertained. This, I see, by your letters written to Pinart, has given you an argument for writing in the same fashion under our permission, which seems to me strange when you are making demonstration that I urge you to proceed more importunately, as much from my hesitancy as for my haste. O Monsieur, how that touches my honour, being a woman as I am. You will think of it at your good leisure; some will mock it at their ease and I am sensible of it to my regret, which notwithstanding is lessened when I imagine that the end tended to bring an end to our long trammels which redouble to such an extent the fastenings of my bonds, that no one will ever be able to loose them. You write of having sent me copies of the letter of the King and the Queen, which I did not see before, except a letter to Pinart, which was only written the 12th of May, a day far distant from the time of your departure from this Realm, whence I see that you have never mentioned it since your arrival in Flanders. Herein I can justify myself, how that I have not delayed shamelessly, as my Ambassador has several times made mention. And I think that the King will repute me as a diligent seeker, which will be always a good reputation for a woman. You can see, if you please, clearly, easily, the hope that I can conceive of a sincere accomplishment of the matter which is solved with such difficulty, or rather cannot be undertaken at all.

For the matter of the money, I am so poor an advocate for my own profit, and so little enjoy husbandry, that I entrust it to those who are wiser than I, who have declared all to Marchaumont, who is of my determination. To whom I have made request to advertise you particularly, being very importunate in this matter, and beg you, with clasped hands, to be willing to weigh in true balance upon what groundwork I go, and you will see that I have not less consideration for your greatness and the preservation of your enterprises than you could yourself wish. Receiving your last letter of news sent by the Queen of Navarre, I am only too beholden to you for the alleviation received thereby. But for my part, I heard nothing of it at the last audience which my Ambassador had with the King, which was the 6th of this month, and I beg you believe that my last advertisement will be found very true, since I received it from a good source, and am greatly astonished that you have not received it, especially as I dispatched it to you as soon as the wind allowed. You will pardon me if I do not easily give credit to news so good, for fear lest deception redouble my disquiet. I keep myself therefore, without being assured hereof, from answering to the name by which you conjure me; only I can tell you that such obligation cannot blind my affection more than your merits have hitherto, which cannot receive increase. And I will compare myself with anyone in having no less affection for you than if the little priest had already performed his office. I will do it in such sort that you cannot justly impute any lack for your part. I could enlarge the answer which I send you by Marchaumont. But I have left this labour to him, begging you to believe that if our marriage were accomplished, I should not thereby benefit England. If by chance God took me out of this world before having children, if ever I had them, you are wise enough to see what a good turn I should have done them, to gain them such good neighbours, if perchance Flanders change masters and the French govern there. Pardon me this frankness. Do not forget my heart, which I risk a little for you in this matter, more than you can imagine, but not more than I already feel, and has solaced me as with the taste of a fine liquor. But when I remember for whom it is, I console myself so much that I am supported by it. For the commission which we shall give you, I shall not wonder so far as to comprehend, if the desire to please you so occupied the spirit of the Queen, that she comprehended the intention of the King to resemble the sum of your desire, not at all according to the interpretation which it can perchance bear. Which to understand . . . (*cetera desunt*)

XXXV. To George Talbot, Earl of Shrewsbury

An example of Elizabeth's letters of condolence.

c. September 5, 1582.

We had thought immediately upon understanding of the death of the Lord Talbot your son, to have sent you our letters of comfort, but that we were loath that they should have been the first messengers unto you of so unpleasant matter as the loss of a son of so great hope and towardness, that might have served to have been a comfortable staff unto you in your old years, and a profitable pillar unto this our estate in time to come, whereof he gave as great hope as any one of his calling within this our Realm; which we know, in respect of the love you bear us, cannot but greatly increase your grief. But herein, we, as his Prince and Sovereign, and you as a loving and natural father, for that we both be interested in the loss (though for several respects), are to lay aside our particular causes of grief, and to remember that God, Who hath been the worker thereof, and doeth all things for the best, is not to be controlled. Besides, if we do duly look into the matter in true course of Christianity, we shall then see that the loss hath wrought so great a gain to the gentleman whom we now lack, as we have rather cause to rejoice than lament; for if the imperfections of this declining age we live in be truly weighed, and the sundry miseries that we are daily subject unto be duly looked into, we shall then find more cause to judge them unhappy that live, than to bewail those as unfortunate that are dead. But, for that the weakness of frail flesh cannot so rest upon that comfort which the happy estate of his change hath wrought but that nature will have her force, we cannot therefore but put you in mind how well God in His singular goodness hath dealt with you, in that He left you behind other sons of great hope, who through the good education that you have carefully given them, and the good gifts of nature they are plentifully endowed withal, are like to prove no less comfortable unto you than serviceable unto us. And, therefore, for your comfort you are to remember that, of four sons that He hath given you, He hath taken only one to Himself. These reasons, which we have thought on and used with good fruit as seems to lessen our own grief, we have thought meet to impart them unto you, and do hope they shall work no less effect in you, whose case we tender as much as our own, having made as great trial of your care and fidelity towards us as ever Prince hath made of servant. And, therefore, we do assure ourself that in this discomfort there is no earthly thing can yield you more comfort than the assurance of our gracious favour towards you; whereof you may make full account to receive the same from us in as full measure as a well-deserving servant and subject may in true gratuity look for at a gracious and thankful Prince's hands.

XXXVI.? PIERRE CLAUSSE, SEIGNEUR DE MARCHAUMONT

Translated from the French

? *March* 1583.

Le fidèle, I send you the very words which I added to the letter to Monsieur. My hand being a little sprained I had great trouble to write so much. 'Permit me, my dearest, to say that I entreat you to consider that if the worst came to pass, and the marriage did not take place, if you think it better to arrange some other league, amity or security on very close terms, when you are present, than any other way; in that case I should not be so much vexed for the fear I have of any dishonour you might receive thereby. Enlighten me therefore, I beg of you, as to your own notions in this matter of coming to some other agreement; although I am sure that none of us will be too much satisfied with it. In my heart I have already [   ]¹ the lot of being dedicated to you more than to any other soever.'

Keep this copy for me till I see you again. I beseech you to write frankly to Monsieur, and let him have a good regard for himself. You understand me; few words to the wise.

God restore you to health.

$.

XXXVII.TO WILLIAM CECIL, LORD BURGHLEY

Burghley, disheartened by the constant worries of the last months and conscious that he was disliked by some of his power-ful colleagues in the Council, wished to resign his office.

¹ The original here reads '*recte*'.

May 8, 1583.

SIR SPIRIT,

I doubt I do nickname you for those of your kind, they say, have no sense. But I have lately seen an *ecce signum*, that if an ass kick you, you feel it too soon. I will recant you from being spirit, if ever I perceive that you disdain not such a feeling. Serve God, fear the King, and be a good fellow to the rest. Let never care appear in you for such a rumour, but let them well know that you desire the righting of such wrong by making known their error, than you to be so silly a soul as to forshow what you ought to do, or not freely deliver what you think meetest, and pass of no man so much, as not to regard her trust who putteth it in you.

God bless you, and long may you last,

Omnino E.R.

XXXVIII. TO JAMES THE SIXTH, KING OF SCOTLAND

James had, after some difficulties, succeeded in freeing himself from the government of the Earls. He wrote to the Queen that he had reason to fear for his own life but promised to maintain amity with her and follow her counsel in his affairs. This resolution he had not been able to fulfil. The Queen accordingly accused him of being false to his word, and sent Walsingham to strengthen the alliance between the two countries.

August 7, 1583.

Among your many studies, my dear Brother and Cousin, I would Isocrates' noble lesson were not forgotten, that wills the Emperor his sovereign to make his words of more account than other men their oaths, as meetest ensigns to show the truest badge of a Prince's arms. It moveth me much to move you, when I behold how diversely sundry wicked paths, and, like all evil illusions, wrapped under the cloak of your best safety, endanger your state and best good. How may it be that you can suppose an honourable answer may be made me when all your doings gainsay your former vows. You deal not with one whose experience can take dross for good payments : nor one that easily will be beguiled. No, no, I mind to set to school your craftiest Councillor. I am sorry to see you bent to wrong yourself in thinking to wrong others: yea, those which if they had not even then taken opportunity to let[1] a ruin that was newly begun, that plot would have perilled you more than a thousand of such mean lives be worth, that persuade you to vouch such deeds to deserve a soul's pardon. Why do you forget what you write to myself with your own hand, showing how dangerous a course the Duke was entered in, though you excused himself to think no harm therein, and yet they that with your safety preserved you from it, you must seem to give them reproach of guilty folk? I hope you more esteem your honour than to give it such a stain, since you have protested so often to have taken these Lords for your most affectionate subjects, and to have done all for your best. To conclude, I beseech you pass no further in this cause till you receive an express messenger, a trusty servant of mine, by whom [I] mean to deal like an affectionate sister with you as [   ] whom you shall see plainly you may perceive honour and contentment with more surety to your rest and state, than all these dissembling Councillors will or can bring you. As knoweth the Lord to Whose most safe keeping I do commit you, with my many commendations to your person.

XXXIX. To Francis, Duke of Anjou

Anjou had failed completely in Flanders. He had received much help from the Queen, but she had no further use for him as husband or as ally.

Translated from the French

September 10, 1583.

Monsieur,

After a long expectation of receiving some news of you and your affairs, Monsieur de Reaux came to visit me from you, bearing only letters quite full of affection and assurance of its continuance for ever, for which I return you an infinity of thanks, since I have heard of the care which you take for fear of some ill impression that I might conceive of your actions. And then he spoke to me in a way that seemed very strange, as desiring to know what will be the help that we shall give for the

---

[1] Let = hinder.

preservation of the Low Countries; telling me that you are assured by the King that he will aid you as well as I. My God, Monsieur, what? are you not mad to believe that the means of keeping our friends is always to weaken them? Whoever has given you the advice has thought to make a blemish on our friendship or to break it altogether; in order by the same means to accomplish their designs and bring you to their desire. Do you not remember, Monsieur, against how many friends I have to prepare? Must I look unto those afar off as much as I neglect the nearest? Is the King, your brother, so weak a prince that he cannot defend you without another neighbour who has enough on her back, or so weakened that he must open a way to his enemies? You will not consider me so unworthy of reigning that I may not fortify myself, forsooth, with the sinews of war while awaiting too much courtesy from those who seek my ruin. I am astonished at the King, your brother, who has given me the precedence in fortifying you in such great need, having commenced before him, and seeing that he does not lack better means with less inconvenience. Pardon me, I beg you, if I tell you that this answer is quite clear, that he would not do anything, thinking that I should have little reason for not giving. So much so that if the King will not speak, and will not do much more than before, such an enterprise will break very soon, and if he be not for himself, I think that such is his determination. There is my opinion. As to you, Monsieur, I think that you are so surrounded with contrary persuasions and such differing humours, doubting so much, and assuring yourself of nothing that you know not where conveniently to turn, as you have reason good enough. Would to God that I were clever enough in wisdom to give you counsel, the best and most assured counsel, and that I had the understanding as I have the will. Then rather I would bear it to you than send it. I hope among other things that you will remember that he is very worthy of tripping who enters a net: do not only take advice; be ruthless; that is enough. I hear to my great regret that the King, the Queen Mother, indeed you yourself, put on me the fault which I have never committed, it always having depended on the King to perfect that of which I cannot make more mention, except to beg you to do me so much

M

justice as to purge me, even by the opinion of your very ministers who know my innocence. For I cannot endure such a wrong, that they bite at and lament my affection for you. I appeal to the King's Ambassador, to Monsieur la Motte, Marchaumont, and Baqueville, how that God will not permit such an agreement, if I cease not ever to love, honour and esteem you, like the dog who being often beaten returns to his master. God keep you from painted counsel, and permit you to follow those who respect you more than themselves.

XL. To Catherine de Medici, Queen Mother of France

On receipt of the news of the death of Anjou, the Queen wrote the following letter to his mother.

Translated from the French

c. July 1584.

Madam,

If the extremity of my misfortune had not equalled my grief for his sake, and had not rendered me unequal to touch with a pen the wound that my heart suffered, it would not be possible that I had so greatly forgotten to visit you with the fellowship of regret that I afford you, which I assure myself cannot exceed mine; for, although you were his mother, yet there remain to you several other children. But for myself, I find no consolation if it be not death, which I hope will make us soon to meet. Madam, if you could see the image of my heart you would there see the picture of a body without a soul; but I will not trouble you more with my plaints, having too many of your own. It remains at this present that I vow and swear to you that I will turn a great part of my love for him to the King, my good brother, and you, assuring you that you will find me the faithfullest daughter and sister that ever Princes had; and for this principal cause that he, to whom I had altogether dedicated myself, belonged to you so near; from whom, if he had had the divine favour of longer life, you would have known it further. Madam, I pray you give [   ] credit to this gentleman who will more amply tell you on my behalf my thoughts in your case, and believe that I will accomplish them faithfully as if I

were your natural daughter. [? As] God please, Whom I pray
to give you long life and all consolation.

Your very affectionate sister and cousin,

ELIZABETH.

XLI. To James the Sixth, King of Scotland

*In order that the young King of Scots might be won over to
amity with England, Sir Edward Wotton with Robert Alexander
was sent as Ambassador to Scotland with a handsome present of
buckhounds and horses in April 1585. King James had, in the
years preceding, been so much at the mercy of the contending
parties in Scotland that his dealings with the Queen had perforce
been ' contrarious '.*

June–July 1585.

RIGHT DEAR BROTHER,

Your gladsome acceptance of my offered amity, together
with the desire you seem to have engraven in your mind to
make merits correspondent, makes me in full opinion that some
enemies to our goodwill shall lose much travel, with making
frustrate their baiting stratagems, which I know to be many
and by sundry means to be explored. I cannot halt with you
so much as to deny that I have seen such evident shows of
your contrarious dealings, that if I made not my reckoning the
better of the months, I might condemn you as unworthy of such
as I mind to show myself toward you, and therefore I am well
pleased to take any colour to defend your honour, and hope that
you will remember, that who seeketh two strings to one bow, they
may shoot strong, but never straight; and if you suppose that
Princes' causes be veiled so covertly that no intelligence may
bewray them, deceive not yourself; we old foxes can find shifts
to save ourselves by others' malice, and come by knowledge of
greatest secret, specially if it touch our freehold. It becometh
therefore all our rank[1] to deal sincerely, lest, if we use it not,
when we do it, we be hardly believed. I write not this, my dear
Brother, for doubt but for remembrances. My Ambassador
writes so much of your honourable treatment of him and of
Alexander, that I believe they be converted Scots. You oblige me
for them, for which I render you a million of most entire thanks,

[1] *Original* ' rencq '.

163

as she that meaneth to deserve many a good thought in your breast through good desert. And for that your request is so honourable, retaining so much reason, I were out of senses if I should not suspend of any hearsay till the answer of your own action, which the actor ought best to know, and so assure yourself I mean and vow to do; with this request that you will afford me the reciproque. And thus, with many petitions to the Almighty for your long life and preservation, I end these scribbled lines.

Your very assured loving sister and cousin,

ELIZABETH R.

XLII. To James the Sixth, King of Scotland

Peaceful negotiations between Queen Elizabeth and King James were suddenly interrupted by the murder, during a border truce, of Lord Francis Russell on 28th July. James was genuinely distressed and wrote at once to the Queen. This letter is her answer and comment on the affair.

August 1585.

RIGHT DEAR BROTHER,

I find too true the French adage, *Qu'un mal ne vint jamais seul*; for as the horrible and sudden murder of my most faithful subject and most valiant Baron was unto me a heartsore and grievous tidings, so was it tenfold redoubled with knowledge that a Scot should dare violate his hands on any of our noble blood, in a peaceable concord, when our friendship should have sent out his hottest beams to the kindling of the entire affection of both Realms; that any of that nation should once dare have had a thought to maculate such a contract of amity. I perceive, by my Ambassador, that your grief is little less than such a hap deserveth, and do perceive that you have not spared your well-favoured to cause him answer such a suspicion. I think myself, therefore, greatly obliged unto your care for my satisfaction, and therein I thank you for being so considerate of your own honour, which, I assure you, lieth a-bleeding in the bowels of many an Englishman, until full reason be made for such a treachery. God send us better luck after our league be finished than this bloody beginning may give calends of, else many a red side will follow such demerits. But I hope you will spare no man that may be doubtful of such a meaning. I mean, not only of the murder, but of the breaking out upon our borderers, which commonly are the beginnings of our quarrels. I doubt nothing of your curious care in this behalf, and for that the Warden of that March hath been the open and common fosterer and companion of the traitor Westmorland and his complices in France and Scotland, I hope you will agree to send him to my hands, where he shall never receive injury nor evil measure. And thus desiring [you] to credit my Ambassador in certain particularities that he shall impart unto you as to myself, I recommend you to God's safe tuition, Who grant you many gladsome years.

> Your most affectionate sister and cousin,
> ELIZABETH R.

XLIII. To James the Sixth, King of Scotland

In 1582 the party favouring Catholicism and alliance with France was in the ascendant in Scotland. Accordingly the Protestant Lords, including Gowrie, Angus, More and Glamis, seized the person of King James, the affair being known as the 'Raid of Ruthven'. James was subsequently rescued, and Gowrie was beheaded; the other Lords took refuge in England, where they were protected by Queen Elizabeth, who refused to give them up. In October 1585 the Lords returned to Scotland (not improbably with the Queen's approval), gathered a force of 8,000 men and occupied Stirling. This letter was written by the Queen to explain and justify her action in allowing the Lords to leave her realm.

November 1585.

RIGHT DEAR BROTHER,

The strangeness of hard accidents that are arrived here of unlooked for, or unsuspected, attempts in Scotland, even by some such as lately issued out of our land, constraineth me, as well for the care we have of your person as of the discharge of our own honour and conscience, to send you immediately this gentleman, one that appertaineth to us in blood,[1] both to offer you all assistance of help as all good endeavour of counsel, and

---

[1] William Knollys, grandson of Mary Boleyn, the Queen's aunt.

to make it plain that we dealt plainly. These Lords making great outcries that I would not or could help them to be restored, I, by their great importunity, yielded, that if I might be freed of my assurance given unto you for their safe keeping, I would consent unto their departure, and so, after your answer, as my thought most honourable, that they might take their way to Germany, with your gracious grant of some livelihood, after a week's space I gave them my passport and so dismissed them, without, I swear unto you, once the sight of any one of them. Now, when I weigh how suddenly, beyond my expectation, this sudden stir ariseth, and fearing lest some evil and wicked person might surmise that this was not without my foresight, I beseech you trust my actions according the measure of my former dealings for your safety, and answerable to the rule of reason, and you shall find that few Princes will agree to constraint of their equals, much less with compulsion of their subjects. Judge of me, therefore, as of a King that carries no abject nature, and think this of me, that, rather than your danger, I will venture mine; and albeit I must confess that it is dangerous for a Prince to irritate too much, through evil advice, the generality of great subjects, so might you ere now have followed my advice, that would never betray you with unsound counsel; and now to conclude, making haste, I pray you be plain with this bearer, that I may know what you would that I should do, without excuse hereafter that constrained you did it, for I dare assure you of his secrecy, and thereof be you bold. For the Lord Russell's death, and other things, I refer me to this gentleman, who I dare promise is of no faction beside my will. God bless you in all safety as I wish myself.

Your true assured cousin and sister,
ELIZABETH R.

Fear not, for your life must be theirs, or else they shall smart well, every mother's son of them.

CHAPTER IV
1586-1590

*In 1585 the Queen decisively took a hand in the affairs of the
Netherlands. The trouble with Spain had been maturing since
1568. In that year Philip the Second of Spain, having insulted
and disgraced Dr. John Mann, the English Agent in Spain,
recalled his own capable ambassador, Guzman de Silva, and
substituted Don Guerau. There were other troubles. Hawkins
and Drake had attacked Spanish trade in the West, and Englishmen openly showed practical sympathy with the revolting
Netherlands. In December 1568 the Queen further complicated
the issue. Certain galleys laden with treasure for Alva, Spanish
Governor of the Netherlands, put in for safety to English ports.
The Queen seized the treasure. Alva made reprisal on English
men, ships and goods in the Netherlands; and the Queen
retaliated on Spanish men and goods in England.*

*In April 1582 Queen Elizabeth negotiated with the Queen
Mother of France the Treaty of Blois, which was, in effect, a
defensive alliance with France against Spain. Moreover not only
did she allow refugees from the Netherlands, where the revolt
against the Spaniards had broken out again, to return to fight
against Alva, she also sent Sir Humphrey Gilbert, ostensibly
without her leave, but actually with secret instructions to seize
and hold Flushing to prevent it falling into the hands of the
French.*

*In the next year the Queen changed her policy, and entered
into a treaty of peace with Alva. Alva was recalled in November
1575. His successor, whose manners were milder, died in 1576,
and was succeeded by Don John of Austria; but before Don John
could take up his governorship the Spanish troops revolted and
sacked Antwerp. The whole country now rose against the
Spaniards. Queen Elizabeth helped the rebels with money and
advice, and the revolt continued till October 1578 when Don
John died. In the same year Anjou entered the country at the
head of a filibustering expedition. Don John was followed by
the Duke of Parma, who in seven months won back the Southern
Provinces. Anjou had been offered the sovereignty of the Low
Countries in 1579, and continued intermittently to give help to
the States; but in 1584 he made a treacherous attempt to take
Antwerp from his own allies, and on its failure fled the country
and shortly after died. In the following year, 1585, William of
Orange died, and at once the United Provinces were disrupted*

*by factions and revolts. Henry III was too much occupied with
his own troubles to give any aid. At last in August 1585 the
Queen declared her policy openly and made a treaty with the
States whereby she promised to aid them with money and men;
and the Earl of Leicester was sent over to take command and
unite the factions.*

*Leicester arrived at Flushing on 10th December, 1585. On
1st January, 1586, he was offered the absolute government of
the Low Countries, which, after some delay, he accepted, and
on 25th January was solemnly installed by proclamation as bearing ' highest and supreme commandment and absolute authority
above and in all matters of warfare'. He neither asked permission of the Queen, nor even informed her of what was happening.
When she heard of Leicester's action, the story was amply
embellished with gossip, as that the Countess of Leicester was
to join him and set up a Court which would rival her own. This
information ' did not a little stir her Majesty to extreme choler
and dislike' of all Leicester's doings, so that she swore with great
oaths that she would have no more Courts under her obeisance
but her own and would revoke Leicester with speed. On
7th February Leicester received from the Council an intimation
that the Queen would disavow his acts. On the 10th she
dispatched Sir Thomas Heneage.*

1. To Sir Thomas Heneage

Detailed instructions for his mission to the Earl of Leicester.

February 10, 1586.

You shall let the Earl understand how highly upon just cause
we are offended with his late acceptation of the government of
those provinces, being done contrary to our commandment
delivered unto him both by ourself in speech and by particular
letters from certain of our Council written unto him in that behalf
by our express direction, which we do repute to be a very great
and strange contempt, least looked for at his hands, being he is
a creature of our own; wherewith we have so much the greater
cause to be offended, for that he hath not had that regard that
became him; to have at the least by his letters acquainted us with
the causes that moved him so contemptuously to break our said

commandment, nor used that diligence that appertained in sending our servant Davison unto us with instructions how to answer the said contempt, which hath greatly aggravated the fault. Though for our own part, we cannot imagine that anything can be alleged by him to excuse so manifest a contempt, at the least to make it appear that there was any such necessity in the matter, as we doubt not that will be greatly prevented, but that the acceptation might have been stayed until our pleasure had been first known.

You shall let him understand, that we hold our honour greatly touched by the said acceptation of that government, and least as we may not with our honour endure, for that it carrieth a manifest appearance of repugnancy to our protestation set out in print by the which we declare that our only intent in sending him over into those parts was to direct and govern the English troops that we had granted to the States for their aid, and to assist them with his advice and counsel for the better ordering both of their civil and martial causes, as is contained in the late contract passed between us and their Commissioners that were here, so as the world may justly thereby conceive.

You shall say unto him, that men of judgement will conceive another course taken by him; that the declaration published by us was but to abuse the world, for that they cannot in reason persuade themselves that a creature of our own, having for that purpose given him express commandment, upon pain of his allegiance,[1] to proceed, all delays and excuses laid apart, to the present demission thereof, considering the great obedience that even from the beginning of our reign hath been generally yielded us by our subjects, would ever have presumed to have accepted of the said government contrary to our commandment, without some secret assent of ours; or at least they will think that there is not now that reverent regard carried to our commandment as [hereto]for hath been, and as in the course of obedience ought to 'be.

For the removing of which hard conceit that the world may justly take, upon consideration either of the said abuse or con-

---

[1] To charge a subject 'on his allegiance' was the most solemn form of command; to disobey such an order was direct treason.

tempt, you shall let him understand that our express pleasure
and commandment is, upon pain of his allegiancy, that all delays
and excuses set apart, without attending any further assembly
of the States than such as shall be provided present with him at
the time of your access there, or in some convenient place, he
shall make an open and public resignation in the place where he
accepted the same absolute government, as a thing done without
our privity and consent contrary to the contract passed between
us and their Commissioners, letting them notwithstanding understand that this direction of ours given unto the said Earl for
the demission of his absolute authority proceedeth not of any
decay or alteration of our own goodwill and favour towards
them, whose well-doing we do no less tender than our own
natural subjects, as it hath manifestly appeared unto them by
our former actions, having for their sakes opposed ourselves
to one of the mightiest Princes of Europe, assuring them, therefore, that we do mean the continuance of the same towards them,
and our intent is, that the said Earl should hold that form of
government both likely to touch us greatly in honour. We see,
you may tell him, no other way but the said election must be
revoked with some such solemnity as the same was published,
and the States and people let understand, that our meaning is
not he shall hold or exercise any other sort of government during
the time of his abode there, than as is expressed in the said contract, which we do purpose inviolately to observe according to
our promise, not doubting but that the assistance they shall receive
that way will be as effectual for their safety and benefit, or rather
more, for some causes best known to ourself, as the other course.

After the delivery of which message to the Earl, we think
meet, to the end the States, or such as shall assist the Earl at the
time of your arrival may know the cause that moveth us to dislike
of the said acceptance and to have the same revoked, that you
shall advertise yourself to them and let them understand that we
find it strange that a nobleman, a minister [of] ours, sent thither
to execute and hold such a course of government as was contained
in the said contract, should without our assent, be pressed to
assent to accept of more large and absolute authority over the
said countries than was accorded on by virtue of the said contract,

especially seeing that ourself being oftentimes pressed by their
Commissioners to accept of the absolute government did always
refuse the same, and therefore by this manner of proceeding we
hold ourself two sundry ways wronged by them, greatly to our
dishonour : the one by provoking a minister of ours to commit
so notorious a contempt against us, the other in that they show
themselves to have a very slender and a weak conceipt of our
judgement by pressing a minister of ours to accept of that which
we refused, as though our long experience in government had not
yet taught us to discover what were fit for us to do in matters
of our State.   And though we cannot think but that this offer of
theirs proceeded of the great goodwill they bear us, and so consequently acknowledge the same with all thankfulness, yet may
it minister cause of suspicion to such as are apt to judge the worst
of things best meant, that the said offer, under colour of goodwill
to us, was made by some, though not by the generality, of a
malicious purpose, supposing the same would have been refused,
and that there would thereby have followed a change and alienation of the hearts of the common sort, when they shall see a plain
refusal of an offer that contained so evident and manifest a staid
argument of their goodwill and devotion towards us.

You shall further let them understand that forasmuch as we
conceive that the said acceptation hath greatly wounded our
honour, for the causes above specified, we have resolved to have
the said Earl's authority revoked, requiring them therefore in
our name to see the same executed out of hand.

And, to the end they may not enter into any hard or jealous
conceit upon knowledge of this our purpose, you shall, on our
behalf, assure them that the promised assistance according to the
contents of this contract, shall be faithfully performed, and that
the said Earl during his abode there, shall second and assist them
with his best advice and counsel accordingly, as is above expressed,
and is also at large contained in our own letters directed to them.

You shall also let the said Earl understand, that whereas by
his instructions he hath special direction, upon his first arrival to
inform himself of the particular state of their forces there, both
by sea and land, as also of their means and ability to maintain
the same and of the likelihood of their continuance of the said

means, we find it very strange that in all this time of his abode there, we hear yet nothing thereof, considering how often he hath otherwise written hither since his arrival there, and that he cannot be ignorant how much it importeth us to have knowledge of these things, which maketh the fault of his slackness therein so much the greater.

And whereas in the late government in those countries, there hath been great abuse committed, as well in the collection of the contributions as in the distribution of the same, which hath bred no little offence and mislike in the people than hindrance in the public service, you shall, in our name, charge both the Earl and such as by the States are appointed to assist him, to have an especial care the said abuses [be] redressed and the offenders punished; for the better performance whereof it shall be necessary that the Earl do press the States to grant him extraordinary power and authority in their name, as well to displace such officers as shall be found to have committed the said abuses, as to take charge of the distribution of the said contributions, which we know may be well enough performed without carrying the title of an absolute governor.

11. To Robert Dudley, Earl of Leicester

Sir Thomas Heneage took over the following letter.

February 10, 1586.

How contemptuously we conceive ourself to have been used by you, you shall by this bearer understand, whom we have expressly sent unto you to charge you withal. We could never have imagined had we not seen it fall out in experience that a man raised up by ourself and extraordinarily favoured by us above any other subject of this land, would have in so contemptible a sort broken our commandment, in a cause that so greatly toucheth us in honour; whereof, although you have showed yourself to make but little accompt, in most undutiful a sort, you may not therefore think that we have so little care of the reparation thereof as we mind to pass so great a wrong in silence unredressed: and, therefore, our express pleasure and commandment is, that all delays and excuses laid apart, you do presently, upon the duty of your allegiance, obey and fulfil whatsoever the bearer hereof shall direct you to do in our name : whereof fail you not, as you will answer the contrary at your uttermost peril.

III. To Sir John Perrot, Lord Deputy of Ireland

A note written at the head of a strong official letter in the Queen's own hand.

April 14, 1586.

Let us have no more such rash unadvised journeys without good ground, as your last fond journey in the North. We marvel that you hanged not such a saucy advertiser as he that made you believe so great a company were coming. I know you do nothing but with a good intent for my service, but yet take better heed ere you use us so again.

IV. To Sir Thomas Heneage

The Council were so greatly alarmed lest the Queen's violence should cause havoc in the Low Countries that Burghley even offered his resignation. Hereupon Heneage ventured, on his own responsibility, to tone down her message to Leicester, and further to promise in her name that the Queen would not make peace with Spain without the consent of the States. When she heard of it, she wrote to him as follows:

April 27, 1586.

What phlegmatical reasons soever were made you; how happened it that you will not remember that when a man hath faulted and committed by abettors thereto that neither the one nor the other will willingly make their own retreat. Jesus : what availeth wit when it fails the owner at greatest need? Do that you are bidden, and leave your considerations for your own affairs : for in some things you had clear commandment, which you did not; and in other none, and did; yea, to the use of those speeches from me that might oblige me to more than I was bound or mind ever to yield. We Princes be wary enough of our bargains. Think you I will be bound by your speech to make no peace for mine own matters without their consent? It is enough that I injure not their country, nor themselves, in making peace for them, without their consent. I am assured of your dutiful thought, but I am utterly at squares with this childish dealing.

v. To Alexander Farnese, Duke of Parma

Secret negotiations between the Queen and Parma had been carried out by means of an Englishman named Bodenham, who was one of Parma's servants, and an Italian merchant, called Augustin Grafigny. Grafigny hinted to Parma that the Queen was prepared to help the Spaniards to regain the maritime provinces of the States. Hereupon Bodenham came to England with a letter from Parma to the Queen, asking her to make definite proposals. The Council heard of it. Bodenham and Grafigny were brought before them and closely examined. Grafigny was asked whether he had received any authority from the Queen and equivocated. Hereupon the Queen wrote a reply to Parma's letters.

Translated from the Italian

July 8, 1586.

The letters which your Excellency has sent us by a certain Agostino Grafigna, accompanied by one William Bodenham, have seemed to us very strange, insomuch as you say therein that you had learnt from the said Grafigna what we had been pleased to commit to him on our behalf, and had heard it with infinite satisfaction. And although we cannot do less than approve of that inclination and the desire of your Excellency to bring matters to some good issue, with the offer of all the means in your power to this end, yet you must know that a great error has been committed in this matter, that in our name, without our knowledge, and contrary to our inclination and in some sort to the prejudice of our honour, any such person as this Grafigna, or indeed any other of much better condition should have had the audacity to begin such a thing in our name or on our part; as if by means of messages sent to your Excellency, we were seeking a treaty with the Catholic King, who, in so many ways, has requited our good offices in so quite contrary a manner, that we have been forced against our natural disposition, to intervene in these actions, for no other cause than for the defence of our state, necessarily joined with the safety of our ancient neighbours in those Low Countries.

And, moreover, when, by our order, Grafigna was asked by some of our Councillors whether he had in the past received any commission from us, or had spoken to your Excellency by direction of any of our Council, he denied it expressly, as you may see from a paper written by him, which we send enclosed. And for more certain proof thereof, he has offered to return into these parts to testify the same.

Then, as to Bodenham's being sent hither by you, we have also caused some of our Council to speak with him, who declared that there was on your part a great inclination to re-establish a peace between us and the Catholic King; to which end (as he says) your Excellency offers to procure authority from the King to treat with us by means of fitting persons, so soon as he should know that we were inclined to lend an ear thereto. As to which we conceive that by our public declaration, the King, as well as your Excellency, may have learned what was then our mind, and is so still, and how important are the reasons which have moved us to interfere in these affairs, not being urged either by ambition, or any desire for the shedding of blood, but only to make safe our own State and to free our ancient neighbours from misery and from slavery. And to these two ends we have directed our actions, with the resolution to continue them, notwithstanding that by indirect means rumours have been spread, chiefly in the Low Countries that we were inclined to a peace, giving heed to the safety and liberty of those our neighbours, who have moved us by compassion for their miseries, and for other just and important causes to aid them and to defend them from perpetual ruin and captivity.

And therefore in this very great wrong has been done to us. For such is our compassion for their miseries that in no manner will we allow their safety to be separated from our own, knowing how the two depend upon each other. And so we pray your Excellency to understand that this is our determination, notwithstanding any sort of rumours falsely spread abroad to the contrary, greatly to our dishonour. Nevertheless, you may be persuaded that if any reasonable conditions of peace should be offered to us

N

which tend to the establishing of our safety and honour and the liberty of our neighbours, we shall no less willingly accept them than unwillingly we have been forced to the contrary, seeing that in no way can we do anything more pleasing to God Almighty than by embracing the peace and safety of Christendom, of which in these times, we who are Princes and Monarchs have chiefly to think. And it is known to the Omnipotent (the God of peace and Searcher of all human hearts) that to this our heart has always been inclined, to whose judgement we appeal against the malice of those tongues which strive to persuade the world of the contrary.

vi. To Robert Dudley, Earl of Leicester

A personal letter, Leicester having been entirely forgiven for the indiscretions of the winter.

July 19, 1586.

Rob, I am afraid you will suppose by my wandering writings that a midsummer moon hath taken large possession of my brains this month, but you must needs take things as they come in my head, though order be left behind me. When I remember your request to have a discreet and honest man that may carry my mind and see how all goes there, I have chosen this bearer, whom you know and have made good trial of. I have fraught him full of my conceits of those country matters, and imparted what way I mind to take, and what is fit for you to use. I am sure you can credit him, and so I will be short with these few notes. First, that Count Maurice and Count Hollocke find themselves trusted of you, esteemed of me and to be carefully regarded if ever peace should happen, and of that assure them on my word that yet never deceived any. And for Norris and other captains that voluntarily without commandment have many years ventured their lives and won our nation honour and themselves fame, [let them] be not discouraged by any means, neither by new-come men nor by old trained soldiers elsewhere. If there be fault in using of soldiers or making of profit by them, let them hear of it without open shame and doubt not but I will chasten them there-for. It frets me not a little that the poor soldier that hourly ventures life should want their due, that well deserve rather reward: and look in whom the fault may duly be proved, let them smart therefore. And if the Treasurer be found untrue or negligent, according to desert he shall be used; though you know my old wont, that love not to discharge from office without desert; God forbid. I pray you let this bearer know what may be learned herein; and for this treasure I have joined Sir Thomas Shirley to see all this money discharged in due sort where it needeth and behoveth. Now will I end that do imagine I talk still with you, and therefore loathly say farewell, ōō,[1] though ever I pray God bless you from all harm and save you from all foes, with my million and legion of thanks for all your pains and cares. As you know, ever the same. E.R.

Let Wilkes see that he is acceptable to you.

If there be anything that Wilkes shall desire answer of, be such as you would have but me to know, write it to myself. You know I can keep both other's counsel and mine own. Mistrust not that anything you would have kept shall be disclosed by me; for although this bearer ask many things, yet may you answer him such as you shall think meet, and write to me the rest.

About this time the affairs of Mary, Queen of Scots, came to a head. Since 1567 she had remained a prisoner, latterly under the charge of Sir Amyas Paulet. In 1586 a number of sympathizers, of whom the chief was Anthony Babington, plotted to murder Queen Elizabeth and set Mary on the throne. Walsingham, however, had succeeded in insinuating one of his own spies into the conspiracy and tapped their correspondence with Mary, so that at the appropriate moment the plotters were arrested, and confessed. They were arraigned and executed in September. Mary's papers were seized and examined, and her complicity established. On 11th October a special commission met at Fotheringhay to try her. The commission adjourned to Westminster and on 25th October pronounced that Mary was guilty. A few days later Parliament petitioned the Queen to have Mary put to death, which she refused, but in December sentence of death was proclaimed.

[1] ōō i.e. ' Two Eyes '—the Queen's nickname for Leicester.

VII. To Sir Amyas Paulet

Paulet was keeper of Mary, Queen of Scots, and had acted with great discretion during the Babington affair. The letter was apparently written when Mary was closely confined after the discovery of the plot.

c. September 1586.

Amyas, my most faithful and careful servant, God reward thee treblefold in the double for thy most troublesome charge so well discharged. If you knew, my Amyas, how kindly, besides most dutifully, my grateful heart accepts and prizes your spotless endeavours and faultless actions, your wise orders and safe regard, performed in so dangerous and crafty a charge, it would ease your travails and rejoice your heart, in which I charge you place this most just thought, that I cannot balance in any weight of my judgement the value that I prize you at, and suppose no treasures to countervail such a faith. If I reward not such deserts, let me lack when I have most need of you; if I acknowledge not such merit, *non omnibus dictum*.

Let your wicked murderess[1] know how, with hearty sorrow, her vile deserts compel these orders; and bid her from me, ask God forgiveness for her treacherous dealings towards the saviour of her life many a year, to the intolerable peril of my own, and yet, not contented with so many forgivenesses, must fault again so horribly, far passing woman's thought, much less a Princess; instead of excusing whereof, not one can sorrow, it being so plainly confessed by the authors of my guiltless death. Let repentance take place, and let not the fiend possess her, so as her better part may not be lost, for which I pray with hands lifted up to Him, that may both save and spill.

With my most loving adieu and prayer for thy long life, your most assured and loving Sovereign, as thereby by good deserts induced.

---

[1] Mary, Queen of Scots.

VIII. To Mary, Queen of Scots

At the opening of the trial of Mary, Queen of Scots, at Fotheringhay on 12th October, 1586, the Commissioners delivered her this personal letter from Queen Elizabeth.

Translated from the French

October 1586.

You have in various ways and manners attempted to take my life and to bring my kingdom to destruction by bloodshed. I have never proceeded so harshly against you, but have, on the contrary, protected and maintained you like myself. These treasons will be proved to you and all made manifest. Yet it is my will, that you answer the nobles and peers of the kingdom as if I were myself present. I therefore require, charge, and command that you make answer for I have been well informed of your arrogance.

Act plainly without reserve, and you will sooner be able to obtain favour of me.

ELIZABETH.

IX. To James the Sixth, King of Scotland

This letter was written when the proceedings against Mary, Queen of Scots, were begun at Fotheringhay. The Kers, whose persons the Queen demands, were implicated in the murder of Lord Francis Russell.

October 15, 1586.

MY DEAR BROTHER,

It hath sufficiently informed me of your singular care of my estate and breathing that you have sent one, in such diligence, to understand the circumstances of the treasons which lately were lewdly attempted and miraculously uttered. Of which I had made participant your Ambassador afore your letters came. And now I am to show you, that, as I have received many writings from you of so great kindness, yet this last was fraughted with so careful passion, and so effectual utterance of all best wishes for my safety, and offer of as much as I could have desired, that I confess, if I should not seek to deserve it, and by merits tie you to continuance, I were evil-worthy such a friend; and, as the thanks my heart yields my pen may scant render you, so shall the owner ever deserve to show it not evil employed, but on such a Prince as shall requite your goodwill, and keep a watchful eye to all doings that may concern you.

And whereas you offer to send me any traitor of mine residing in your land, I shall not fail but expect th' accomplishment of the same in case any such shall be, and require you, in the meantime, that speedy deliverance may be made of the Kers, which toucheth both my conscience and honour.

I thank God that you beware so soon of Jesuits, that have been the source of all these treacheries in this Realm, and will spread like an evil weed, if at the first they be not weeded out. I would I had had Prometheus for companion, for Epimetheus had like to have been mine too soon. What religion is this, that they say the way to salvation is to kill the Prince for a merit meritorious? This is that they have all confessed without torture or menace. I swear it, on my word.

Far be it from Scotland to harbour any such, and therefore I wish your good providence may be duly executed, for else laws resemble cobwebs, whence great bees get out by breaking, and small flies stick fast for weakness.

As concerning the retarding of your answers to all points of your Ambassador's charge, you had received them or now, but that matters of that weight that I am sure you would willingly know cannot as yet receive a conclusion, and till that Master Douglas doth tarry; and with his return I hope you shall receive honourable requital of his amicable embassade, so as you shall have no cause to regret his arrival; as knoweth the Lord, Whom ever I beseech to send you many joyful days of reign and life.

Your most assured loving and faithful sister and cousin,

ELIZABETH R.

I must give you thanks for this poor subject of mine, for whom I will not stick to do all pleasure for your request, and would wish him under the ground if he should not serve you with greatest faith that any servant may. I have willed him tell you some things from me; I beseech you hear them favourably.

X. To HENRY III, KING OF FRANCE

On 6th January, 1587, Monsieur de Bellievre, Ambassador Extraordinary from Henry III, was received in audience by the Queen when he pleaded the cause of Mary, Queen of Scots. His concluding words were threatening, which moved Queen Elizabeth to ask whether this language was in the orders of his master; she also demanded to see the signed authority of the King. This letter of protest was the result.

January 1587.

SIR, MY GOOD BROTHER,

The old ground, on which I have often based my letters, appears to me so changed at present, that I am compelled to alter the style, and instead of returning thanks, to use complaints. My God! how could you be so unreasonable as to reproach the injured party, and to compass the death of an innocent one by allowing her to become the prey of a murderess? But, without reference to my rank, which is nowise inferior to your own, nor to my friendship to you, most sincere, for I have wellnigh forfeited all reputation among the Princes of my own religion, by neglecting them in order to prevent disturbances in your dominions; exposed to dangers such as scarcely any Prince ever was before; expecting, at least, some ostensible reasons and offers for security against the daily danger, for the epilogue of this whole negotiation : you are, in spite of all this, so blinded by the words of those who I pray may not ruin you, that instead of a thousand thanks, which I had merited for such singular services, Monsieur de Bellievre has addressed language to my ears, which, in truth, I know not well how to interpret. For, that you should be angry at my saving my own life, seems to me the threat of an enemy, which, I assure you, will never put me in fear, but is the shortest way to make me dispatch the cause of so much mischief. Let me, I pray you, understand in what sense I am to take these words; for I will not live an hour to endure that any Prince whatsoever should boast that he had humbled me into drinking such a cup as that. Monsieur de Bellievre has, indeed, somewhat softened his language, by adding that you in nowise wish any danger to accrue to me, and still less to cause me any. I therefore write you these few words, and if it please you to act accordingly, you shall never find a truer friend; but if otherwise, I neither am in so low a place, nor govern realms so inconsiderable, that I should in right and honour, yield to any living Prince who would injure me, and I doubt not, by the grace of God, to make my cause good for my own security.

I beseech you to think rather of the means of maintaining than of diminishing my friendship. Your Realm, my good brother, cannot abide many enemies. Give not the rein in God's name to wild horses, lest they should shake you from your saddle. I say this to you out of a true and upright heart, and implore the Creator to grant you long and happy life.

ELIZABETH.

XI. To James the Sixth, King of Scotland

The condemnation of Mary, Queen of Scots, aroused great feeling in Scotland, and James dispatched commissioners to intercede for his mother and to discuss his own rights of succession to the English throne. Whilst Mary's fate was still uncertain a new conspiracy was reported to the Council by William Stafford, brother to Sir Edward Stafford, Ambassador in France, who declared that Chasteauneuf, the French Ambassador in London, had tried to persuade him to have the Queen murdered. Chasteauneuf retorted that the true story was that Stafford had made the proposal to him and that he had forborn to send him bound to the Queen out of love for his family. Whatever may be the truth of the story, it so greatly increased the clamour for Mary's death that the Queen was persuaded to sign the warrant for her execution on 1st February.

January 1587.

I find myself so troubled lest sinister tales might delude you, my good brother, that I have willingly found out this messenger, whom I know most sincere to you and a true subject to me, to carry unto you my most sincere meaning toward you, and to request this just desire, that you never doubt my entire goodwill in your behalf; and do protest, that, if you knew, even since the arrival of your Commissioners (which if they liest, they may tell you), the extreme danger my life was in, by an Ambassador's honest silence, if not invention, and such good complices as have themselves, by God's permission, unfolded the whole conspiracy,

184

and have avouched it before his face, though it be the peril of their own lives, yet voluntarily, one of them never being suspected brake it with a Councillor to make me acquainted therewith. You may see whither I keep the serpent that poisons me, when they confess to have reward. By saving of her life they would have had mine. Do I not make myself, trow ye, a goodly prey for every wretch to devour? Transfigure yourself into my state, and suppose what you ought to do, and thereafter weigh my life, and reject the care of murder, and shun all baits that may untie our amities, and let all men know, that Princes know best their own laws, and misjudge not that you know not. For my part, I will not live to wrong the meanest. And so I conclude you with your own words, you will prosecute or mislike as much those that seek my ruin as if they sought your heart blood, and would I had none in mine if I would not do the like; as God knoweth, to Whom I make my humble prayers to inspire you with best desires.

Your most affectionate sister and cousin,
ELIZABETH R.

I am sending you a gentleman forthwith, the other being fallen sick, who I trust shall yield you good reason of my actions.

XII. TO JAMES THE SIXTH, KING OF SCOTLAND

Apparently written about the time that the Queen signed the warrant for Mary's execution. James's commissioners had proposed that Mary should be transferred into the custody of some neutral Prince.

c. February 1587.

Be not carried away, my dear brother, with the lewd persuasions of such as instead of informing you of my too needful and helpless cause of defending the breath that God hath given me, to be better spent than spilt by the bloody invention of traitors' hands, may perhaps make you believe, that either the offence was not so great, or if that cannot serve them, for the over-manifest trial which in public and by the greatest and most in this land hath been manifestly proved, yet they will make that her life may be saved and mine safe, which would God were true, for when you make view of my long danger endured these four, nay five, months' time to make a taste of, the greatest wits amongst mine own, and then of the French, and last of you, will grant that if need were not more than my malice she should not have her merits.

And now for a good conclusion of my long-tarried-for answer. Your Commissioners tell me, that I may trust her in the hand of some indifferent Prince, and have all her cousins and allies promise she will no more seek my ruin. Dear brother and cousin, weigh in true and equal balance whether they lack not much good ground when such stuff serves for their building. Suppose you I am so mad to trust my life in another's hand and send it out of my own? If the young Master of Gray, for currying favour with you, might fortune say it, yet old Master Melville hath years enough to teach him more wisdom than tell a Prince of any judgement such a contrarious, frivolous, maimed reason. Let your Councillors, for your honour, discharge their duty so much to you as to declare the absurdity of such our offer; and, for your part, I do assure myself too much of your wisdom as, though like a most natural good son you charged them to seek all means they could devise with wit or judgement to save her life, yet I cannot, nor do not, allege any fault to you of these persuasions, for I take it that you will remember, that advice or desires ought ever agree with the surety of the party sent to and honour of the sender, which when both you weigh, I doubt not but your wisdom will excuse my need, and wait my necessity, and not accuse me either of malice or of hate.

And now to conclude. Make account, I pray you, of my firm friendship, love, and care, of which you may make sure account, as one that never minds to fail from my word, nor swerve from our league, but will increase, by all good means, any action that may make true show of my stable amity; from which, my dear brother, let no sinister whisperers, nor busy troublers of Princes' States, persuade to leave your surest, and stick to unstable stays. Suppose them to be but the echoes to such whose stipendiaries they be, and will do more for their gain than your good. And so, God hold you ever in His blessed keeping, and make you see your true friends. Excuse my not writing sooner, for pain in one of my eyes was only the cause.

Your most assured loving sister and cousin,
ELIZABETH R.

Although she signed the warrant for Mary's execution, Queen Elizabeth was unwilling to give orders for its dispatch. Hereupon Burghley invited those of the Council who were available to meet him, and together they resolved to send the warrant on their own responsibility. It was sent from London on 4th February, and reached Fotheringhay on the following evening. On the 7th the Earls of Shrewsbury and Kent, who were charged with the duty of supervising the business, warned Mary to prepare for death on the following day. On the 9th the news of her execution reached London, and was received by the Queen with surprise and horror. Next day she expressed her detestation of the act to Hatton; and on the 10th she summoned the Council, rated them and ordered them out of her sight. Davison, her Secretary, she sent to the Tower. Four days later she wrote to James to declare her innocence of Mary's death. This letter has been very generally condemned as a typical example of the Queen's hypocrisy, and her whole action as timid and inexcusable.

Queen Elizabeth was no great stickler for truth, but her letter seems to express her true feelings at the moment. She certainly wished Mary dead, but she shrank, very naturally, from the irrevocable act. Not only was she naturally merciful, but she realized that though Mary's execution was legal and justifiable it was not necessarily so expedient as some of the Council thought; the deed would arouse detestation in all the Courts of Europe, and, by killing her cousin, she would bring on herself a war sanctioned by religion and give her enemies a legitimate argument for her own death. Nor was her instinct necessarily wrong. Had Mary been spared, it is not likely that she would have outlived Elizabeth and the long war with Spain would probably have been avoided. As it was, by their action the Council exposed her unawares to the general hatred of Christendom, so that her horror was genuine and her anger comprehensible. Historians, who can view these far-off matters without passion and without anxiety, do not always make sufficient allowance for the Queen's difficulty.

XIII. TO JAMES THE SIXTH, KING OF SCOTLAND

Written when the Queen had received the unexpected news of the execution of Mary, Queen of Scots.

February 14, 1587.

My dear Brother, I would you knew (though not felt) the extreme dolor that overwhelms my mind, for that miserable accident which (far contrary to my meaning) hath befallen. I have now sent this kinsman of mine, whom ere now it hath pleased you to favour, to instruct you truly of that which is too irksome for my pen to tell you. I beseech you that as God and many more know, how innocent I am in this case : so you will believe me, that if I had bid aught I would have bid by it. I am not so base minded that fear of any living creature or Prince should make me afraid to do that were just; or done, to deny the same. I am not of so base a lineage, nor carry so vile a mind. But, as not to disguise, fits not a King, so will I never dissemble my actions, but cause them show even as I meant them. Thus assuring yourself of me, that as I know this was deserved, yet if I had meant it I would never lay it on others' shoulders; no more will I not damnify myself that thought it not.

The circumstance it may please you to have of this bearer. And for your part, think you have not in the world a more loving kinswoman, nor a more dear friend than myself; nor any that will watch more carefully to preserve you and your estate. And who shall otherwise persuade you, judge them more partial to others than you. And thus in haste I leave to trouble you : beseeching God to send you a long reign. The 14th of February, 1586.

Your most assured loving sister and cousin,

ELIZAB. R.

XIV. TO ROBERT DUDLEY, EARL OF LEICESTER

In July 1587 Sluys, although heroically defended, was captured by the Duke of Parma. The Queen laid the blame on her allies, and, tired of the continual expenses of the forces in the Low Countries, and realizing the dangers that might follow if the enemy held a port so near to England, was anxious to make peace.

Finding by certain letters lately written to certain of our Council that the Duke of Parma both before the rendition of Sluys and since, continueth his former disposition to proceed in the treaty of peace for which purpose he hath sent hither a safe conduct for such Commissioners as we shall like to use in that service, whereof we send to you a copy. We have thought good considering the broken state of things therewith do threaten nothing but the ruin of those countries, the great touch of honour we have received by the loss of Sluys through the malice or other foul error of the States, and such as ought to have succoured it and the little hope we have of better success in times to come, to yield to the said treaty. And for that by the contract between us and the States of those countries, it is agreed that we shall not treat of anything with the King of Spain that may concern them without their privity. We think very [well] you should acquaint the States General with this our disposition and the urgent reasons leading us thereto, letting them understand at the time of the assembly that although the Duke of Parma hath above six months past made an overture unto us of peace with good authority to him given for the same from the King of Spain, referring the choice of the time, place, and quality of the person to us.

Yet did we not think it meet to enter over suddenly into a matter of so great weight, as well in respect of some doubt and scrupules that were laid before us that might move us to doubt some sound meaning, as also that we understood how great they of that country did dislike to enter into any treaty at all of peace. But now entering on the one side into consideration of the hard success that these wars are accompanied withal which groweth chiefly in respect of the contempt of public authority; lack of union among themselves and how unable they show themselves to be for lack of means to maintain and continue the wars as they ought to be maintained: and considering on the other side the great forces of Spain is now preparing both in Spain, Italy and Germany, the great provision he hath also made of treasure for the prosecuting of the wars in those countries, and also the great preparation he hath made by sea, being a thing likely that having so convenient a port as the town of Sluys is, he will draw his navy down thither with intent to assail them both by land and sea.

We cannot but advise them to concur with us in taking profit of this overture made unto us by the said Duke, for that otherwise we do not see how they shall be able to hold out but shall by the neglecting of the same obstinately persevere in a course that will work their open ruin whereof though through their unthankfulness, and sundry indignities offered unto us, the contempt of our government under yourself and misusage of our subjects, with daily loss of our subjects, for their price we have no great reason to be so careful as we have been and yet are. Yet considering the ancient intelligences that hath been between our countries and those there, and the great goodwill we understand the people generally do bear towards us, we would be loath to leave anything sudden that might tend to their good and conservation, even as though they were our own.

And whereas we are given to understand that certain illdisposed persons of those countries hearing of the overtures of peace that have been made to us by the said Duke have borne the people in hand that we had a meaning to make our peace apart, and to have delivered such towns of theirs as were in our possession into the King of Spain's hands, you shall let them know that besides the regard of our own honour, who have always carried ourself in such sort as hath appertained to one of our place and quality, we ourself are not ignorant that any peace made with disadvantageable conditions to their peril and danger cannot be with our safety, and, therefore, you shall conclude that in case they shall not be content to take profit of our advice in this behalf, but shall show themselves enemies or adversaries to all treaties of peace, we cannot but impute it to proceed of the ambition of some few of those that now have rule that seek still to continue the government in their own hands without care of the conservation of the generality whatsoever show they make to the contrary, which ought to lead us, seeing how greatly our honour both hath and shall be interested besides the consumption of our treasure and the lives of our subjects by taking part with persons obstinately bent to overthrow themselves and those countries to take some such way of counsel as shall be for our honour and safety.

And for that it is to be doubted that Count Hollocke and Maurice for their particulars will seek by all means and practices they can to impeach and hinder the said treaty, we think it very meet that you should by some such instruments as you shall think fit cause them to let understand that notwithstanding their strange manner of usage towards us, yet a special care shall be had in the said treaty to provide both for their benefit and safety as we shall understand from them to be expedient. It shall be also meet for you that you do make choice of some fit person to dispose the minds both of the State General and of the Council of State to embrace the said treaty when the overture shall be made.

And in case you shall find them inclinable to concur with us in the said overture, then shall you require them with all speed to make choice of certain Deputies or Commissioners of theirs to concur with ours in the said treaty : letting them also understand that the said Duke of Parma to the end the treaty may proceed with better success hath made offer unto us to yield to a cessation of arms having put us also in hope that such forces as are now preparing in Italy amounting to this number 15,000 footmen at the least shall be stayed so as such forces as are to be drawn to them from foreign parts may also be stayed which we see not but will prove beneficial to them. And therefore do look that they shall assent thereunto with falling out according to our expectation we think it meet for that the said Duke is content, as we have signified by our other letters unto you to treat about the said cessation of armies with such as you shall depute for that purpose that you shall send our servant, Henry Killigrew, or some other whom you shall think meet with some one whom the State shall appoint to win with him in that behalf.

xv. To James the Sixth, King of Scotland

For some time after the death of Mary, Queen of Scots, feelings between the English and Scots were bitter; but, with the increasing danger from Spain, it was very necessary to secure neutrality from the north. Henry Carey, Lord Hunsdon, was therefore sent on a mission to James to persuade him not to listen to the offers of the Spaniards. On Hunsdon's return the Queen resumed her letters with James.

c. May 11, 1588.

My pen, my dear brother, hath remained so long dry as I suppose it hardly would have taken ink again, but, mollified by the good justice that with your own person you have been pleased to execute, together with the large assurance that your words have given to some of my ministers, which all doth make me ready to drink most willingly a large draught of the river of Lethe, never minding to think of unkindness, but to turn my eyes to the making up of that sure amity and staunch goodwill which may be presently concluded in ending our league, that so unhappily, to my heart's grief, was delayed and differed, assuring you, on the faith of a Christian and word of a King, that my heart cannot accuse my conscience of one thought that might infringe our friendship, or let so good a work. God the cherisher[1] of all hearts ever so have misericord of my soul as my innocency in that matter deserveth, and no otherwise; which invocation were too dangerous for a guilty conscience; as I have commanded this bearer more at large to tell you. And for your part, my dear brother, think, and that with most truth, that if I find you willing to embrace it, you shall find of me the carefullest Prince of your quiet government, ready to assist you with force, with treasure, counsel, or anything you shall have need of, as much as in honour you can require, or upon cause you shall need. You may the more soundly trust my vows, for never yet were they stained, neither will I make you the first on whom I shall bestow untruth, which God will not suffer me to live unto.

I have millions of thanks to render you, that so frankly told to Carey such offers as were made you, which I doubt not but you shall ever have cause to rejoice that you refuse; for where they mean to weaken your surest friend, be you assured they intended to subject you and yours. For you see how they deal even with their own in all countries lesser than their own, and therefore God, for your best, I assure myself, will not let you fall into such

[1] In the original ' chersar '.

an apert danger, under the cloak, for all that, of harming other and advancing you: but I hope you will take Ulysses' wax to save you from such sirens. It were most honourable for you, if so it please you, to let them know that you never sent for their horse, though some of your Lords (too bold with you in many their notions and over saucy in this) made them believe you consented to their message, which they themselves desired your pardon for. This will make them fear you more hereafter, and make them afraid to attempt you to weaken your assured friend. If I deserve not your amity persecute me as your foe; but being yours, use me like a Prince who feareth none but God.

Your most assured loving sister and cousin,

ELIZABETH R.

XVI. TO JAMES THE SIXTH, KING OF SCOTLAND

In the summer of 1588 the long expected Armada set sail from Spain, and was sighted off the coast of England on the 19th July. After a week's intermittent fighting, the fleet reached Calais on the 27th, whence it was driven out on the 29th by the action of the fireships. On the 30th there was fighting all day, but on the 31st the south wind rose, and the Spanish ships were driven northward by the tempest which followed. There was thus considerable danger lest the Spaniards should land in Scotland, and by uniting with the Scottish Catholics cause trouble to both kingdoms. In the exultation of victory the Queen wrote to James, warning him of this danger. The 'rare young man and a wise' who carried the letter was Sir Robert Sidney, younger brother of Sir Philip.

August 1588.

Now may appear, my dear Brother, how malice conjoined with might strivest to make a shameful end to a villainous beginning, for, by God's singular favour, having their fleet well beaten in our Narrow Seas, and pressing with all violence, to achieve some watering place, to continue their pretended invasion, the winds have carried them to your coasts, where I doubt not they shall receive small succour and less welcome; unless those Lords that, so traitors like, would belie their own Prince, and promise another King relief in your name, be suffered to live at liberty, to dishonour you, peril you, and advance some other (which God

o

forbid you suffer them live to do). Therefore I send you this gentleman, a rare young man and a wise, to declare unto you my full opinion in this great cause, as one that never will abuse you to serve my own turn; nor will you do aught that myself would not perform if I were in your place. You may assure yourself that, for my part, I doubt no whit but that all this tyrannical, proud and brainsick attempt will be the beginning, though not the end, of the ruin of that King, that, most unkingly, even in the midst of treating peace, begins this wrongful war. He hath procured my greatest glory that meant my sorest wrack, and hath so dimmed the light of his sunshine, that who hath a will to obtain shame, let them keep his forces company. But for all this, for your self sake, let not the friends of Spain be suffered to yield them force; for though I fear not in the end the sequel, yet if, by leaving them unhelped, you may increase the English hearts unto you, you shall not do the worst deed for your behalf; for if aught should be done, your excuse will play the *boiteux*;[1] if you make not sure work with the likely men to do it. Look well unto it, I beseech you.

The necessity of this matter makes my scribbling the more speedy, hoping that you will measure my good affection with the right balance of my actions, which to you shall be ever such as I have professed, not doubting of the reciproque of your behalf, according as my last messenger unto you hath at large signified, for the which I render you a million of grateful thanks together, for the last general prohibition to your subjects not to foster nor aid our general foe, of which I doubt not the observation if the ringleaders be safe in your hands; as knoweth God, Who ever have you in His blessed keeping, with many happy years of reign.

Your most assured loving sister and cousin,

ELIZABETH R.

In April 1589 Sir Francis Drake and Sir John Norris led a naval expedition to Portugal to assist Don Antonio, Pretender to the throne, to recover Portugal from the Spaniards. The Earl of Essex (now aged twenty-one), contrary to the Queen's command, slipped away from the Court to take part in the expedition,

---

[1] *Boiteux*, ' cripple '; i.e. ' your excuse will be lame '.

accompanied by Sir Roger Williams. He embarked on the Swiftsure (a ship of the Navy Royal), and set sail, but did not join the fleet until it was at sea so that the letters recalling him to Court could not reach him until it was too late. The expedition, known as the 'Portugal voyage', was disappointing, for though the Spaniards were handsomely defeated in their own country, the Portuguese did not support Don Antonio, and of some 12,000 soldiers and sailors, half died of disease. The moral effect, however, was considerable, for (in Camden's words) ' England reaped this benefit by this voyage, that from this time forward it feared nothing from Spain but took greater heart and courage against the Spaniards '.

XVII.To Robert Devereux, Earl of Essex

The Queen was highly indignant when she heard that Essex had left Court contrary to her command, and wrote to recall him. He did not, however, receive the letter until the beginning of June when he returned home, and was forgiven.

April 15, 1589.

Essex,

Your sudden and undutiful departure from our presence and your place of attendance, you may easily conceive how offensive it is, and ought to be, unto us. Our great favours, bestowed on you without deserts, hath drawn you thus to neglect and forget your duty; for other constructions we cannot make of those your strange actions. Not meaning, therefore, to tolerate this your disordered part, we gave directions to some of our Privy Council to let you know our express pleasure for your immediate repair hither; which you have not performed, as your duty doth bind you, increasing greatly thereby your former offence and undutiful behaviour, in departing in such sort without our privity, having so special office of attendance and charge near our person. We do therefore charge and command you forthwith, upon receipt of these our letters, all excuses and delays set apart, to make your present and immediate repair unto us, to understand our further pleasure. Whereof see you fail not, as you will be loath to incur our indignation, and will answer for the contrary at your uttermost peril.

XVIII. To Thomas Bodley

Thomas Bodley was English Agent in the Low Countries from 1589 to 1596 when he retired from public life and devoted himself to the collection of his famous library. This letter is one of a number of official communications to the United Provinces. Ostend was a constant embarrassment as it was costly to hold and dangerous to lose.

May 3, 1589.

Where we have heretofore at sundry times caused the States there to understand that we had found the keeping of Ostend to be more chargeable unto us than we minded to continue, as well for the great decays of the fortifications by breaches made by the seas, as also by the often attempts made to besiege it. And, therefore, did require them to have regard thereto, and to see the decays repaired in convenient time, and to take the town into their own charge and defence; to which motions and warnings we hitherto have had no direct answers, as yourself partly knoweth, and so also we are here directly informed by the Lord Willoughby that in January last he did deliver to them the copy of our letters written to him in that behalf, and did require answer thereto but they only made answer to some other part of that our letters concerning their contentation for Sir John Norris to have some numbers of footmen and horsemen of our Army without giving any answer to the matter of Ostend, wherewith we have been somewhat offended with the Lord Willoughby for neglecting of that matter by leaving it unanswered.

Now, therefore, you shall let them know how much we do mislike to be thus used, in a matter of such importance, to receive no manner of answer. And, further, you shall let them plainly understand that we mind not to continue such a burdenous charge as this is, being also an extraordinary matter for us to maintain such a town as this is, subject both to the rages of the sea, and to the daily attempts of the enemy, and therefore you shall require them to use no further delay, but to take the town into their own government and defence, which doth properly belong to the general State of the Provinces United whereof that of Flanders is one. And if they shall not presently give order for the resuming thereof into their own charge, you shall say that we shall be compelled upon their refusal to think of some other means to be quit of the charge, and to withdraw our forces and abandon the town, which we shall be sorry to do, but yet we are excusable in reason, considering we have so many times notified this our purpose, and do now peremptorily warn them of our resolution. And if they shall upon conference with you, use some allegations, as that ' they are not able presently to take it into their charge, but that they will do their best to repair it ', or that ' they will hereafter accept it ', you shall allow no such dilatory answers but after your misliking and reproving of such delays you shall require to have either some better answer, or else an act of their refusal, whereupon we may with our honour abandon it and withdraw our people, for you shall resolutely affirm that we mind to do. And of your doing herein you shall speedily send us answer.

And yet so use all this matter in secret manner, as the knowledge thereof come not to the enemy before we may execute our resolution. You shall remember to the States that they did agree when Sir John Norris had obtained leave to have the numbers of horsemen and footmen out of the country that if in their absence there should be any need of succours for want of them then the States would supply for succouring of any place needful. And of this also the Lord Willoughby did make mention in January last so as either for Ostend or any other place that shall need of succour, we look they will give reasonable aid. And these our letters shall be your sufficient warrant and discharge in this behalf.

xix. To Sir John Norris and Sir Francis Drake

Written when certain news of Essex's departure in the Swiftsure *had reached Court. Sir Roger Williams was not executed, but forgiven, and in 1591 was sent out in command of the little Dieppe expeditionary force.*

May 4, 1589.

Trusty and well beloved, we greet you well. Although we doubt not but of yourselves you have so thoroughly weighed the heinousness of the offence lately committed by Sir Roger Williams, that you have both discharged him from the place and charge which was appointed him in that army, and committed the same to some other meet person (as we doubt not but you have choice of as sufficient as he is), and that you have also laid punishment upon him according to his desert; yet w‸ would not but you should also know from ourself, by these our special letters, our just wrath and indignation against him, and lay before you his intolerable contempt against ourself, and the authority you have from us, in that he forsook the army, and conveyed away also one of our principal ships from the rest of the fleet. In which points his offence is in so high a degree, that the same deserveth by all laws to be punished by death, which if you have not already done (and whereunto we know your authority as General doth warrant you) then we will and command you that you sequester him from all charge and service, and cause him to be safely kept, so as he slip not away until you shall know our further pleasure therein, as you will answer to the contrary at your perils; for as we have authority to rule, so we look to be obeyed, and to have obedience directly and surely continued unto us, and so look to be answered herein at your hands. Otherwise we will think you unworthy of the authority you have, and that you know not how to use it. In the meantime we have also found it strange, that, before your departing from Plymouth, you should either be so careless, or suffer yourselves so easily to be abused, that any of our ships, much more a principal ship, should be in such manner conveyed away from the rest of the fleet, and afterwards, also being so near as Falmouth (as we understood) should not by your commandment and direction be stayed; a matter which we cannot but remember unto you, and yet we do hope that you are no partakers of the offence that is committed.

And if Essex be now come into the company of the fleet, we straitly charge you that, all dilatory excuse set apart, you do forthwith cause him to be sent back hither in safe manner; which if you do not, you shall look to answer for the same to your smart, for these be no childish actions, nor matters wherein you are to deal by cunning of devises, to seek evasions, as the customs of lawyers is; neither will we be so satisfied at your hands. Therefore consider well of your doings herein.

XX. To James the Sixth, King of Scotland

In 1589 King James was betrothed to the Princess Anne of Denmark. Hereupon the Queen wrote to congratulate him.

September 1589.

As no tidings, my dear Brother, can ever come out of season to me that may breed you honour or contentment, so this last news, though sudden, of the approaching near of your coming Queen, bids me so much to bode you all the best blessings that the Mighty God can send you, in witness thereof to salute you both with an Ambassador, and some tokens, for sign of the happiness I wish that feast, and the gladness my heart should have received if it were as lawful to honour it with my presence as it is sure I bless it with my orisons. And for that the speed of such a bargain was far greater than the expectation of her arrival, you will, I trust, blame yourself, and impute no neglect to me, that my messengers come after the solemnities; for I assure you, but for my honour sake, my will would have hied their post with smaller company than fits my place. And in the meanwhile let it content you to give me so much right as to assure yourself no witness there of so princely a pact shall wish it more success, nor greater lasting joy than myself, that wisheth sign King no longer while than to see the performance of such alliance, having besides yourself, which is the principal, an inward zeal, which, since my childhood, I have born to the parents of your honourable Queen, to whom I desire all felicity, and never shall scrape from my memory the entire love they bare me; as knoweth God, Who ever bless and guide you.

Your most assured loving sister and cousin,

ELIZABETH.

XXI. To Lady Drury

Written on the death of Sir William Drury, killed in action in France.

1589.

Be well ware, my Bess, you strive not with divine ordinance, nor grudge at irremediable harms, lest you offend the highest Lord, and no whit amend your married hap. Heap not your harms where help there is none; but since you may not that you would wish that you can enjoy with comfort, a King for his power, and a Queen for her love, who leaves not now to protect you when your case requires care, and minds not to omit whatever may be best for you and yours.

Your most loving careful sovereign,

E.R.

XXII. To Lady Paget

Another specimen of the Queen's letters of sympathy, sent on the death of the Lady Paget's daughter, Lady Crompton.

Undated.

Call to mind, good Kate, how hardly we Princes can brook of crossing of our commands; how ireful will the Highest Power be (may you be sure) when murmurings shall be made of his pleasingest will? Let Nature therefore not hurt herself, but give place to the giver. Though this lesson be from a silly vicar, yet it is sent from a loving Sovereign.

XXIII. To James the Sixth, King of Scotland

The arrival of King James's bride was long delayed by contrary winds. James therefore in romantic and chivalrous manner went to fetch her. During his absence the Catholic Lords began to cause trouble.

1590.

Although my faith stands me, my dear Brother, in so good stead, as, without assurance by anyone [but] your own handwork, I do believe that God hath, of His goodness more than your heed, prospered to good end your untimely and, if I dare tell truth, evil-seasoned journey, yet I may no longer, though my courage could stay me till you first began, that best hath course to acknowledge thankfulness, stay but let you know, what humble sacrifice of thanks I yield to the Omnipotent for your safest stop for all your hard course, and am so bold to challenge some part of that surety to my heartiest orisons poured out of no feigned lips, which best is pleasing to His ears. And do beseech the same to send you, in this noble-raced lineage, such lasting joy as the continuance may yield you both happy.

And now to talk with you freely as paper may utter conceit. Accept my hourly care for your broken country, too too much infected with the malady of strangers' humours, and to receive no medicine so well compounded as if the owner make the mixture appropriated to the quality of the sickness. Know you, my dear Brother, for certain, that those ulcers that were too much skinned with the doulceness of your applications were but falsely shaded, and were within filled with such venom as hath burst out since your departure with most lewd offers to another King to enter your land, with declaration of their assured performance of their by-passed helps, and numbers great to undertake either part. If with my eyes I had not viewed these treasons, I would be ashamed to write them you. And shall I tell you my thought herein? I assure you, you are well worthy of such traitors, that, when you knew them, and had them, you betrayed your own surety in favouring their lives. Good Lord! who but yourself would have left such people to be able to do you wrong. Give order with speed that such scape not your correction, and hie your return, that is more your honour than another man's land, without you mind to make you seem innocent of your Realm's ruin, when absence will serve but for your bad excuse. Seld recovers Kings their dominion when greater possesses it; yea, such as their own scarce may endure for your tyranny.

My dear Brother, you see how far my entire care draws me out of the limits that another's affairs should pluck me to, but all such error I hope you will impute to affection, not my curiosity, and bear with overplain imputation, since it springs of so good a root. I crave of you, for your own best, to authorize, yea, animate, your faithfullest and guiltless of this conspiracy, that the fear not to apprehend in time (I pray God not too late), all such as any way they may suspect or know to be partakers of this faction. Believe no more to dandle such babies as may, or they come to honesty, shake your chair, for you have had too sour experience what such vain opinions hath bred you. I will not fail, from time to other, to warn such as I may think most clear of this infection of all my knowledge in this dangerous season, daring so much in your absence as to animate them not to linger this great matter till your return, for I know that were too late; the days that they have given are shorter than to expect so long. If my prayers were not more than my good [writing], I should be sorry to retain your eyes on so rude scribbling, wherefore I end, with my incessant prayers to God for your safe keeping and joyful return.

Your most affectionate loving sister and cousin,
ELIZABETH R.

After the finishing of my letter, there came to my hands an overture that makes me suppose it could not, nor durst not, have been offered me without your consent, albeit for it I neither saw your commission nor received from you one word thereof, but for all that, it makes me see your sight serves you not alone for present view, but makes you to behold the state of distant countries which do feel the smart of my undeserved hate, and makes the innocent blood call for revenge of evil-framed injuries. And though my conscience cannot accuse my thoughts to have by any cause procured such an enemy, and that he hath too plainly sought my life and kingdom, yet I think myself obliged to you that would make end of so unjust a war, and acknowledge the dead King of famous memory more happy in such faithful councillors than I see many Kings in their living servants. And for that they offer me, I will ever chronicle them among the just fulfillers of true trust. And albeit my wrongs be such as nature of a King ought rather, for their particular, die than not revenge, yet the top of my courage shall never overstretch my heart from care of Christian blood, and for that alone, no fear of him, I protest to God, from Whom both just quarrel, faithful subjects, and valiant acts I doubt not will depend : yet, am I thus content that you shall follow the well-devised method, and if he will give plain grant without a guileful meaning, I will make known that in me the lack of so good a work shall never be found.

XXIV. To James the Sixth, King of Scotland

At this time the doctrines of the English Presbyterians were causing much anxiety to the Queen and Council. Two months

*later Thomas Cartwright, the most influential of their leaders,
was brought before the Ecclesiastical Commissioners, and charged,
amongst other offences, with renouncing the ecclesiastical orders
of the Church of England as anti-Christian and unlawful; with
establishing an Eldership which exercised right of censure,
admonition and excommunication; with criticizing the government and officials of the Church of England, and claiming that
the Eldership was a Divine Institution and the only lawful
Church government; with summoning synods at various places;
and in general with creating a religious organization opposed to
the Establishment. As Cartwright and many of his followers
were men of undoubted purity and piety in their lives, they won
a considerable following.*

*Queen Elizabeth had no great patience with the subtleties of
theologians; she objected not so much to the religious beliefs of
the Presbyterians as to the logical and practical results of their
doctrines. Civil and Ecclesiastical government were two aspects
of one State, and the claim to disobey the one implied a right to
disobey the other. Extreme Puritans indeed claimed that in all
matters of doctrine, morality and even civil policy the final
authority lay with the national synod of their own adherents.
Magistrates and even Kings were to be subject to their control;
and if they refused to obey the decisions of the synod they were
to be deposed.*

*Hearing that the Scottish Presbyterians were sheltering
refugees and publicly praying for their persecuted English
brethren, the Queen wrote to King James.*

July 6, 1590.

Greater promises, more affection, and grants of more
acknowledgings of received good turns, my dear Brother, none
can better remember than this gentleman by your charge hath
made me understand; whereby I think all my endeavours well
recompensed, that see them so well acknowledged; and do trust
that my counsels, if they so much content you, will serve for
memorials to turn your actions to serve the turn of your safe
government, and make the lookers-on honour your worth, and
reverence such a ruler.

And lest fair semblance, that easily may beguile, do not breed
your ignorance of such persons as either pretend religion or dissemble devotion, let me warn you that there is risen, both in your
Realm and mine, a sect of perilous consequence, such as would

have no Kings but a presbytery, and take our place while they enjoy our privilege, with a shade of God's Word, which none is judged to follow right without by their censure they be so deemed. Yea, look we well unto them. When they have made in our people's hearts a doubt of our religion, and that we err if they say so, what perilous issue this may make I rather think than mind to write. *Sapienti pauca.* I pray you stop the mouths, or make shorter the tongues, of such ministers as dare presume to make orison in their pulpits for the persecuted in England for the Gospel.

Suppose you, my dear Brother, that I can tolerate such scandals of my sincere government? No. I hope, howsoever you be pleased to bear with their audacity towards yourself, yet you will not suffer a strange King receive that indignity at such caterpillars' hand, that instead of fruit, I am afraid will stuff your Realm with venom. Of this I have particularized more to this bearer, together with other answers to his charge, beseeching you to hear them, and not to give more harbour-room to vagabond traitors and seditious inventors, but to return them to me, or banish them your land. And thus with my many thanks for your honourable entertainment of my late embassade, I commit you to God, Who ever preserve you from all evil counsel, and send you grace to follow the best.

Your most assured loving sister and cousin,

Elizabeth R.

CHAPTER V
1591-1603

In the early 1590's the Queen took a hand in French affairs. By the death of the Duke of Anjou, Henry of Navarre became heir to the French King, Henry the Third, but, since he was a Protestant, the Catholics formed a League to compel Henry III to submit to their demands. Henry III effected the murder of the Duke of Guise, the Catholic leader, but was himself murdered on 1st August, 1589. The League refused to recognize Henry of Navarre as their King, and civil war followed. The Spaniards came to the help of the Leaguers; the Queen helped Henry with money, arms and men, and at the battle of Arques the Leaguers were put to flight. In 1590 further Spanish reinforcements arrived which overran Picardy and Brittany. In 1591 two small English expeditions were sent over, the first into Brittany under Sir John Norris, the second into Normandy under command of Sir Roger Williams. The Normandy force was soon afterwards entrusted to the Earl of Essex, who was, however, ordered to consult the older and experienced soldiers and Sir Henry Unton, the Ambassador.

1.To William Cecil, Lord Burghley

In May 1591 the Queen was entertained by Burghley at Theobalds. Burghley was now over seventy years old, and, feeling the affairs of State too great a burden, wished to retire into private life. Hereupon the Queen addressed him this mock charter.

May 10, 1591.

Elizabetha Anglorum id est a nitore angelorum Regina formosissima et felicissima: To the disconsolate and retired sprite, the eremite of Theobalds, and to all other disaffected souls, claiming by, from, or under the said eremite, sendeth greeting. Where, in our High Court of Chancery it is given us to understand that you, Sir Eremite, the abandonate of Nature's fair works, and Servant to Heaven's wonders, have (for the space of two years and two months) possessed yourself of fair Theobalds with her sweet rosary the same time, the recreation of our right trusty and right well beloved, Sir William Cecil, Knight, leaving to him the old rude repose, wherein twice five years (at his cost) your contemplate life was relieved, which place and fate inevitable hath brought griefs innumerable (for lower grief biddeth no compare), suffering your solitary eye to bring into her house desolation and mourning, joys' destroyers and annoy friends; whereby Paradise is grown wilderness, and for green grass are comen grey hairs, with cruel banishment from the fruit of long labour, the possession whereof he hath holden many years, the want of the mean profit thereof (health and gladness) having been greatly to his hindrance; which toucheth us most in the interest we have in his faithful service; besides the law of his loving neighbours and friends, infinite, as by the record of their countenances most plainly may appear.

We upon advised consideration have command you, eremite, to your old cave, too good for the forsaken, too bad for our worthily beloved Councillor. And because we greatly tender your comfort, we have given power to our Chancellor, to make out such and so many writs, as to him shall be thought good, to abjure Desolations and Mourning (the consumer of sweetness) to the frozen seas and deserts of Arabia Petrosa, upon pain of 500 despites to their terror, and contempt of their torments, if they attempt any part of your house again : Enjoining you to the enjoyment of your own house, and delight without memory of any mortal accident, or wretched adversary.

And for that you have been so good a servant to common tranquillity, we command Solace to give the full and pacific possession of all and every part thereof : not departing until our favour (that ever hath inclined to your meek nature) have assured you peace in the possession thereof. Wherein we command all causes within the Prerogative of our High Favour to give you no interruption. And this under the pain aforesaid they shall not omit. *Teste me ipsa apud Theobalds, 10ᵐᵒ die Maii, regni nostri 33°.*

11. To Henry the Fourth, King of France

When Essex was sent over to Normandy, the Queen wrote to the French King to warn him that Essex was impetuous, and at the same time to treat her soldiers with tact and consideration.

Translated from the French

July 27, 1591.

According to the promise which I have always kept in your behalf, my dearest brother, I send 4,000 men to your aid, with a Lieutenant who appears to me very competent. His quality, and the place he holds about me, are such, that it is not customary to permit him to be absent from me; but all these reasons I have forgotten on the present occasion, preferring, to our own necessity and convenience, the gratification of your wish; for which cause, I doubt not, you will respond, with an honourable and careful respect for your greatness, by giving him a favourable reception. In regard to his many merits, you may be assured, if (which most I fear) the rashness of his youth does not make him too precipitate, you will never have cause to doubt his boldness in your service, for he has given too frequent proofs that he regards no peril, be it what it may; and you are entreated to bear in mind, that he is too impetuous to be given the reins.

But, my God, how can I dream of making any reasonable requests to you, seeing you are so careless of your own life. I must appear a very foolish creature; only, I repeat to you, that he will require the bridle rather than the spur. Nevertheless, I hope he will be found to possess skill enough to lead his troops on to do you worthy service; and I dare promise that our subjects are so well disposed, and have hearts so valiant, that they will serve you to ruin all your foes, if their good fortune corresponds with their desires. And now, for the wages of all these forces, I must make you two requests: the first, on which depends their lives, your heart being such that nothing ought to be omitted that regards them, that you will cherish them, not as those who serve as mercenaries, but freely from good affection; also that you will not carry them into too great danger. You are so wise a Prince, that I am assured you will not forget that our two nations have not often accorded so well but they would remember their ancient quarrels, not considering themselves of the same country, but separated by a mighty deep; and that you will so bear it in hand, that no inconveniences shall arise when they arrive. I have, on my part, inculcated good lessons on my people, which, I am assured, they will observe.

And now, not to fatigue you with too long a letter, I will conclude with this advice : that, in approaching our coasts, you would not forget to *débouche* the way to Parma in all directions where he might enter, for I am assured that he has received orders to press towards the Low Countries rather than to France.

Your very assured good sister and cousin,

E.R.

III. To Sir Henry Unton, Ambassador in France

The main purpose of the English assistance to Henry IV was to prevent the Spaniards from occupying the ports in Normandy and Brittany. Unton was instructed to remind the King of his promises, most of which, indeed, he was quite unable to fulfil.

Chichester, August 22, 1591.

Upon knowledge given us of your continuing sick of an ague at Dieppe, whereof we heard nothing until the coming of this bearer, Thomas Smith, from thence, we found ourselves much grieved therewith, for that the same hath happened to you in a strange country, although we hope you shall be shortly recovered, which the messenger reported you were towards. And finding now that our forces were sent thither in such haste as they are inutile, because the King with his forces hath not been ready there, as was formerly promised by him and his ministers when they provoked us thereto, though in very truth we did always fear the ready performance of their promises when we understood that the King had directed himself to the siege of a town far off, from whence he knew not how to remove; yet such was the importunity of the King and his Ambassadors here, and the inclination of our Council to give more credit to the promises than we ourselves hoped to be performed with that speed that was promised, as we were in a manner led thereunto against our own opinion. And yet now leaving all new debate thereof, because of that which is past, we find it most necessary that all means be used to delay no more time, but seriously and with celerity to amend this error.

And therefore, though by the King's absence and your sickness you cannot presently, as our Ambassador, show to him these preposterous actions in sending our forces thither as an aid to his in those parts, where his was not come, as were promised; yet we require you, by advice of Grimston, or by some other ways, if your health will not suffer you to go to him, to make choice of some of his Council that are noted men of experience and fidelity and direct your letters to them, with such earnest reasons as the cause requireth : and specially the King to ponder the weight of our last letters, which were sent to you as well for the accelerating of this action for Rouen, as for further succours of Bretagne, to which we daily hear the King of Spain sendeth new forces.   And amongst other reasons to be used, you may say also that we ourselves do well consider how dangerous it shall be to divide his forces, at the least so to esloin himself from this action of Rouen, as for further succours of Bretagne, as by lack of his presence the enterprise must be more doubtful; specially consider-ing he hath lost such opportunity of time past since he determined it, having neglected occasion, which is figured bald, and being once past cannot be recovered.

You shall not omit to let him know that for our great kind-ness many ways showed to him, and specially by yielding to him the services, yea the hazard of the lives of so many of our subjects, we do firmly hope that he will have no less respect to them for putting them to desperate hazards than he will have to his own subjects.

These reasons and arguments you may use, as proceeding from our writing from our own mouth and from our own heart, presuming that where we have so urgent and great reasons either to write or speak earnestly, the King will interpret the same in good part.   And so we end; wishing you to have care of your own health, which we desire as much to hear of as any friend you have, excepting your own wife.

IV. To Sir Thomas Leighton and Henry Killigrew

Soon after reaching his army, Essex left the troops and with a small escort rode through hostile country to meet Henry, narrowly escaping capture on his way back.   The Queen was doubly annoyed.   The King was not fulfilling his promise to recapture Rouen, and Essex had left his command without leave.

September 2, 1591.

ELIZABETH R.

Right trusty and well beloved, we greet you well. Although we hope that both of you will have due regard of such directions as by your own mouth hath been severally delivered to you for the counselling and advising of our cousin, the Earl of Essex, General of our army there; yet some cause we have to doubt of you, Henry Killigrew, that being sent over with the Earl and present when he departed with our army to the French King without our knowledge, we know not whether you did advise him from that journey until we had allowed thereof or no, or what you did therein we know not; but what you ought to have done we think yourself cannot be ignorant. And now where he is, or what he doth, or what he is to do, we are ignorant also; for since his going from his charge we never heard word from him. But omitting this error past, now we think it meet you should understand how more errors are committed, for hither came Monsieur de Reaux, as you, Leighton, do know, but after your departure after he had been seven days in our Realm, passing by us within less than two miles, at length he came; and with letters written before Noyon was taken, he declared certain causes of the King's absence from these parts at this time, when by accord between him and us, upon the arrival of our forces, he should have come with his army into those quarters to have besieged Rouen, whereas it [is] seen our forces have been there about one month at our great charges and to no purpose, without any appearance of forces provided on the King's part. And further, he hath made request that we should command the Earl of Essex to employ our forces to some other purpose, as the French King should find it good for himself. And though the said de Reau hath used many arguments to persuade us thereunto, yet considering we perceiving what inconveniences and inestimable charge these motions would drive us, and have contrary to all reason and honour the intention we had in yielding to these succours is meant to be frustrate, we have flatly denied to assent thereunto, and have so advertised the said Earl by your letters, with charge that he do only obey our commandment, and use our advices, and observe the purposes for the which we sent him, and as was solemnly accorded between the French King and us, and his army to join with us to the besieging of Rouen, and that only for the space of two months, whereof one month is already past, and but one remaining, wherein which time we find no reason to think that anything of moment can be done to the town after so large delay given to the enemy to fortify it.

And yet because on our part nothing shall be omitted that we have promised, we are content that our forces shall continue to the end of the second month, to be accompted from the time of their arrival; and after that time our full purpose is they shall be revoked, against which time shipping shall be provided to transport them into our Realm.   But if it should happen, which we think unlikely, that the French King shall presently and without delay attempt to besiege it, and that before the end of the second month, it may be probable that the continuance of our forces for the space of one month, or forty days more, might help to bring the enterprise to effect, we shall be contented that either the whole or part thereof shall remain so as it may be made certain and plain beforehand that the French King will make like good payment to them weekly, as we have done during their abode; for otherwise we will not have any of them to abide longer than until they may be shipped after the end of the second month, wherein we will have you not to be abused by any promises of words, but by certainty of pay, whereof we may doubt how the French King shall perform that, considering in the time of the Lord Willoughby promises were made of payment to our forces for their longer abiding than was at the first intended, yet the pay which they had, though it was named to be the French King's pay, was with our money lent here to his Ambassadors being parcel of greater sums due to us.   Nevertheless yet you may seek to understand of Monsieur Saldagne and others there, whither the money collected and granted to the King by the Parliament of Caen hath been reported to be granted conditionally that the King should enterprise to take Rouen, may not in part be assured to pay our forces for the surplusage of the time they shall serve; whereof if good assurance may be had for ready weekly payments, we shall be more willing to have them continue to the only purpose for the winning of Rouen or Newhaven,[1] but for no other purpose. And hereof you shall confer with our General; and as you shall find this matter probable, to be duly performed, so you shall treat thereof with the King's Council there, and speedily advertise us what may be hoped for and with what assurance the same may be performed, because according to that which you shall advertise us, the shipping may be sent against the end of the next month or otherwise stayed.

From Lichfield, the 2 of September, 1591.

[Postscript written with the Lord Treasurer's own hand]

By the Queen's commandment I do let you understand that her Majesty hearing after this letter signed, that her Majesty's Ambassador was not yet departed from Dieppe, would have you impart this her letter to him, and to use his advice and credit as her Majesty's Ambassador, with any pertaining there to the King. And so I have by her Majesty's commandment advertised him of her pleasure.

v. To Sir Henry Unton and Sir Thomas Leighton

The Queen rebuked Unton and Leighton for disobeying her orders.

September 25, 1591.

Trusty and well beloved, we greet you well. Although, upon the hearing of your letters lately sent hither we perceive that you gave advice and consent to the Earl of Essex, upon the Marshal Biron's request, to go meet him on the way, to consult about the siege of Gournay, and that you, the Ambassador, and Leighton did accompany him thither, for which your attempt therein, and for your further advice given to carry our forces thither to Gournay, and the hasty sending them thither, we commanded our Treasurer to declare to you how we misliked those your inconsiderate actions, directly contrary to our former letters written to you, by which we signified our mind to have the Earl and our forces to return, and not to continue longer than to the end of the two months; yet the more we think of these your

---

[1] i.e. Le Havre.

errors in counselling of the Earl, or assenting to him, contrary to our direction, the greater we find your fault to be, and find it necessary that you should so understand the same to be by your own letters, letting you to understand that we conceived better both of your discretions and dutifulness, when we sent you thither, than thus, after knowledge given you of our determination for their return, as soon as shipping might come for them after the end of the two months, to give counsel to remove them farther into France many days marches from the seaside, and that, to the siege of a town of strength never mentioned to us before, and uncertain how long the siege might continue, and altogether uncertain how our people should be paid after the end of the two months, which was to expire within eight or nine days after your consent. Such a counsel, notwithstanding any discourses made to you by the Marshal of the necessity of the besieging that place, cannot be defended, at the least not to be executed without first having our allowance. And therefore let this be a warning to you hereafter, by no persuasions of a stranger to assent unto anything on our part that shall appear contrary to our determination, without our privity and allowance.

And as to you, our Ambassadors, going to Louviers, we find it strange, not knowing for what cause you should go any way forward to follow the French King, from whom we have received such cause of discontentment, as yourself doth well know, except the world should see that by your following of him to remote parts we should in a sort grace him for his disgracing of us, and our General and people; considering when we sent you thither, our meaning was that you should have found him there near Rouen, according to his promise. And therefore we will you rather to return back to some place free from infection, where you may remain without danger to your health; and when he shall come towards Rouen, whereof we see no certainty, then it shall be sufficient enough for you to go to him; if otherwise we shall not find it more convenient to revoke you.

And to the intent none of you may allege ignorance of the just causes of our discontentment, but may, as cause shall be given to any of you upon speech with any of the French King's Council that shall seem to mislike of the revocation of our forces, be informed to answer therein; we have commanded a memorial to be made in writing containing some special points, which we have both sent to the Earl of Essex for his instruction, and have commanded the like to be sent to you; which writing containeth nothing but truth, and that which cannot be denied by the King nor any his ministers.

vi. To Robert Devereux, Earl of Essex

The expedition to Normandy was originally sanctioned for two months only, but as the French King was making good progress against the rebels and had at last begun the siege of Rouen, the Queen agreed to allow her army to remain. At the same time she rebuked Essex for rashness. Essex was more concerned with winning a reputation for bravery than strategy in the field.

Oatlands, October 4, 1591.

Whereby sundry our late letters, some to yourself, and some to our Ambassador, and Sir Thomas Leighton, we declared our pleasure to be, that both you and our forces should return from thence after the end of the two months, according as was accorded afore your going thither; and having showed and sent to you in writing very good causes, which moved us thereto, such as, if you have weighed them with a mind and judgement not blinded with vain persuasions, either of yourself or of such others, as do accompany you with their glorious windy discourses, you would have readily assented thereto. Yea, besides the regard of our honour, which hath been overmuch blemished by the King's actions, even for your own reputation, you would, without our commandment, at the end of two months, which was the time limited for your charge, have returned.

But yet, since our commandment sent for your return, which we doubt not but you have disposed yourself according to your duty to have performed, we have lately considered, that since the winning of Gournay in so short a time, whereof we are very glad, and that we perceive the attempt of Caudebec, and the besieging also of Rouen is begun, and like well to succeed; wherein also we certainly understand that our people, not only with their own proper forces, but with a reputation of them, are

like to give great furtherance, and their revocation great
hindrance; and that also other the forces of the King, which are
promised to be shortly brought thither by himself, as we are
made to believe, might percase be discomforted, upon report of
the revocation of ours; and so also to enterprise against Rouen
and Newhaven might fall to the ground; and the enemies' forces,
which are to come from sundry places, might have more comfort
to come towards Rouen to raise the siege thereof.

For these considerations only, and not to pleasure the King
at all, how earnest soever he hath and may be to intreat us to stay
our forces there for some longer time than by covenant we have
been bound, we are content, that if the King shall make due payment to our army there for the time of their abode, after the two
months expired, then, notwithstanding our former commandments, you and our forces shall, and may remain for one month
longer, or   days so as they shall be employed only to
recover Rouen and Newhaven, and for no other service, and yet
we think it meet, that such of our forces as are grown by any
sickness infections unable to serve, should be dismissed and sent
home; but not to come to our City of London, nor to populous
towns, but for avoiding of further infection.   And this our contentation, with the causes thereof, you shall impart to the Marshal
Biron, and to others of the King's Council there, so as they may
understand, that herein we. have more regard of the common
cause to be relieved, and the dangers avoided, than particularly
to gratify the King therein, whose strange actions towards us in
many of his proceedings, contrary to our many advices for his
own weal, hate bred in us a great misliking, such as though his
affairs may hereby receive advancement, yet we will not require
any thanks from him for the same.

Finally considering the former enterprise at Rouen, whereby
besides the loss of Devereux,[1] there might have happened a great
loss of our people, yea of the most principal persons, was such as
we had reason in our former letters to condemn it of rash ends;
yet now, understanding that since our censure thereof, and the
general misliking by many others, Roger Williams hath presumed
in an audacious and foolish manner by writing to command, yea,

[1] Walter Devereux, Essex's younger brother.

to extol it, as thereby apparently manifesting himself to have been the author or principal persuader thereof, so as we have just cause to doubt that he may, continuing in his error, commit the like offence again, the rather considering he hath the principal office of the field as Marshal, and thereby, and by the credit he presumeth to have with you our General, we do think it very convenient to avoid all such like occasions by his dangerous advices or rash directions : And therefore we will and command you, that no action of any moment be attempted by his advice, either privately or publicly, without the assent of Sir Thomas Leighton, and some other of the captains of most discretion and understanding. And so we require you to observe this our commandment; for otherwise it were better for our service that he were displaced, notwithstanding we know he can serve well in his kind.

VII. To Henry the Fourth, King of France

Henry had promised to undertake the siege of Rouen in person, and the Queen was indignant because he had not as yet fulfilled his promise.

November 9, 1591.

My pen has never touched paper which was subject to so strange an argument as to show a new accident in a friendship much injured by him whose sole support has been ministered by the party most offended. From our enemies we were expecting nothing but every evil dealing, and our friends lend us as much; what difference do we find? I am astonished that any one, who is so much beholden to us for aid in his need, should pay his most assured friend in such base coin. Can you imagine that the softness of my sex deprives me of the courage to resent a public affront? The royal blood I boast could not brook, from the mightiest Prince in Christendom, such treatment as you have within the last three months offered to me. Be not displeased if I tell you roundly, that if thus you treat your friends, who freely, and from pure affection, are serving you at a most important time, they will fail you hereafter at your greatest need. I would instantly have withdrawn my troops, had it not appeared to me that your ruin would have been the result, if the others, led by my· example, and apprehending similar treatment, should desert you. This consideration induces me to allow them to remain a little longer; blushing, meantime, that I am made to the world the spectacle of a despised princess. I beseech the Creator to inspire you with a better way of preserving your friends.

Your sister, who merits better treatment than she has had,

E.R.

VIII. To Robert Devereux, Earl of Essex

The Queen authorized Essex to return to report on the state of affairs in France, again rebuking him for rashness.

December 23, 1591.

Having received your letters of the 18th of this month, we expected thoroughly to understand particularly what reason we should have to continue our force with the French King underneath your charge, for which purpose you only pretended to us to be desirous to go over, with an offer to make your repair hither presently upon the true view of the state of things there, and the likelihood of their amendment or present declination.

To this your earnest and vehement desire we were contented to assent, rather by the persuasion of divers that saw your judgement so transported with the humour of the journey, than that, by our own observation of all the course of this action, we had not apprehended both the untoward proceedings hitherto, and thoroughly foreseen the unlikelihood of any good to come hereafter, especially in such an action as had received his greatest wound, even in his first beginning, for want of timely proceeding, which all wise men do account the half gained in any action of importance.

Immediately upon your departure, before your arrival there, we received letters from the King declaring the desperateness of his estate and the nature of his demands, so unreasonable, or rather so impossible to be performed, if we could have been contented to have been further exhausted by his endless devices, as we did much marvel to see a Prince so much to forget his friends, and could not but be offended with any that would presume to recommend the same. He assured us of the entrance of the Duke of Parma, and that he would most certainly be at Rouen within fifteen days, and therefore if he had not then 5,000 men to meet him, he did not only expect little good, but rather quite the contrary, for so are the very words of his own letter. This seemed so strange to all that know the proceedings herein, as they never expected letters from you, but your immediate personal repair, wherein you should have showed there a resolute judgement no longer to be led on, and here have confirmed that which your words assured us, and those which wished you best have most expected.

We hear besides, to our no small wonder, how little the King regards the hazard of our men, and how you, our General, at all times refuse not to run with them to all service of greatest peril, but even, like the forlorn hope[1] of a battle, to bring them to the slaughter. And therefore in regard that divers gentlemen of good quality, dear to their parents and blood, should not be vainly consumed to the grief of such as were contented to suffer them to go there for our service, we do command you to send them back although yourself should stay; which for our own part, notwithstanding daily entreating to revoke you, we are determined not to do so long as one man is left behind; only this we are content to let you know, that if at last you shall be so well advised as to think how dishonourable it is for you to tarry with so mean a charge, after so many men consumed so little to the purpose they went sent for, with many other absurd defects, which blemish the honour of the place you hold under us as our General, we shall right well allow of your judgement to return as a thing very fit and necessary to be performed, and hereby do authorize you to leave our said companies with the Marshal and Serjeant-Major, without putting Sir Thomas Leighton to any further trouble in this hard time of the winter, so great an enemy to his infirmity; of which our pleasure, leaving other particularities to be answered by our Treasurer, we have thought good to acquaint you by our own handwriting.

[1] The ' forlorn hope ', i.e. the small body of men preceding the vanguard.

IX. TO JAMES THE SIXTH, KING OF SCOTLAND

*In 1592 James was considerably troubled by the rebellion of
Francis Hepburn, Earl of Bothwell, insomuch that he was compelled to flee from place to place to avoid capture. The Queen
rebuked him for lack of kingly qualities.*

September 11, 1592.

The dear care, my dear Brother, that ever I carried, from your
infancy, of your prosperous estate and quiet, could not permit
hear of so many, yea so traitorous attempts, without unspeakable
dolour and unexpressful woe, of which to be [by] your own
messenger ascertained, breeds my infinite thanks, with many a
grateful thought for so kind a part. To redouble crimes so oft,
I say with your pardon, most to your charge, which never durst
have been renewed if the first had received the condign reward;
for slacking of due correction engenders the bold minds for new
crimes. And if my counsels had as well been followed as they
were truly meant, your subjects had now better known their
King, and you no more need of further justice. You find by
sour experience what this neglect hath bred you.

I hear of so uncouth a way taken by some of your conventions,
yea, agreed to by yourself, that I must [wonder] how you will
be clerk to such lessons. Must a King be prescribed what
Councillors he will take as if you were their ward? Shall you
be obliged to tie or undo what they list make or revoke? O
Lord, what strange dreams hear I, that would God they were so,
for then at my waking I should find them fables. If you mean,
therefore, to reign, I exhort you to show you worthy the place,
which never can be surely settled without a steady course held to
make you loved and feared. I assure myself many have escaped
your hands more for dread of your remissness than for love of the
escaped; so oft they see you cherishing some men for open crimes,
and so they mistrust more their revenge than your assurance. My
affection for you best lies on this, my plainness, whose patience
is too much moved with these like everlasting faults.

And since it likes you to demand my counsel, I find so many
ways your state so unjointed, that it needs a skilfuller bone-
setter than I to join each part in his right place. But to fulfil

your will, take, in short, these few words: For all whoso you know the assailers of your courts, the shameful attempters of your sacred decree, if ever you pardon, I will never be the suitor. Who to peril a King were inventors or actors, they should crack a halter if I were King. Such is my charity. Who under pretence of bettering your estate, endangers the King, or needs will be his schoolmasters, if I might appoint their university they should be assigned to learn first to obey; so should they better teach you next. I am not so unskilful of a kingly rule that I would wink at no fault, yet would be open-eyed at public indignity. Neither should all have the whip though some were scourged. But if, like a toy, of a King's life so oft endangered nought shall follow but a scorn, what sequel I may doubt of such contempt I dread to think and dare not name. The rest I bequeath to the trust of your faithful servant, and pray the Almighty God to inspire you in time, afore too late, to cut their combs whose crest may danger you. I am void of malice, God is judge. I know them not. Forgive this too too long a writing.

x. To James the Sixth, King of Scotland

In January 1593 a Scottish gentleman, George Ker, brother to the Abbot of Newbottle, was taken whilst endeavouring to leave Scotland for Spain. In his luggage various blank papers were found signed and sealed by the Catholic Earls of Huntly, Errol and Angus. Ker was put to the torture of the boots and revealed a plot of the Catholic Lords who were to be joined by Spanish troops; the blank papers were, he confessed, to have been filled up by him later, according to verbal instructions already received. The letter was written by the Queen when the first news of the conspiracy reached her.

January 1593.

My most dear Brother,

Wonders and marvels do so assail my conceit, as that the long expecting of your needful answers to matters of such weight as my late letters carried needs not seem strange. Though I know they ought be more regarded, and speedily performed, yet such I see the eminent danger and wellnigh ready approach of your state's ruin, your life's peril, and neighbour's wrong, as I may not (to keep you company) neglect what I should, though you forget that you ought. I am sorry I am driven from warning to heed, and from too much trust to seek a true way how your deeds, not your words, may make me assurance that you be no way guilty of your own decay and other danger. Receive, therefore, in short, what course I mind to hold, and how you may make bold of my unfeigned love and ever constant regard.

You know, my dear Brother, that, since you first breathed, I regarded always to conserve it as my womb it had been you bear.[1] Yea, I withstood the hands and helps of a mighty King to make you safe, even gained by the blood of many my dear subjects' lives. I made myself the bulwark betwixt you and your harms when many a wile was invented to steal you from your land, and making other possess your soil. When your best holds were in my hands, did I retain them? Nay, I both conserved them and rendered them to you. Could I endure (though to my great expense) that foreigners should have footing in your kingdom, albeit there was then some lawful semblance to make other suppose (that cared not as I did) that there was no danger meant? No. I never left till all the French that kept their life parted from your soil, and so it pleased the Highest to bless me in that action, as you have ever since reigned void of other nation than your own. Now, to preserve this, you have overslipped so many sundry and dangerous attempts, in neither uniting with them when you knew them, nor cutting them off when you had them, that if you haste no better now than heretofore, it will be too late to help when none shall avail you.

Let me remember you how well I was thanked, or he rewarded, that once brought all the letters of all those wicked conspirators of the Spanish faction, even the selfsame that still you have, to your eminent peril, conserved in their estates. Was I not so much doubted as it was thought an Italian[2] invention to make you hold me dearer, and contrived of malice, not done by cause : and, in that respect, the poor man, that knew no more of his taking but as if thieves had assailed him, he most cruelly suffered so guiltless a martyrdom as his tormentors doubted his life : so sore had he the ' boots ' when they were evil-worthy life

---

[1] i.e. as if I had been your mother.
[2] i.e. subtle.

that bade it. See what good encouragement I received for many watchful cases for your best safety! Well, did this so discomfort my goodwill as, for all this, did I not ever serve for your true espial, even when you left your land and yours ready, wellnigh, to receive such foreign forces as they required and were promised? Which, if you had been pleased to know, was and is too evident to be proved. But what of all this, if he who most ought, did naught to assure him, or to requite them?

Now, of late, a lewd fellow hath been apprehended with letters and instructions. I pray God he be so well handled as he may confess all his knowledge in the Spanish conspiracy, and that you use not this man as slightly as you done the ringleaders of this treason. I vow, if you do not rake it to the bottom, you will verify what many a wise man hath (viewing your proceedings) judged of your guiltiness of your own wrack; with a warning, that they will you no harm in enabling you with so rich a protector, that will prove, in the end, a destroyer.

I have beheld, of late, a strange, dishonourable, and danger-ous pardon, which if it be true, you have not only neglected yourself but wronged me, that have too much procured your good to be so evil-guerdoned with such a wrong, as to have a free forgiveness of aught conspired against my person and estate. Suppose you, my dear brother, that these be not rather ensigns of an enemy than the taste of a friend? I require, therefore, to all this, a resolute answer, which I challenge of right, that may be deeds, both by speedy apprehension with busy regard, and not in sort as public rumour may precede present action, but rather that they be entrapped or they do look therefor; for I may make deem you would not have [them] taken, and what will follow then, you shall see when best you look. Think me, I pray you, not ignorant what becometh a King to do, and that will I never omit; praying you to trust Bowes in the rest as myself. I am ashamed that so disordered courses makes my pen exceed a letter, and so drives me to molest your eyes with my too long scribbling, and therefore end, with my earnest prayers to God that He will inspire you to do, in best time, all for your best.

Your loving, affectionate sister,

ELIZABETH R.

XI. To Henry the Fourth, King of France

In spite of the aid given him by the Queen, Henry was unable to make any progress against his enemies. In the summer 1593, he was converted to Catholicism and made terms with his Catholic rebels. The Queen was horrified, not only lest his immortal soul should perish everlastingly, but more immediately lest he should join the Spaniards and repudiate his debts to her. Her fears were not realized, as Henry declared war on Spain and endeavoured to eject the Spaniards from his country.

Translated from the French

July 1593.

Ah what griefs, what regret, what groanings I feel in my soul at the sound of such news as Morlains has recounted. My God, is it possible that any earthly respect should efface that terror wherewith Divine fear threatens us? Can we reasonably even expect a good issue from an act so iniquitous? He who has for many years preserved you by His hand, can you imagine that He allows you to go alone in the greatest need? Ah, it is dangerous to do ill that good may come of it. Yet I hope that sounder inspiration shall come to you. In the meantime I shall not cease to set you in the foremost rank of my devotions that the hands of Esau undo not the blessing of Jacob. And where you promise me all friendship and faith, I confess that I have dearly merited it, and of that I shall not repent, provided that you will not change your father : otherwise I shall be to you but a bastard sister, or at least not of the same father. For I shall prefer always the natural to the adopted, as God best knows, Who guides you to the right way of the best feeling. Your very assured sister, if it be after the old manner; with the new, I have nothing to do.

E.R.

XII. To James the Sixth, King of Scotland

In the early weeks of 1593, King James advanced against the Catholic Lords, who fled, leaving their estates in his hands. When the Parliament met in June, it was proposed to bring in an act of attainder against the rebels, but James refused, and his Advocate, Master David Makgill, declared that the evidence against them

R

*was insufficient. A few weeks later Bothwell succeeded in
secretly entering the palace and appeared before James with
drawn sword and the King was once more a virtual captive.
James thought that Bothwell intended to murder him, but Bothwell declared his loyalty, and it was at length agreed between
them that Bothwell should stand his trial for attempting to
procure the King's death. Pending the trial Bothwell retired
into England nominally to seek Elizabeth's advice and betook
himself to Durham, where he made himself the guest of Dr.
Toby Mathew, the Dean. Bothwell returned to Scotland and
was duly acquitted. But Catholic help was now at hand; James
was freed of the domination of Bothwell; and it was even
rumoured that he was intending to turn Catholic.*

October 7, 1593.

MY DEAR BROTHER,

If the variableness of Scottish affairs had not inured me with
too old a custom, I should never leave wondering at such strange
and uncouth actions, but I have so oft with careful eyes foreseen
the evil-coming harms, and with my watch foremet with chiefest
attempts, and see them either not believed or not redressed, that
I wax faint under such burden and weary of fruitless labour.
One while, I receive a writ of oblivion and forgiveness; then, a
revocation with new additions of later consideration; sometimes,
some you call traitors with proclaim, and anon, there must be
no proof allowed, though never so apparent, against them. Yea,
if one lewd advocate, perchance hired for the nonce, dare
pronounce a sentence for them, though one of like state deny the
same, his word must not take place. It seems a paradox to me,
that, if of two pleaders one be for the King, the equal number
shall not serve for a King. I muse how any so lewd a man hath
been chosen for such a place, as durst come in open view to plead
against his master. Their office is, as to do right, so do the
sovereign no wrong. If he had doubted, as no honest man could,
he ought been absent rather than there to play so unfitting a part,
though secretly he had told it you. He is happy he is no Englishman. You should have heard other news of him then.

Old Melville, I perceive, hath told you a piece of a tale and
left out the principal. My words were these, ' I hear say the
offending Lords hope by their friends to escape their pain : I

suppose your King too wise to be so unmindful of his peril to suffer unprosecuted such as would tral [*sic*] their country to strangers' courtesy, having known it so plain and so long, for this is not their first offence.   But if his power served not to apprehend, yet to condemn I doubted not, for if ever he would pardon them, which I could hardly counsel, yet I could not think, without some obligation to some other Prince, that for their request he would do it.'

Now to this great cause that touches us both so much.   First, consider of what profession they be; next, to whom they have made vow for religion, the which I can christen treason, under what cloak soever.   I have oft told you I was never horseleech for blood, but rather than your overtrust should peril the creditor, I would wish them their worst desert.   Then how to credit that so oft hath deceived?   My brains be too shallow to fathom that bottom.   How hardly remedies be applied to help inveterated maladies.   I have small skill of such surgery.   In fine, I see neither judgement, counsel, nor sure affection in so betraying advice as to give yourself such a lash that they shall be both uncondemned and saved.   What thanks may they give your mercy when no crime is tried?   ·What bond shall tie their proffered loyalty if no precedent offences past be acknowledged by confession?   Shall they leave to adhere to that party which they never made?   Or what oath shall be sure to such as their profession scarce thinks lawful for a trust?   I vow to the living Lord that no malice to any nor turbulent spirit, but your true surety and Realm's freedom, enforceth my so plain discourse, which cannot omit that there be left so great a blot to your honour as the receiving them uncondemned to your grace.

And for Bothwell, Jesus! did ever any muse more than I, that you could so quietly put up so temerarious indigne a fact, and yet by your hand receive assurance that all was pardoned and finished.   I refer me to my own letters what doom I gave thereof. And now to hear all revoked, and either scanted or denied, and the wheel to turn to as ill a spoke.   I can say, bad is the best, but yet of evils the least is to be taken.   And if I were in your place, I would, or he departed, make him try himself no suitor for their favour whose persons let him prosecute; so shall you best know him. For there be liars if deeply they have not sought him or now.

But that I weigh most is the small regard that your sure party may make you, when they see you adhere to your own foes, abandoning the others' service. I fear me the fame blows too far that you will not pursue the side of which you be, whatso your words do sound. And this conceit may breed, if not already, more unsound hearts than all the patching of these bad matters can work you pleasure. You are supposed (I must be plain for dissemble I will not) to have received this heretical opinion, that foreign force shall strengthen you, not endanger you, and that all these Lords seek your greatness not your decay. O how wicked Sirens' songs! which, in first show, please; in end ruins and destroys. May enough of God's reason befall you to resist so destroying advice, and be so well lightened as not so dark a cloud may dim you from the sight of your best good, which cannot be more shunned than by the not yielding to so betraying deceit; from the which I will incessantly pray for your deliverance, wishing you many days of reign and long.

Your most assured Sister,

ELIZABETH R.

XIII. TO JAMES THE SIXTH, KING OF SCOTLAND

In the spring of 1594, James having now strengthened his position, began to take action against the Catholic Lords. Bothwell tried to take advantage of his distraction, and with a force largely recruited from the English Border marched on Edinburgh, but finding that the King was too strong for him, retired again into England. As there was every reason to suppose that Queen Elizabeth had actively supported Bothwell, James was indignant. He sent Edward Bruce, a minister of the Kirk, openly to invite her to be godmother to his first born son (afterwards Henry, Prince of Wales) but privately to protest at her action in a vigorous and sarcastic letter, in which he gave her back some of her own sentiments. 'So many unexpected murders, Madame and dearest Sister,' he began, ' have of late so overshadowed my eyes and mind, and dazzled so all my senses, as in truth I neither know what I should say, nor where at first to begin; but, thinking it best to take a pattern of yourself, since I deal with you, I must,

repeating the first words of your last letter, only the sex changed,
say " I rue my sight that views the evident spectacle of a seduced
Queen." '   He went on to threaten her, with the Virgilian tag
'Flectere si nequeo superos, Acheronta movebo.'   The Queen
was indignant but embarrassed, and took great care over the
wording of her reply.   The letter sent differs considerably from
her own first draft which survives.

May 1594.

Though by the effects, I seld see, my good Brother, that
ever my advices be followed, yet that you have vouchsafed to give
them the reading I well understand, as having made some of them
the theme of your last, though, God knows, applied far away
from their true sense or right desert; for if I sin in abuse, I claim
you the author of my deceit, in believing more good than sequele
hath told me.   For I have great wrong if you suppose that any
persuasion from whomsoever can make me have one evil opinion
of your actions, if themselves be not the cause.   I confess that
divers be the affections of many men, some to one, some to
another, but my rule of trust shall never fail me, when it is
grounded, not on the sands of every man's humour, but on the
steady rock of approved fact.   I should condemn my wicked disposition to found any amity promised upon so tickle ground that
others' hate might break the bounds of my love, and upon others'
judgements to build my confidence.   For Bothwell's bold and
unruly entrance into my borders, I am so far from guilt of such
a fault as I protest if I had received an answer in seventeen weeks'
space of my letter that contained his offer to reveal unto you the
treason of the Lords with foreigners, I could soon have banished
him from thence; and next, he came with your own hand to
warrant that no offence was imputed, which made the borderers
readier to receive him; but after I had not left unpunished some
of his receipters I could not have believed they durst have procured the pain due for such desert, and mind to make them afraid
to venture such a crime again; and if order now given to all the
Wardens do not suffice, I vow their bodies and purses shall well
suffer therefor.

I will not trouble you with recital of what this gentleman
hath heard in all the other points, but this toucheth me so near

as I must answer, that my deserts to you have been so sincere as shall never need a threat of hell to her that hath ever procured your bliss. And, that you may know I am that Prince that never can endure a menace at my enemy's hand, much less of one so dearly treated, I will give you this bond, that affection and kind treatment shall ever prevail, but fear or doubt shall never procure aught from me; and do avow, that if you do aught by foreigners, which I know in the end worst for yourself and country, it shall be the worst aid that ever King had, and I fear may make me do more than you will call back in haste. Dear Brother, use such a friend, therefore, as she is worthy, and give her ever cause to remain such a one as her affection hath ever merited, whose rashness is not such as neglect their own so near if they will not forgo their best and shun their own mishaps, whom none can at my hand procure but your own facts. Thus, hoping that this bearer will tell you my faithful meaning and sincere professions, with all the rest that I have committed to him, I leave this scribbling, beseeching God ever more to preserve you.

Your most affectionate sister and cousin,

ELIZABETH R.

XIV. To Ernestus, Archduke of Austria, Governor of the Spanish Netherlands

In 1594 several plots against the Queen's life were discovered, the most sensational being that of Dr. Roderigo Lopez, who was condemned for compassing the Queen's death by poison at the instigation of the Spanish King and his ministers. In order to ventilate her annoyance at such unkingly conduct, she proposed to send Sir Thomas Wilkes to the Archduke with proofs of the Spaniards' complicity, and a special messenger was sent to demand a safe conduct for Wilkes. The messenger returned with a letter from the Archduke in which he said that he expected to have nothing propounded which might be to the disservice of the King of Spain. He committed the further offence of addressing himself simply ' to the Queen of England ', without any of her titles of honour. This letter is her reply to the insult.

c. October 20, 1594.

We have received a letter, signed by you the 14 of October, which was brought to us by him that carried our letter dated the 11 September; which, being considered by us for the form of the direction within your letter, we see so different in style and title from that which is due to us, as being a Sovereign Queen of Realms, and that both by the Emperors, your grandfather, your father and brother, yea, by all Kings and Potentates in their letters, hath from the beginning of our reign been attributed to us; and also adding thereto the consideration of a special clause in your letter that you do trust that we will not cause anything to be proposed to you *au desservice* of the King, your lord and uncle, we are now sorry that we did write to you in such friendly manner as we did, having no reciproque regard of us by you in your letters, and have cause also to forbear to impart that which we meant in a friendly manner you might understand, as being a Governor under the King of Spain, and assisted by some persons as Councillors with you, which was that we had sundry matters to declare to you, which, being true, touched the King, your uncle's, honour, either to suffer great lack thereby or by some good means to discharge himself thereof. And in like sort for certain others, his principal ministers with you, it should have appeared by what good proofs they were to be charged with certain detestable facts to be abhorred by all good Christians. And now that by your writing you seem to be unwilling to hear of anything to the deservice of the King, how far you will interpret to concern the deservice of the King, we know not; and therefore we mean not to trouble you herewith otherwise than we mind to publish the matters to the world, as the same are proved or affirmed, without any sinister additions, and then we shall expect such issue thereof both by you, under whose governance such detestable acts have been attempted, and by the King of Spain, whom the same doth so nearly touch as in reason he ought to discharge himself of the same being imputed to him by his own ministers. Which if he shall not, we mind otherwise, by God's favour, to procure a redress thereof by such other course as hitherto we have forborne.

xv. To Henry the Fourth, King of France

On 17th December, 1594, a young man named Jean Chastel, a member of the Jesuit College at Claremont, attempted to murder the French King with a poniard. As a result the Jesuits were forthwith ordered to quit France. The Queen wrote to congratulate Henry on his escape.

Translated from the French

c. December 1594.

The courteous and honourable reception, my beloved brother, which you have been pleased to vouchsafe to this gentleman, together with the wish you have testified of showing the same good offices to me, render me so infinitely obliged to you, that words fail me in my attempts to demonstrate my veritable thoughts in regard to you. I entreat you to believe that I should think myself too happy, if fortune should ever send an hour in which I could, by speech, express to you all the blessings and felicity that my heart wishes you; and among the rest, that God may accord to you the grace to make a difference between those that never fail you, and spirits ever restless. It appears to me that gratitude is sacrifice pleasant in the sight of the Eternal, Who has extended His mercy more than once to guard you in so narrow an escape, that never Prince had a greater; which, when I heard, I had as much joy as horror of the peril thereof. And I have rendered very humble thanks, on my bended knees, where solely it was due, and thought that He had sent you this wicked herald to render you more chary of your person, and make your officers of your chamber take more care. I have no need to remind you of some shops where fine drugs are forthcoming, and it is not enough to be of their religion. You stayed long enough among the Huguenots at first to make them think of the difference, and you may well fear. You will pardon always the faults of good affection, which renders me so bold in your behalf; and I am very glad to hear that you dare, without the licence of licentiates, do so much for your surety and honour to crush this single seed, which has sown more tares in a dozen years than all Christian princes can exterminate in as many ages. God grant that they may be uprooted out of your dominions! Yet no phrenatique can lead you to such just reasoning. I make no doubt but that the Divine hand will avert from you all bad designs, as I supplicate very humbly, and recommend myself a thousand times to your good graces.

Your very affectionate sister,
ELIZABETH.

XVI. TO THE MOSLEM EMPEROR

A formal letter on behalf of Sigismund, Vayrod of Transylvania.

Translated from the Latin

February 9, 1595.

Sigismund, the Most Illustrious Vayrod of Transylvania, a Prince very friendly to us, hath sent us in these days an Ambassador with letters whereby he hath informed us of the state of his Province, and hath sought that we might by our intercession alleviate his affairs, which in no mean measure are thrown into confusion by your Imperial Majesty. For the fame of your Majesty's goodwill towards us is noised abroad amongst all the Princes of Europe, whereon relying they often implore our aid in their affairs. This therefore we could by no reason deny him, not only because of the ancient union of the friendship of his family towards us, as also because of the form of the Christian religion which he practises with us, having rejected the superstition of the Pope of Rome and the worship of images.

Since therefore he avers that himself and the state of Transylvania to be aggrieved in certain matters by your ministers contrary to the terms of the treaty and even against the desire of your Majesty, we especially ask your Majesty that it may please you mercifully to incline your exalted ears to his humble prayers, and having heard his complaints through fit persons, as shall appear, to grant them relief according to law and right.

Which thing because of the conformity of the religion of his state with us and our ancient friendship with his family, and his necessity, we vehemently beg with our whole heart of your Imperial Majesty.

May the Best and Greatest God, Creator of the Heaven and Earth, keep your Majesty safe and unharmed.

> Given at our Palace in our City of London, the 9th day of February, in the year of our Saviour Jesus Christ 1594 [-5], the 36th year of our reign.

XVII. To Sir Francis Drake and Sir John Hawkins

In the summer of 1595 Drake and Hawkins collected an expedition which was intended to seize the Spanish treasure at Panama. It consisted of six ships of the Queen's navy, twenty-one other ships and barks, and 2,500 men. Sir Thomas Basker-ville accompanied them as general of the land forces. The expedition was much criticized; rumours of a new Spanish armada were constant, and it was felt that to send away so large a fleet at such a critical time was a rash proceeding hardly counter-balanced by the hope of booty. Contrary winds delayed the departure of the fleet.

August 1, 1595.

We have returned you this gentleman[1] with as much expedition as the consideration of such an affair would permit us, with some instructions in writing signed by our Council agreeable to our directions, which our pleasure is should be followed by you for the present action; requiring you both, in these and all other things which he shall impart unto you, to give him full and ample credit. By this our sending one so near unto us thus suddenly after his former painful journey (to whom you are not a little beholding for his report of the exceeding care and pains of you and our servant Baskerville for all things belonging to our service), we trust that you very well conceive that we are full of care for you as persons to whom we wish all happy and prosperous success, no doubting but you will think that if we do not much rely upon your faith, valour and judgement, we would not commit to you so great a charge, and especially in such a time, considering the nature of this action, where matter of money is one of our least adventures in comparison of the rest. And therefore be thus persuaded, that our extraordinary experience of your former merits is the only and chiefest cause of this so extra-

[1] Sir Thomas Gorges.

ordinary an affiance in those courses to which you have conducted us both for the honour and benefit of our estate, which we assure ourselves shall so be managed by you as conclusion of your actions shall prove the great and general expectation of the beginning; wherein we doubt not but you will affix your surest anchorhold, as well as we do in all things, in God's good favour and providence, Who can and will direct both your counsels and actions to the good of our estate and your particular honour and reputation.   There is nothing more acceptable to us, nor any greater argument of your discretions and affections to our service, than the report which this gentleman delivereth of both yours and Sir Thomas Baskerville's good and mutual conjunction of love and kindness.

XVIII. To Sir Francis Drake and Sir John Hawkins

As usual on such occasions the Queen was nervous and apprehensive, and constantly changing her mind. The contrary winds still prevented the fleet from sailing. On the 28th August they weighed anchor in Plymouth Sound. Neither Drake nor Hawkins came back, and the expedition, having failed in its object, returned in the following May, having lost heavily by disease.

August 16, 1595.

We have received your letters of the 11th, whereof we are not satisfied for the principal matters whereof we gave you direction by ours, neither for your forbearing to go upon the coast of Spain to meet with the Spanish forces that might issue thence, neither yet by your refusal to spend a month to the meeting with the Indian fleet; but though we are content to pass over your answers to these two points, yet we can no ways allow your uncertain and frivolous answer to our notion to have knowledge in what time we might hope of your return, in that you have used words altogether uncertain, without answering either our opinion or according to your former promise that the voyage might be performed in six or seven months.   And for proof of the probability thereof, in our opinion, we sent you an information given us by men of credit, within what time the voyage might be reasonably made, with God's favour and reasonable winds, whereof you have made no mention, but passed it over with all uncertainty; wherein we have cause to doubt whether you have taken to heart or had regard to our former reasons expressly contained in our letters, which as dutiful subjects you ought to have done, having neither limited any time certain by your own judgement, nor answering the time expressed by us. And though you may say that no person can make assurance of such matter without God's sufferance to have wind meet therefor, yet you might so have said that, with God's favour, having no let by wind, you had a full intention to have finished the journey within the space of six or seven months, as at the first you did promise; or, enlarging yourselves with two months more, your voyage might be ended by the end of April, or at the furthest by middest May, which is nine months. But considering you have not herein answered us, as you ought to have done, we cannot assent to your departure without you shall presently herein satisfy us, in showing your intention fully in what time you shall mind to finish the voyage, having, with God's favour, a reasonable wind to further you. And so we charge you, upon your allegiance, to make us a direct answer, either that you mind and purpose by all your means possible to finish your voyage in the time by us aforementioned, which if you shall upon your allegiance assure us that you mind so certainly to do, then we are content that with the next good wind you may depart, or else make you an account that the journey shall stay; for the breaking whereof the disgrace shall be yours; and to diminish the loss for the charges sustained, you shall consider how the chargeable provisions may be dispersed with least loss, and the companies also discharged, so as the loss betwixt us and you may be made as little as can be devised; and therein we charge you hereby advertise us with speed of your opinion for order to be given accordingly.

XIX. To Henry the Fourth, King of France

Don Antonio, the unfortunate Pretender to the throne of Portugal, lived for some years in England after the failure of the 'Portugal Voyage'. Then he went over to Paris, where he died in poverty on 12th August, 1595. The French King had granted him a pension which was not paid. Queen Elizabeth now wrote to King Henry on behalf of the children.

Translated from the French

c. August 1595.

If the spirit of one departed could disturb a living friend, I should fear that the late King Anthony (whose soul may God pardon) would pursue me in all places, if I did not perform his last request, which charged me, by all our friendship, that I should remind you after his death of the good and honourable offers which you made to him while living, that you might be pleased to fulfil them in the persons of his orphans and son, which I must own to be an office worthy of such a Prince, who will not forget, I feel assured, the wishes of him who can no longer himself return thanks, and that you will not omit the opportunity of being crowned with that true glory, which shall sound the trumpet to your honour.

I am not so presumptuous as to prescribe to you what it befits you to do, but submit the case to your sound judgement, as you must know, better than any one else, what will be most suitable to the state of your realm. Only having acquitted myself of my charge, I implore you to treat this desolate Prince so well, that he may know who it is that has written for him, and have him in your good favour, praying the Lord God to preserve you for many years, which is the desire of

Your very affectionate sister,

ELIZABETH.

xx. To Frances, Countess of Hertford

The Earl of Hertford's troubles have already been shown in the letter printed on page 35. His first wife died in 1567. The present Countess was Frances, daughter of Lord Howard of Effingham. The Queen at this time was much irritated because the question of her successor was being publicly discussed by gossips. Father Parsons, the Jesuit, had written a book called A Conference about the Succession to the Crown of England, *which he dedicated to the Earl of Essex. A copy of the book had just reached the Queen, who showed it to Essex. About the same time she heard that the Earl of Hertford had secretly caused a record to be put into the Court of Arches to prove his former marriage lawful and his children legitimate. He was therefore sent to the Tower. His Countess was so distressed that the Queen wrote her the following:*

November 5, 1595.

GOOD FRANCES,

We do well understand your disposition to be troubled with sudden impressions, even in matters of little moment, as we would not forget you in this accident of your Lord's misfortune, and therefore have thought it not amiss, even by our own hand-writing, your brother being absent whom otherwise we would have used, to assure you of the continuance of our former grace to yourself, and to preserve your spirit from those perturbations which love to the person offending, and apprehension of the matter so far unexpected, might daily breed in your body and mind. To acquaint you with all the particular circumstances of his offence now [is] not convenient; neither could it aught avail you, who have been ignorant of all those causes; but (to prevent any apprehension that this crime is in its nature more pernicious and malicious than as an act of lewd and proud contempt against our own direct prohibition) we have vouchsafed to cause a ticket to be shown you by this gentleman, which may suffer to resolve you from further doubting what it is not, and so satisfy your mind for caring for that which care remedies not, it being a matter both proved by record, and confessed with repentance.

And therefore as you ought well to know how far it is from our desire to pick out fault in such as his, so believe that we (who are slow to rigour towards the meanest) will use no more severity than is requisite for others' caution in like cases, and it shall stand with honour and necessity. And for yourself, as you will quickly judge when you understand it, that his offence can have on you no colour of imputation; so do we assure you that though for any of his faults you should not be one jot the less esteemed, yet we will say that for your sake in this or in anything else he shall find himself without your suit [   ] the better used. Trust therefore (good Frank) to this assurance, as the voice of that Prince to whose pure and constant mind you are no stranger, and comfort yourself that you have served one who wisheth still your good, and care for the contrary.

And for a farewell, observe this rule of us, that seeing griefs and troubles in this world make haste enough unsent for to surprise us, that there can be no folly greater than by fearing that which is not, nor by overgrieving for that which needs not, to overthrow at one instant the health of mind and body, which once being lost, the rest of our life is labour and sorrow, a work to God unacceptable, and to our friends discomfortable.

XXI. TO JAMES THE SIXTH, KING OF SCOTLAND

In January 1596 the Queen again sent Sir Robert Bowes as her special Ambassador to Scotland bearing two letters, one for the King and the other for the Queen. There had been quarrels between King James and Queen Anne over the guardianship of the young Prince, which the King insisted on entrusting to the Earl of Mar. In her letter to the King, Queen Elizabeth refers to the reliable reports which were coming in that the Spaniards were again proposing to invade England, and commends the King for a proclamation to his subjects calling upon them to resist the common enemy.

January [?28], 1596.

MY DEAR BROTHER,

If the wracked state, and well-nigh ruined, of this poor gentleman, through the faithless trust of deceiving servants, in looking every week of the ending of his troubles [had not occasioned me to delay], I could not have left my pen so long dry, but would have filled it to you with matter full of truth, and memorials of my cares, which never are at rest for your best avail, and meant to warn you of such occurrence as other nations afford me; especially, such as might touch the safety of our countries, and honours of ourselves. Although I do not doubt, as now I do perceive, that you should think them now overstale for news, being by good espials not made ignorant of our enemies' drifts, whose scope have their bounds while either lives in reign, but the ever guider of best actions, and readiest ruiner of wicked acts, will, I doubt not, cool their heat, abate their pride, and confound their force. I am not such a weakly nor of so base a courage, that ever I mean break one slumber for their malice, nor once dream of their victory, whose ground-

work is of so slipper foundation that the hold of such edifice will
be overturned with his own guilt. I may not deny but
Epimetheus is no companion for a King. With Prometheus,
therefore, I mind to follow that after-wish condemn not for judgement, and thereafter prepare such means and power, that, I fear
not, shall be so marshalled as shall make us no scorn to the
world, nor delight to our foes; in some such sort as I hear you
have begun; whose praise, if I should not lessen in praising, I
could more dilate, but this much I must tell you, that I cannot
imagine how you could by any more glorious means set out your
care for your land, your love to your neighbours, your hate to
such wrongful invaders, than with your pen and charge to your
subjects you have uttered, in words of such effect and matter, of
such weight, as, in honest deemers, it may mar the fashion of
devilish machines,[1] and craze the hearts of treason-minding men.
In me it hath set a deep impression of a cousin-like zeal, that
mixeth not his loss with her decay, and joyeth not that she should
perish first, in hope of better fare; which, as it is ever unsure,
so seld is it not a wind-shaked blast. But your so speedy care
for threats, that they may not arrive to deeds, doth assure me
that they shall have no just cause that should make such a scruple.
Receive, therefore, dear Brother, both my censure, and my thanks
therefor, as she that will not suffer you to go one foot beyond
her in busy inquiring and narrow searching what fitteth best for
my counsel, or my warning for that may concern your safety or
estate, as I have charged this my Ambassador to tell you more at
length, as time and cause shall invite me, not omitting to beseech
you, that as I know him most obsequious in aught that may concern you, so it will please you to shadow him with your grace
against the spirits of such as may fortune envy him but shall
never match him. Thus I end my tedious scribbling, which you
will the rather pardon for to recompense the long space that my
writing hath not spoken with you, praying the Everliving God
ever to preserve you from sinister counsel, and all else may ever
befall you may prosper.

Your most affectionate sister and cousin,

ELIZABETH R.

---

[1] i.e. 'machinations'.

XXII. To Anne, Queen of Scots

With the previous letter, Sir Robert Bowes bore a letter for Queen Anne. This letter is typical of the Queen's correspondence. The bulk of it is in her Secretary's hand, the postscript is her own, and the real message is to be delivered verbally by the bearer.

January 28, 1596.

By a servant of ours of such trust as is this gentleman, well known to you, whom now we do return to exercise his charge of Ambassador towards the King, our brother, we would not omit to salute you, with assurance of the continuance of such kindness as we have always professed towards you, although the good intelligence heretofore offered on your part have of late passed under greater silence. And yet, sweet is our inclination still to hold a firm correspondency with you upon all occasions, whereby we may demonstrate our care towards yourself and the King, our brother. We have given in charge to this our faithful servant, sincerely attached to the preservation of perfect amity between both Kingdoms, both freely to impart with you and carefully to deliver over to us, such things as you shall at any time think meet for our understanding, who never will be found behind with any offices of true kindness and affection.

[*Postscript in the Queen's hand*]·

Sister, I beseech you let a few of your own lines satisfy me in some one point that is boasted of against you, which this bearer will tell you.

XXIII. To the Emperor, Rudolph the Second

Thomas Arundel, son of Sir Matthew Arundel, went abroad as a soldier of Fortune to serve under the Emperor against the Turks, and so greatly distinguished himself that the Emperor created him Count (i.e. Earl) of the Holy Roman Empire. He returned to England, in circumstances described in the letter, with letters from the Emperor to Queen Elizabeth. The Queen was always unwilling to allow her subjects to accept titles and honours from foreign rulers. She was so angry that she caused Arundel to be restrained and proposed to take away his title. He retorted (in a letter to Cecil) that if the Queen were to take upon herself

*to unmake a Count of the Empire, it would cause great offence
amongst the German Princes. The Queen accordingly wrote to
the Emperor to explain her attitude in the matter.*

March 1596.

We have received letters from your Majesty, dated the 30th of
the month of December, in commendation of a subject of ours
named Thomas Arundel, a gentleman whom we recommended
to your Majesty certain years past at his desire to travel beyond
seas; which letters of yours came not to our hands before the
6th of this month of March, by reason the said Thomas Arundel
in his coming hither by sea suffered shipwreck and was forced
to save his life by swimming. But hearing by report that he
pretended to have a title to be an Earl of the Empire (a matter
very strange unto us and not credited), whereto he alleged that
he was by a grant under your Majesty's Seal of the Empire
preferred and created, although the same original grant was, as
he said, lost in the seas with other his goods at the shipwreck,
we entering into a further consideration of this his allegation,
pretending that he should now come home as an Earl that when
he went from hence was but a private gentleman without any
title of honour, and but the son of an ancient gentleman that
now liveth without other degree than to be *eques auratus*; adding
thereto also of our certain knowledge, that there was never any
example in this age nor of any former time that any natural
born subject of this kingdom was ever preferred by any, either
Emperor or other King in Christendom, to such high title of
honour; neither yet do we think it convenient or agreeable to
reason that any subject to a Prince Sovereign should receive any
honour whereby to be bound to do service to a Prince to whom
he is not a born subject, without some former allowance of his
natural Lord and Prince, to whom he is wholly and solely bound
by his natural birth, to serve with his life, blood, lands, goods,
and all his earthly power without exception or reservation to
any other Prince: upon which considerations we thought him
worthy of great reprehension either for seeking or accepting
such a dignity without our knowledge. And hearing of this his
report that he had brought such a grant from your Majesty
(though the original with your seal was lost), we did command

him to forbear to come to our presence, or to challenge to himself any such title of dignity as never any subject of our realm had accepted. And for further satisfaction of a number of our good subjects of greater degree than he was that grudged against him for such an extraordinary title, we committed him for a show of correction to custody, restraining him of his liberty, whereto he yielded obediently, confessing his error herein. But yet when we do perceive by the said grant, as also by his own relation, that your good will towards us (whom false reports had sought to render suspicious), together with his service done against the common enemy of Christ, hath been the cause that your Majesty hath so graciously entreated and accepted this gentleman upon our commendation, and hath with such an excess of honour rewarded his service, for which we shall better esteem him and all those that adventured in that action: we cannot but by these our letters give your Majesty our most hearty thanks, and do require you not to think but that we do greatly allow of your Majesty's noble nature in offering to a subject of ours both such a reward for his service, and do most kindly interpret it as an overt testimony of your love and kindness to ourself, whereof we shall ever be most desirous to make requital: Not doubting but your Majesty will in your wisdom allow of the reasons above expressed, the rather that we are informed by some that have seen a clause in a copy of your Majesty's original grant in these words, *Serenissimæ tamen Principis et Dominæ Elizabethæ, Reginæ Angliæ, Franciæ et Hiberniæ, sororis et consanguinæ nostræ charissimæ, iuribus et superioritatibus semper illæsis ac salvis.* By which special words we see plainly how your Majesty had due respect to us, as a Queen Sovereign, to have our royal superiority preserved in such manner as we will always observe to your Imperial Majesty, either in the like occasion or any other good office fit for us to perform.

XXIV. To Robert Devereux, Earl of Essex

*Throughout the winter and spring of 1595-6 great prepara-
tions were being made for a combined naval and military
expedition against Spain. At the beginning of April news came
that the Cardinal Archduke of Austria had suddenly abandoned
the siege of La Fere and was preparing to assault Calais. Essex
and Lord Charles Howard, the Lord Admiral, hastened down to
Dover, intending to collect all available troops and ships; but the
Queen hesitated and haggled over the terms on which her help
should be given. Essex's commission was dispatched to him on
the 13th April.*

April 13, 1596.

Whereas we have already given commission to you, and to
our Admiral of England, to transport an army for our service
beyond the seas, and have given you commission for the said
service to levy 3,000 soldiers here in England to be added to
2,000 more to be brought out of the Low Countries, having now
present occasion to levy the forces to the number of 6,000 men
for the relief of Calais to be taken out of our counties of Kent,
Sussex, Middlesex, Surrey, Essex, and our City of London, we
do hereby give you authority with all expedition to transport
the said number now last levied by our Commission in the shires
abovesaid for that only purpose to join with such forces as shall
come with our good brother the French King to be employed for
that action of succouring the Citadel of Calais now besieged, if
you shall find that our said army shall be able to arrive in time
to perform the same, for it is now our only purpose to employ
these numbers to the succouring of that place and to no other,
especially at this time, when so many other great, important
burdens lie upon us and our Realm. For doing whereof this
shall be your sufficient warrant, together with the advice of our
said Admiral, when he shall be with you, according to the tenour
of our former Commission under our Great Seal of England.

XXV. To Robert Devereux, Earl of Essex

*On the 14th April the noise of the cannonade was heard in
London; the order to embark was given; but just as the troops*

*were all on board news came on the evening of the 15th that
Calais had fallen.*

April 14, 1596.

As distant as I am from your abode, yet my ears serves me too
well to hear that terrible battery that methinks sounds for relief
at my hands; wherefore rather than for lack of timely aid it should
be wholly lost, go you on, in God's Blessed Name, as far as that
place where you may soonest relieve it, with as much caution as
so great a trust requires.   But I charge you, without the mere loss
of it, do in no wise peril so fair an army for another Prince's town.
God cover you under His safest wings, and let all peril go without your compass.   Believe Cecil in the rest.

From the *Due Repulse*, where this day I have been, and
render a million of thanks to Grove for his precious present.

XXVI. To Robert Devereux, Earl of Essex

*The great expedition to Cadiz, after some weeks spent in
training the troops and collecting supplies at Plymouth, after one
false start set out on 3rd June.   Just before they sailed the Queen
sent a prayer, which she had composed for their good success,
with the following brief letter:*

May 1596.

I make this humble bill of requests to Him that all makes
and does, that with His benign Hand He will shadow you so,
as all harm may light beside you, and all that may be best hap
to your share; that your return may make you better, and me
gladder.   Let your companion, my most faithful Charles, be sure
that his name is not left out in this petition.   God bless you both,
as I would be if I were there, which, whether I wish or not, He
alone doth know.

XXVII. To Henry the Fourth, King of France

*On 29th August, 1596, the league offensive and defensive,
made between the Queen and the French King, was solemnly
ratified at Greenwich, the King being represented by the Duke
of Bouillon.*

245

Translated from the French

c. September 1, 1596.

Although I have always considered that voluntary good will, not bound by other band than sincere affection, should be sufficient for a sure foundation of long duration, yet understanding the great desire which you had that a league should be made public between us two, I have consented to it, and, according to the custom between great Princes, I have thereto added my faith and word, which as they have never yet received spot, so, if God please, I have the sincere will to keep them in the same way. And although I have advanced the old custom of Kings to be the first to begin the match, I hope that you will not consider me shameless, being of my sex, to commence the dance of love, having no fear that you will give me a mock for such haste, but that you will measure thereby that I shall never be slack in honouring you. I have received by the Duke of Bouillon your letters all full of protestations of faithful love for me, with an ardent desire to honour me with your presence, a thing which would remove from you all credit in your ministers, who have abused you, I suspect, by so much praise of what, when you shall be ocular judge, you will find answers not at all to the half of what they make you believe, who disgrace me in thinking to advance my respect. But one thing you will find that they have never falsified, if they represent to you the purity of my assured friendship, and the lively feeling for any honourable chance that befalls you, with a promptness to aid you as my opportunities will permit me; as I doubt not that Sieur de Bouillon will represent to you, to whose sufficiency I commit myself.

XXVIII. TO HENRY THE FOURTH, KING OF FRANCE

The Queen having ratified her part of the new league, the Earl of Shrewsbury was sent over to receive, on her behalf, Henry's oath. The letter which was now sent was drafted by the Earl of Essex.

Translated from the French

c. September 1596.

Having completely finished for my part the final conclusion of our league with the ceremonies fitting such an act, and having forestalled with my precedence the sequel which invited me to such haste, I do doubt not at all that you will deign to second this fact with your promise given to the Earl whom I have ordered to receive it as given to me. And by this means you will overshadow, if you do not entirely cover, my error, if I may call it so, who was the first to present you my promise, assuring you that if all pacts were as unviolated as this will be on my side, every one would be astonished to see such constant friendship in this century. As for you, I imagine that never in a heart so generous will lodge me one single thought of ingratitude, so I persuade myself that I shall have no reason to repent of having honoured, favoured, and aided such a Prince as will not only think of what is fitting for himself but will take care of what belongs to me.

XXIX. To Sir Robert Carey

Sir Robert Carey was a deputy warden of the Scottish Border. There had been much trouble on the Border, and the wardens were ordered to meet the wardens of the Scottish King to negotiate. Carey was disgruntled because his pay was in arrears and because he had heard that the wardenship of the East Marches was not to be bestowed on himself. He was therefore unwilling to act until he had received proper authority.

June 7, 1597.

And where we find by divers letters written to our Council, both the Treasurer and the Secretary, how unwilling you are to deal in causes, because you have not yet your patent: We do wish you once again to leave this course of peremptory writing, and do command you to do as you ought, for we that can judge what is fit for you, will do things as we please, and when we please. Let these things therefore be performed by you, which you shall find by the Treaty you ought to do, and without any further importunity, and as William Bowes and Robert Bowes shall at any time direct you. And that being ended, you shall then know what shall become of you. And for all that you do or shall herein, we do hereby give you full power and authority, which is warrant good enough we trust for a greater matter.

xxx. To Robert Devereux, Earl of Essex

In the summer of 1597 another expedition against the Spaniards was prepared, but the weather was very bad throughout July and August. The fleet set out from Plymouth on 10th July, but was caught in a violent storm and scattered. Though no ships were lost, much repair was necessary. This letter was written when the Queen heard of Essex's disappointment.

July 8, 1597.

Eyes of youth have sharp sight, but commonly not so deep as those of elder age, which makes me marvel less at rash attempts and headstrong counsels, which give not leisure to judgement's warning, nor heed advice, but make a laughter at the one, and despise with scorn the last. This have I not heard but seen, and thereof can witness bear; yet I cannot be so lewd of nature to suppose the scope was not good. Now, so the race was run, and do more condemn the granters than the offerer, for when I see the admirable work of the Eastern wind, so long to last beyond the custom of nature, I see, as in a crystal, the right figure of my folly, that ventured supernatural haps upon the point of frenetical imputation : but it pleaseth His goodness to strengthen our weakness, and warns us to use wit when we have it hereafter; foreseen haps breed no wonder, no more doth your short returned post before his time. But for answer; if your full fed men were not more fitted by your desired rate, that purse should not be thinned at the bottom, that daily by lightening is made too thin already; but if more heed were taken how, than haste what, we needed not such by reckonings. Kings have the honour to be titled earthly gods, and therefore breeds our shame, if we disgrace so much our name, as though too far short, yet some piece of proportion were not in us, not even to reward desert, by the rule of their merit, but bear with weakness, and help to lift from ground the wellnigh falling man. This, at this present, makes me like the lunatic man that keeps a smack of the remain of his frenzy's freak, helped well thereto by the influence of *Sol in Leone*, that makes me yield for company to a larger proportion than a wiser in my place would ever grant unto, with this caveat, that this lunatic goodness make you not bold to keep too many that you have, and much less taken in more to heap more errors to our mercy; also, that you trust not to the grace of your crazed vessel, that to the ocean may fortune be, too humble; foresee and prevent it now in time, afore too late; you vex me too much with small regard of what I scape or did. Admit that by miracle it would do well, yet venture not such wonders where such approachful mischief might betide you. There remains that you, after your perilous first attempt, do not aggravate that danger with another in a farther off climate, which must cost blows of good store; let character serve your turn, and be content when you are well, which hath not ever been your property. Of this no more, but for all my moods I forget not my tenses, in which I see no leisure for aught but petitions, to fortify with best forwardness the wants of this army, and in the same include your safe return, and grant you wisdom to discern betwixt *verisimile* and *fieri potest*. Forget not to salute with great favour good Thomas and faithful Mountjoy. I am too like the common faction that forget to give thanks for what I received, but I was so loath to take that I had wellnigh forgot to thank, but receive them now with millions, and the rest keeps the dearest.

XXXI. To Robert Devereux, Earl of Essex

The setback in July kept Essex and his ships in Plymouth until 17th August, when once again the fleet set out. The season was now too far advanced for an attempt on the Spanish coast, and the expedition made for the Azores in the hope of intercepting the Spanish treasure fleet.

July 24, 1597.

How irksome long toil, much danger and heart's care may seem to the feeler's part, when they, that only hears reports of what might be full of evil chance or danger's stroke, are so filled with doubts of unfortunate sequel, you may well suppose the weight of these balances, but remember that who doth their best shall never receive the blame that accidents may bring, neither shall you find us so rigorous a judge as to verdict enterprises by events; so the root be sound, what blasts soever withers the fruits, no condemnation shall light in their share. Make of this fleet

I charge you a match, which being afire runs *in extremum*, with good caution of such points as my signed letter gives you. Adieu, with many good wishes to yourself, not forgetting good Thomas Mountjoy, with your joined Council, and tell them that no occasion shall be made by us wherefrom they have not part.

E.R.

XXXII. To Lady Norris

Written to Lady Norris on receipt of the news that Sir John Norris, her son, had died in Ireland. Norris was one of the Queen's most distinguished and able soldiers. After much active service, he was placed in command of English expeditions to Brittany in 1591 and 1594. In 1595 he was sent over to take command in Ireland.

September 22, 1597.

ELIZABETH REGINA

[*In the Queen's hand.*] Mine own Crow, harm not thyself for bootless help; but show a good example to comfort your dolorous yokefellow.

Although we have deferred long to represent unto you our grieved thoughts, because we liked full ill to yield you the first reflection of misfortune, whom we have always sought to cherish and comfort; yet, knowing now that necessity must bring it to your ears, and nature consequently must move both grief and passions in your heart, we resolved no longer to smother either our care for your sorrow, or the sympathy of our grief for his love, wherein, if it be true that society in sorrow works diminution, we do assure you, by this true messenger of our mind, that nature can have stirred no more dolorous affection in you as a mother for a dear son, than gratefulness and memory of his services past hath wrought in us, his Sovereign, apprehension of our miss of so worthy a servant. But now that Nature's common work is done, and he that was born to die hath paid his tribute, let that Christian discretion stay the flux of your immoderate grieving, which hath instructed you both by example and knowledge, that nothing of this kind hath happened but by God's divine Providence. And let these lines from your gracious and loving Sovereign serve to assure you, that there shall ever appear the lively characters of you and yours that are left, in valuing all their faithful and honest endeavours. More at this time we will not write of this unsilent subject; but have dispatched this gentleman to visit both your Lord and you, to condole with you the true sense of your love; and to pray you that the world may see, that what time cureth in weak minds, that discretion and moderation helpeth in you in this accident, where there is so just cause to demonstrate true patience and moderation.

Given at our Manor of Richmond, the 22nd of September, 1597.

XXXIII. To Robert Devereux, Earl of Essex

Little news had been received of the doings of Essex's fleet, which had now been gone two months. Instructions, together with the latest available information, were accordingly sent for his recall. Essex probably did not receive the letter, for on the 28th October news reached the Court that he had landed at Plymouth.

October 16, 1597.

Since we received first advice of your arrival at the Islands (by a letter bearing date 17 September directed to our Secretary) we have heard by another general letter of the 27th of the same that you had been on land in some of those islands to refresh yourselves; and, when that messenger parted, you were purposed to take in St. Michael, and after some part of October spent in that height, to begin to set sail for England to avoid the danger of our Navy by tarrying on till the depth of winter which is ever subject to storms and darkness. We cannot deny but we do wish the safe return of you and our fleet under your charge as a Prince that knows the value of such our dear and beloved servants, neither can mislike these second cogitations of yours concerning the returning; but when we do look back to the beginning of this action which hath stirred so great expectation in the world and charged us so deeply, we cannot but be sorry to foresee already how near all our expectations, and your great hopes are to a faithless conclusion. And therefore, seeing neither the action at Ferrol could not prosper nor the carrack be taken, if now the Indian fleet should be missed in regard of your being forced to return before the fleet should come homewards, we should think ourselves in much worse case than when the action did begin; not only in point of honour and charge but also of safety; as in all this time that fleet in Ferrol hath had his time for gathering and reinforcing, thereby fully accommodated for the pursuits of any of his former malicious purposes at such time as he shall please, since you can well consider that our navy under your charge must needs be far out of repair and so of far less power for our defence when time shall require.

And therefore, seeing it shall not be wisdom, now so much is done already, to leave anything undone which carrieth probability of good success to grace the work begun, as having lately understood that order was sent from Spain to stay the fleet of treasure from coming home until December, and then to be transported in twelve small galleons, without any other wafting[1] we have thought good to request you, upon receipt of this letter, immediately to call a Council of War and to consider with their advice how to draw out of your whole fleet some few of our own ships, accompanied with some other of the merchants' ships, and to devise to see and send out of the whole victualled. Which being done, we do require you to direct as many as you shall think fit to tarry out as long as they possibly can for intercepting those ships with treasure; a matter wherein the enemy will use no precaution when they shall know that our fleet is returned. And therefore our meaning is not, in regard of the necessity of the great care and circumspection which is to be used in bringing home of our fleet and army, that either you or any of those great officers under you should tarry abroad, yet may you find others, principal gentlemen of quality and experience that have especial charge under you, to command that fleet and to proceed according to such instruction as you shall leave them. To whom now that we have represented careful thoughts both for the satisfaction of the world's expectation, not only in the sender but in the actor, we do refer all further consideration to your discretion, to whom the particular state of all things is best known. And to this only make this further addition, that we have some advertisement that the Spanish fleet intends to lie for you in your return with hope

---

[1] For ' wasting ' in the Calendar.

to cut off some part of the stragglers from our fleet, though haply they dare not encounter with the gross. 'And therefore we request you to bethink yourself both to prevent the same in the bringing home of the fleet which shall come in your company; and in the directing those ships which you shall leave behind you, to be watchful of any such practice against themselves. More we have not at this time but to wish you as good hap as our most careful heart hath hourly begged at God's Hands for all their safety that have exposed themselves to danger out of their zeal to do us service.

xxxiv. To Robert Devereux, Earl of Essex

When Essex reached Plymouth he found the west country in great excitement. The Spanish fleet had been discovered, and a straggler taken from which it appeared that their rendezvous was Falmouth. The troops in all the southern counties were being mustered, and hurried preparations made for defence. Essex immediately offered to take command of the situation, and the following letter of instructions was dispatched to him.

October 28, 1597.

We have seen your letters hourly written to our Secretary, and thereby perceive your care and diligence, which we do well allow. And for direction, in this uncertainty of the Spanish purposes, whether it be for our realm of Ireland or England that they mean to make their descent, we do determine that you shall thus proceed. First, you shall put in readiness, and draw forth as you see cause by the opinion of such commanders as we have formerly assigned you, all such forces as you can to encounter the Spanish navy; and for the better strengthening of ourself upon our own coast, we have commanded such ships as can be here drawn out to be also furnished to lie in the Narrow Seas, to join with the fleet under your charge.

Secondly, for the matter of Ireland, you shall first understand that upon the death of our Deputy (an accident to us of no small grief) we have constituted General of our army our cousin, the Earl of Ormond, with two justices for the better government of the civil policy of the Kingdom. But if it shall appear to you that the army is there descended and that our coast is free from danger, we do then give you authority with all speed to make after them with such forces by land and sea as you shall find necessary; and we do give you full authority to command the said army in such form as by your commission already under our Great Seal you have. And when you shall be arrived, because we know not whether you shall have cause to join your forces with our cousin, the Earl of Ormond, already constituted General of our army there, we are pleased that, when he shall be joined with you, you shall have the superior commandment; and in your absence, wheresoever he is, he to be the principal commander in the army.

And now that we have thus directed you provisionally how you shall proceed in these occasions whereof we have advertisement daily from you, we must again say this unto you as a matter fit to be reiterated and deeply imprinted, namely, that seeing already by your late leaving the coast upon an uncertain probability that no army would come forth of Ferrol till March, you have given the enemy leisure and courage to attempt us, and left as unprovided to resist them with that provision which is necessary for so important an action, you do take good heed, according to your duty and allegiance, that you do not in any case upon any probability or light advertisements once adventure to leave our own coast to transport our forces to Ireland, whereby our own Kingdom may be open to serious dangers: but that you do proceed in this great affair according to the rules of advised deliberation as well as affections of zeal and diligence. For treasure, for victual and what may be fit for us to send, you shall find that you serve a Prince neither void of care nor judgement what to do that is fit in cases of this consequence. Of all which particulars we do advertise you by the hands of our ministers, to which we further refer you.

XXXV. TO THE EMPEROR OF ETHIOPIA

' The letters of the Queen's most Excellent Majesty sent by one Laurence Aldersey unto the Emperor of Æthiopia, 1597.'

To the Most Invincible and Puissant King of the Abassens, the Mighty Emperor of Æthiopia, the Higher and the Lower

November 5, 1597.

Elizabeth by the Grace of God, Queen of England, France and Ireland, Defender of the Faith, &c. To the Most High and Mighty Emperor of Æthiopia, greeting. Whereas it is a matter requisite and well beseeming all Kings and Princes of what lands or nations soever, be they never so much dissevered in place or differing in customs and laws, to maintain and preserve the common society of mankind, and, as occasion shall be offered, to perform mutual duties of charity and benevolence; we for that cause conceiving most undoubted hope of your princely fidelity and courtesy, have given unto this our subject, Laurence Aldersey, intending to travel into your dominions, these our letters to be delivered without fail unto your Highness, to the end they may be a testimony of our goodwill towards you and of the said subject his departure from England. Who, after his travels in many foreign countries, being as yet inflamed with a desire more thoroughly to survey and contemplate the world, and now at length to undertake a long and dangerous journey into your territories and regions : both the said Laurence thought, and ourselves also deemed, that it would very much avail him, as well for his own safety as for the attaining of your favour, if, being protected with our Broad Seal, he might transport unto your Highness a testimony of our loving affection, and of his departure from hence. For sithence Almighty God, the Highest Creator and Governor of the World, hath allotted unto Kings and Princes, his Vicegerents over the face of the whole earth, their designed portions and limits to be ruled and administered by them; and by this His gift hath established among them a certain law of brotherly kindness, and an eternal league by them to be observed : it will not (we hope) seem unpleasant unto your Highness, when you shall have intelligence of our loving letters sent so huge a distance over sea and land, even from the farthest Realm of England unto you in Æthiopia. On the other side ourselves shall take great solace and delight, when, as by the relation of our own subjects, the renown of your name shall be brought unto us from the fountains of Nilus, and from those regions which are situate under the Southern Tropic. May it please you therefore of your princely clemency to vouchsafe so much favour on this our subject, that he may, under the safeguard and protection of your name, enter into your Highness's dominions, and there remain safe and free from danger. Which favour and courtesy we do likewise most earnestly request at the hands of other Princes, through whose Seigniories our said subject is to pass; and we shall esteem it as done unto ourself, and for our honour's sake.

Neither do we require any greater favour in this behalf, than we are upon the like occasion most ready to grant unto the subjects of all Princes and the people of all nations travelling into our dominions.

Given at London the fifth day of November, in the thirty and ninth year of our reign; and in the year of our Lord, 1597.

XXXVI. To Thomas Butler, Earl of Ormonde

In the course of a long official letter to Ormonde, then Lord Deputy, occurs the following passage, which is typical of the Queen's attitude towards God and the rebels in Ireland.

December 29, 1597.

We are not so alienated from hearkening to such submission as may tend to the sparing effusion of Christian blood, but that we can be content, in imitation of God Almighty (Whose minister we are here on earth, and Who forgiveth all sins) to receive the penitent and humble submission of those traitors that pretend to crave it; wherein we doubt not but you, that are of noble blood and birth, will so carry all things in the manner of your proceedings, as our honour may be specially preserved in all your actions, seeing you do know that you now represent our own person, and have to do with inferior people and base rebels: to whose submission if we in substance shall be content to condescend, we will look to have the same implored in such reverent form as becometh our vassals and such heinous offenders to use, with bended knees and hearts humbled; not as if one Prince did treat with another upon even terms of honour or advantage in using words of peace or war, but of rebellion in them, and mercy in us; for rather than ever it shall appear to the world that in any such sort we will give way to any of their pride, we will cast off either sense or feeling of pity or compassion, and, upon what price soever, prosecute them to the last hour.

XXXVII. To James the Sixth, King of Scotland

King James in addressing his Parliament (which met at Edinburgh on 13th December, 1597) had spoken his mind over freely on the Queen. She therefore sent Sir William Bowes with the following letter of expostulation.

January 4, 1598.

When the first blast of a strange unused and seld heard of sound had pierced my ears, I supposed that flying fame, who with swift quills oft passeth with the worst, had brought report of some untruth; but when too too many records in your open parliament were witnesses of such pronounced words, not more to my disgrace than to your dishonour, who did forget that (above all other regard) a Prince's word ought utter naught of any, much less of a King, than such as to which Truth might say, ' Amen.' But[1] your neglecting all care of yourself (what danger of reproach, besides somewhat else, might light upon [you]), you have chosen so unseemly a theme to charge your only careful friend withal, of such matter as (were you not amazed in all senses) could not have been expected at your hands; of such imagined untruths as never were once thought of in our time. I do wonder what evil spirits have possessed you, to set forth so infamous devices, void of any show of truth. I am sorry that you have so wilfully fallen from your best stay, and will needs throw yourself into the hurlpool of bottomless discredit. Was the haste so great to hie to such opprobry, as that you would pronounce a never-thought-of action afore you had but asked the question of her that best could tell it? I see well we two be of very different natures, for I vow to God I would not corrupt my tongue with an unknown report of the greatest foe I have,

---

[1] i.e. besides.

much less could I detract my best-deserving friends with a spot so foul as scarcely may ever be out-razed. Could you root the desire of gifts of your subjects upon no better ground than this quagmire, which to pass you scarcely may, without the slip of your own disgrace? Shall embassage be sent to foreign Princes laden with instructions of your rash advised charge? I assure you the travail of your crazed words shall pass the bounds of too many lands, with an imputation of such levity, as when the true sunshine of my sincere dealing and extraordinary care ever for your safety and honour shall overshade too far the dim and misty clouds of false invectives. I never yet loved you so little as not to moan your infamous dealings which you are in mind. We see that myself shall possess more Princes witness of my causeless injuries, which I could have wished had passed no seas, to testify such memorials of your wrongs. Bethink you of such dealings, and set your labour upon such mends as best may. Though not right, yet salve some piece of this overship. And be assured that you deal with such a King as will bear no wrongs and indure [no] infamy. The examples have been so lately seen as they can hardly be forgotten, of a far mightier and potenter Prince than many Europe hath. Look you not therefore that without large amends I may or will slupper up such indignities. We have sent this bearer, Bowes, whom you may safely credit, to signify such particularities as fits not a letter's talk. And so I recommend you to a better mind and more advised conclusions. Praying God to guide you for your best, and deliver you from sinister advice, as descrieth

Your more readier Sister than yourself hath done, for that is fit,

ELIZABETH R.

XXXVIII. TO JAMES THE SIXTH, KING OF SCOTLAND

In the spring of 1598 a certain Valentine Thomas, a Border thief, was captured and brought to London. Here he declared that he had been promised great rewards by King James to murder Queen Elizabeth. James was very indignant and demanded that his good name should be cleared, nor would he be satisfied until public declaration had been made (in the

*December following) that Thomas's charges were utterly repudi-
ated. Thomas remained in the Tower until June 1603 when
he was tried for high treason and executed.*

July 1, 1598.

MY DEAR BROTHER,

Suppose not that my silence hath any other root than hating
to make an argument of my writing to you that should molest
you or trouble me, being most desirous that no mention might
once be made of so villainous an act, especially that might but
in word touch a sacred person. But now I see that so lavishly
it hath been used [by the] author thereof, that I can refrain no
longer to make you partaker thereof sincerely, from the beginning
to this hour, of all that hath proceeded. And for more speed
have sent charge with Bowes, to utter all without fraud or guile,
assuring you that few things have displeased me more since our
first amities. And charge you in God's name to believe, that I
am not of so viperous a nature to suppose or have thereof a
thought against you, but shall make the deviser have his desert,
more for that than for aught else. Referring my self to the true
trust of this gentleman, to whom I beseech you give full affiance
in all he shall assure you on my behalf. And so God I beseech
to prosper you with all His Graces, as doth desire,

Your most affectionate Sister.

XXXIX. TO SIR ROBERT CECIL

*The following note in the Queen's hand, which is undated,
probably refers to the Valentine Thomas affair. Cecil's father,
Lord Burghley, died on 4th August, 1598, after a few days' illness. Sir Dru Drury was Lieutenant of the Tower. This is
one of the very few personal notes to a minister which survive.*

c. August 1598.

Let the Lords after their examination sequester him to his
chamber, and let Dru Drury be with him till their doings have
been declared me, and then I like well these warrants, saving
that three be the least that such a matter deserves. And therefore, instead of your father that never was with them, the Lord
Chamberlain may be inserted who was one, for I like not err in
such a case. E.R.

To the Ελφε.

XL. To the Lords Justices Loftus and Gardener, the Earl of
Ormonde, and the rest of the Council of Ireland

*In August 1598 Sir Henry Bagnal, the Marshal, with the
available troops, consisting of about 300 cavalry and 3,500
infantry, set out from Armagh to relieve the fort at the Blackwater
which was encircled by the rebels. On the 14th Bagnal's force
was ambushed and completely routed by Tyrone, with the loss
of the Marshal, many officers and about 2,000 men. The survivors took refuge in Armagh. Tyrone, however, instead of
following up his victory and annihilating the English force,
allowed them to depart on terms. On first receipt of the news
of the disaster, the Council at Dublin sent an abject letter to
Tyrone, appealing for mercy. The Queen now appointed Sir
Richard Bingham to take command in Ireland. Bingham had
been Governor of Connaught two years before and had quarrelled
with Sir John Norris. He was accused of misgovernment and
summoned by Norris to take his trial, but having small chance
of a just hearing he fled to England.*

*This letter, which is one of many similar complaints from the
Queen, explains some of the reasons for the Irish muddle. The
Government was hopelessly corrupt, every official lining his own
pocket at the Queen's expense. The captains of companies were
as bad as the rest. Amongst other abuses, they did not report
casualties but pocketed their pay. When the muster masters
came round to check the nominal rolls, they hired men from the
enemy to fill up the gaps in their ranks, who afterwards absconded
with their borrowed arms to Tyrone.*

September 12, 1598.

Having been moved by divers letters from yourselves amongst
other your lacks to supply that Council with some principal
persons of experience and judgement because you found yourselves unprovided of such as were able either to advise or execute
in so many actions of importance, as by the several rebellions in
that Kingdom were necessary, we are pleased to make choice of our
servant Richard Bingham, Knight, whom we have also appointed
to be Marshal of that Realm, to repair hither for the better
furtherance of our service; of whose experience and sufficiency
every way, because it is so well known to yourselves, we need
say now no more than this, that he doth return with our favour
and gracious opinion, of which we do require you to take notice,

and to use him and hear him lovingly and friendly, in all things concerning our service. Wherein we know that you, our cousin of Ormonde, our Lieutenant, will find great ease and contentment every way, it being neither fit nor possible that you should spend your body in all services at all times; and yet we must plainly tell you that we did much mislike (seeing this late action was undertaken) that you did not above all other things attend it, thereby to have directed and countenanced the same. For it was strange to us, when almost the whole forces of our Kingdom were drawn to a head, and a main blow like to be stroken for our honour against the capital rebel, that you, whose person would have better daunted the traitors, and would have carried with it another manner of reputation, and strength of the nobility of the Kingdom, should employ yourself in an action of less importance, and leave that to so mean a conduction. And therefore, whosoever of our Council should dissuade you from that course, lacked both judgement and affection to our service and did that which is repugnant to the writings of divers of the best and greatest of them in that Kingdom. With which particularity we will not now trouble ourselves further, because we are so uncertainly informed of the circumstances of that action; only this we may not hide, that it doth not a little trouble us to find so hard effect of all things from thence, considering the notable supplies of men, treasure, and victuals, more plentifully sent than ever heretofore; wherein, although we do not deny but many things concur to make that State more difficult to be recovered than in former time, yet is there no person, be he never of so vulgar judgements, but doth plainly see notorious errors in that Government. Amongst which we have observed this proceeding for one, upon divers certificates, that, when there was great opportunities for lack of pay for the common soldier, occasioned by contrariety of winds, which kept back the treasure, we did never find that any one of the principal officers did ever forbear taking up their own allowance aforehand, in as plentiful manner as ever they did, a matter wherein they showed small consideration of the necessity of the time, when they were sure that at the next treasure they might be holpen. And for the numbers there maintained, we have great cause to be displeased with this great abuse, from which hath ensued notorious mischiefs, by the captains entertaining of the Irish, only to cover their frauds, and to make gain by licensing English to depart, whereby not only the places which ought to be defended by them are wasted and spoiled in their absence, but also at all times of service they are ready to turn our own arms against our own armies; as hath lately fallen out in this late accident at the Blackwater; wherein we may not pass over this foul error to our dishonour, when you of our Council framed such a letter to the traitor, after the defeat, as never was read the like, either in form or substance, for baseness, being such as we persuade ourself, if you shall peruse it again, when you are yourselves, that you will be ashamed of your own absurdities, and grieved that any fear or rashness should ever make you authors of an action so much to your Sovereign's dishonour, and to the increasing of the traitor's insolency. For other things past, we have well observed, that all the journeys and attempts upon the North have had these successes, that not only our armies have come back with loss, or doing nothing, but in their absence other parts of our Kingdom have been left to be spoiled and wasted by the rebels; and though the universality of the rebellion may be used as a reason of the mischief, yet it is almost a miracle that with the charges of an army of eight or nine thousand men, the principal rebels of Leinster and Wexford, and other places, should not be mastered, though the capital rebels have not there been reduced, a matter cried out on by all that either write or come out of Ireland, so as there can be no more token of ill carriage of all things, than where no one thing is reformed. With these things we cannot forbear to charge you in generalities, to the end that you may examine all particulars curiously, and attend the reformation. For the present we think fit only to prescribe you this much, that with all such forces as you have, and shall have by the late increase of those that were appointed for Lough Foyle, you see all our frontier towns strengthened and provided to defend themselves, especially those that are maritime in all places, because you can well consider that those must be staples of victuals, and retreat for such forces as shall be sent at any time to his prosecution. In the meantime you shall follow the wars of Leinster, which is in the heart of our Kingdom, this winter, to the end that those inward provinces of the Realm may be freed; and, above all things, seeing you have these late supplies of 4,000 men (when the last of Lough Foyle shall be arrived), and that your own book did certify so great numbers in pay before those supplies, that you do use all convenient means to clear our army of the Irish, and so to order it, as for this winter it may be reduced to a list of eight thousand; which numbers, as in all men's opinions they are more than ever were seen needful there, so if we shall pay them, and not have them, we think yourselves will imagine that we shall have no small cause to be offended, having often written hereof, without any answer returned what is done in it. Further also, yourselves well know that, though some soldiers may run from the army to the rebel, it being upon the same continent (which are not many), yet all the rest must return by sea, which is not easy, if such good orders were taken as should be, that no soldier were suffered to embark in any our port towns, without good warrant for their passage.

[*Postscript.*] Since the writing of this letter, we have understood that your letter, which we heard from you was sent to the traitor by you, hath since been stayed by accident; whereof, for our own honour, we are very glad, though, for yourselves, the former purpose still deserves the same imputation.

xli. To Robert Devereux, Earl of Essex

Essex had been so critical of the mismanagement of the Irish war that in the autumn of 1598 he was made Lord Deputy of Ireland, and in March 1599 he set out in command of an army of 16,000. He was no more successful than his predecessors. The army was frittered away in minor engagements, and the advance against Tyrone himself, which was to have been the main purpose of the campaign, was constantly postponed. The Queen was highly dissatisfied, and a series of severe letters were sent to Essex. The main heads of her displeasure were that Essex was accomplishing nothing, and that his failure was blemishing her reputation in the eyes of other Princes; that the Irish war was ruinously expensive; that he had created a number of new knights out of all proportion to the successes gained; and that he had, in direct opposition to her wishes, made the Earl of Southampton his Master of Horse. The Queen's annoyance with Southampton was mostly due to his marriage; in the previous summer he had seduced, and then secretly married, one of her Maids of Honour.

July 19, 1599

We have perceived by your letters to our Council, brought by Henry Carey, that you are arrived in Dublin after your journey into Munster; where, though it seemeth by the words of your letter that you had spent divers days in taking an account of all things that have passed since you left that place, yet have you in this dispatch given us small light either when, or in what order, you intend particularly to proceed to the northern action, wherein, if you compare the time that is run on, and the excessive charges that is spent, with the effects of anything wrought by this voyage (howsoever we may remain satisfied with your own particular cares and travails of body and mind), yet you must needs think that we, that have the eyes of foreign Princes upon our actions, and have the hearts of people to comfort and cherish, who groan under the burden of continual levies and impositions, which are occasioned by these late actions, can little please yourself hitherto with anything that hath been effected. For what can be more true (if things be rightly examined) than that your two months' journey hath brought in never a capital rebel, against whom it had been worthy to have adventured one thousand men. For of their two comings in, that were brought unto you by Ormonde (namely, Montgarrett and Cahir), whereupon ensued the taking of Cahir Castle, full well do we know that you would long since have scorned to have allowed it for any great matter in others to have taken an Irish hold from a rabble of rogues, with such force as you had, and with the help of the cannon, which was always able in Ireland to make his passage where it pleased. And, therefore, more than that, you have now learned, upon our expenses, by knowledge of the country, that those things are true, which we have heretofore told you, if you would have believed us, how far different things would prove than from your expectation. There is little public benefit made to us of any things happened in this action, which the President, with any convenient addition to his numbers by you, might not have effected, either now or hereafter, in a time more seasonable, when it should less have hindered the other enterprise, on which depends our greatest expectation. Whereunto we will add this one thing, that doth more displease us than any charge or expense that happens, which is, that it must be the Queen of England's fortune (who hath held down the greatest enemy she had) to make a base bush kern to be accounted so famous a rebel, as to be a person against whom so many thousands of foot and horse, besides the force of all the nobility of that kingdom, must be thought too little to be employed. For we must now remember unto you, that our cousin of Ormonde, by his own relation when you arrived, assured us that he had delivered you a charge of a kingdom, without either town of ours maritime, or inland, or possessed by the traitors. But we did ever think that Tyrone would please himself to see such a portion of our fair army, and led by the person of our General, to me harassed out and adventured in encountering those base rogues, who were no way strengthened by foreign armies, but only by such of his offal, as he was contented to spare and let slip from himself; while she hath lived at his pleasure, hath spoiled all where our army should come, and preserved for himself what he thought necessary. Little do you know how he hath blazed in foreign parts the defeat of regiments, the death of captains, and loss of men of quality in every corner; and how little he seemeth to value their power, who use it so as it is likely to spend itself. It is, therefore, apparent that all places require not one and the selfsame knowledge, and that drafts and surprises would have found better success than public and notorious marches; though where the rebel attends you with greater forces, it is necessary that you carry our army in the form you use.

But it doth sound hardly in the ears of the world, that in a time when there is a question to save a kingdom, and in a country where experience giveth so great advantage to all enterprises, regiments should be committed to young gentlemen that rather desire to do well than know how to perform it. A matter wherein we must note that you have made both us and our Council so great strangers, as to this day (but by reports) we know not who they be that spend our treasure and carry places of note in our army. Wherein you know we did by our instructions direct you as soon as you should be arrived, seeing you used reasons, why it could not be done so conveniently beforehand. These things we would pass over, but that we see your pen flatters you with phrases, that here you are defeated, that you are disgraced from hence in your friends' fortune, that poor Ireland suffers in you; still exclaiming against the effects of your own causes. For if it be not enough that you have all, and more than that which was agreed on before you went, concerning public service, but that you must, by your voluntary actions there in particular things (which you know full well are contrary to our will and liking) raise an opinion that there is any person that dare displease us, either by experience of our former tolerations, or with a conceit to avoid blame by distinctions; then must we not hide from you (how much soever we do esteem you, for those good things which are in you), but that our honour hath dwelt too long with us, to leave that point now uncleared, that whosoever it be that you do clad with any honours or places wherein the world may read the least suspicion of neglect or contempt of our commandments, we will never make dainty to set on such shadows as shall quickly eclipse any of those lustres. And, therefore, although by your letter we found your purpose to go northward, on which depends the main part of our service, and which we expected long since should have been performed yet because we do hear it bruited (besides the words of your letter, written with your own hand, which carries some such sense), that you who allege such weakness in our army by being travailed with you, and find so great and important affairs to digest at Dublin, will yet engage yourself personally into Offally (being our Lieutenant), when you have there so many inferiors able enough to victual a fort, or seek revenge of those that have lately prospered against our forces; and when we call to mind how far the sun hath run his course, what dependeth upon the timely plantation of our garrisons in the north, and how great a scandal it would be to our honour to leave that proud rebel unassailed, when we have, with so great an expectation of our enemies, engaged ourself so far in the action, so as without that be done, all these former courses will prove like *via nauis in mari*; besides that our power, which hitherto hath been dreaded by potent enemies, will now be even held contemptible amongst our rebels; we must now plainly charge you, according to the duty you owe us, so to unite soundness of judgement to the zeal you have to do us service, and with all speed to pass thither in such order, as the axe may be put to the root of that tree, which hath been the treasonable stock from whence so many poisoned plants and grafts have been devised. By which proceeding of yours, we may neither have cause to repent our employment of yourself for omitting these opportunities to shorten the war, nor receive, in the eye of the world, imputation of too much weakness in ourself to begin a work without better foresight. What would be the end of our excessive charge, the adventure of our people's lives, and the holding up of our own greatness, against a wretch whom we have raised from the dust, and who could never prosper, if the charges we have been put to were orderly employed?

For the matter of Southampton, it is strange to us that his continuance or displacing should work so great an alteration, either in yourself (valuing our commandments as you ought), or in the disposition of our army, where all the commanders cannot be ignorant that we not only not allowed of your desire for him, but did expressly forbid it; and being such a one whose counsel[1] can be of little, and experience of less use; [yea, such a one [as], were he not lately fastened to yourself by an accident, wherein, for our usage of yours, we deserve thanks, you would have used many of your old lively arguments against him for any such ability or commandment][2]; it is, therefore, strange to us, that knowing his work by your report, and your own disposition from yourself in that point, will dare thus to value your own pleasing in things unnecessary, and think by your private arguments to carry for your own glory a matter wherein our pleasure to the contrary is made notorious. And where you say further that divers, or the most, of the voluntary gentlemen are so discouraged thereby, as they begin to desire passports, and prepare to return, we cannot as yet be persuaded but that the love of our service, and the duty which they owe us, have been as strong motives to these their travails and hazards as any affection to the Earl of Southampton, or any other. If it prove otherwise which

[1] For 'experience'.
[2] This passage in brackets is crossed out in the contemporary copy.

we will not so much wrong ourself as to suspect, we shall have the less cause, either to acknowledge or reward it.

XLII. To Lord Henry Norris and Lady Norris

Of the sons of Lord and Lady Norris, four had already died in the Queen's service in Ireland, William in 1579, Sir John in 1597 (see p. 250), Henry and Sir Thomas in 1599. Only Sir Edward now survived, whom the Queen caused to be recalled from Ireland to comfort his sorrowing parents.

September 6, 1599.

Right trusty and well beloved, and right dear and well beloved, we greet you well. The bitter accident lately befallen you, which is the cause of our writing seeing it touches you both with equal smart, and our desire that all the comfort which we wish to you may reach to each of you with like effect is the cause that we have coupled you together in our letter. We were loath to have written at all because in such accidents (for the most part) the offering of comfort is but the presenting of fresh occasion of sorrow. But yet being well persuaded of your constant resolution, grounded as well on the experience of other like mishaps, which your years have seen as also chiefly upon your religious obedience to the work of His hands, Whose strokes are unavoidable, we could not forbear to do our part, partly because we conceive that we shall therein propose ourself for our example to you, our loss in political respect . . . being no less than yours in natural consideration. And partly by giving you assurance that whatsoever from us may minister comfort by demonstrating towards [   ] of you the value we made of the departed shall not fail to be employed to your best contentments; assuring you that this hard hap of yours shall rather serve us for matter to increase our care of you than any way to abate it. And because we know it would be some stay to your sorrows to have him in your eyes who is in foreign parts, we will give order that as soon as possibly he may leave his charge in good sort, he shall be with you to yield you all duty and service he may.

XLIII. To Sir Walter Ralegh

In the late summer of 1599 there was a great alarm that the Spaniards were again planning the invasion of England. The reports were so persistent that the musters in the counties were mobilized and concentrated in London. Heroic measures for defence were proposed. By the end of August it was clear that the alarm was false, and the musters were dismissed. There was much speculative gossip and criticism of the Council. The following letter, directed to Ralegh as Warden of the Stannaries, expresses the Queen's appreciation of the zeal of the musters, and endeavours to soothe their annoyance at being called up for service at harvest time.

September 12, 1599.

We have with great content understood from you of the great forwardliness and dutiful disposition of our subjects of these parts in performance of these commandments and directions as we or our councils in our name have lately cause to give for their defence upon the apprehensions that were conceived of some attempts intended by the Spaniard upon that coast. In which executing of their duties upon all like occasions . . . we doubt not but themselves do understand that they work their own safety by resisting such mischiefs as conquests and invasions by malicious enemies do threaten yet forasmuch as we do account our [. . . illegible] self principally interested in the well-doing of our subjects we cannot but rejoice to full the part and members of that body whereof God hath made us the supreme head apt and ready to perform these offices and duties which to them belong for preventing of these [those] evils whereof the least that might befall them would as less grieve us than themselves, of which our affection towards them and acceptation of their late travail we pray you that they may be by you informed giving them from us full assurance that they shall ever find at our hands those effects of love and care which may be expected from a Prince that can mark a true judgement difference of her subjects' affections and duties towards her.

XLIV. To Robert Devereux, Earl of Essex

Roused by the indignant letters of the Queen, Essex at last determined to go against Tyrone. On 21st August he summoned

*a Council of War at Dublin at which the captains all opposed
the expedition; the army was now reduced to less than 4,000;
moral was bad; and there was very little chance of success.
Essex therefore drew up a memorandum of this resolution, which
the captains signed, which he sent over in care of his secretary,
Henry Cuffe, who was to inform the Queen that he had determined nevertheless to advance against Tyrone. This letter was
written after the Queen had received Cuffe in audience.*

September 14, 1599.

Having sufficiently declared unto you before this time how
little the manner of your proceedings hath answered either our
direction or the world's expectation, and finding now by your
letters by Cuff a course more strange, if strange may be, we are
doubtful what to prescribe you at any time, or what to build upon
your writing unto us in anything. For we have clearly discerned
of late, what you have ever to this hour possessed us with expectation, that you would proceed as we have directed you; but your
actions always shows the contrary, though carried in such sort,
as we were sure to have no time to countermand them. Before
your departure, no man's counsel was held sound, which persuaded not presently the main prosecution in Ulster; all was
nothing without that; and nothing was too much for that. This
drew on the sudden transportation of so many thousands, to be
carried over with you; and, when you arrived, we were charged
with more than the list on which we resolved, by the number of
300 horsemen above the thousand, which was assented to, which
were only to be in pay during service in Ulster. We have been
also put in charge ever since the first journey, the pretence of
which voyage, [as] appeared by your letters, was to do some
present service in the interim, whiles that grew more commodious
the main prosecution. For which purpose you did importune
with great earnestness that all manner of provisions might be
hastened to Dublin against your return. Of this resolution to
defer your going into Ulster you may well think that we would
have made stay, if you had given us more time by warning, or
if we could have imagined, by the contents of your own writing,
that you would have spent nine weeks abroad, and your return
when the third part of July was spent; and that you had under-

stood our mislike of your former course, and made your excuse
of undertaking it, only in respect of your conformity to the
Council's opinions, with great protestations, of haste to the north.
Then we received another letter of new reasons to suspend that
journey yet awhile, and to draw the army into Offally, the fruit
whereof at your homecoming was nothing else but new relations
of further missing of our army, and greater difficulties to perform
the Ulster wars.   Then followed from you and the Council a
new demand of two thousand men, to which if we would assent,
you would speedily undertake what we had so often commanded.
When that was granted, and your going onward promised by
divers letters, we received by this bearer new fresh advertisement,
that all you can do is to go to the frontiers, and that you have
provided only twenty days' victuals.   In which kind of proceeding we must deal plain with you and that Council that it were
more proper for them to leave troubling themselves with instruct-
ing us by what rules our power and their obedience are limited,
and bethink them of the courses that have been only derived
from their counsel, and how to answer this part of theirs, to train
us into a new expense for one end, and to employ it to another,
to which we never would have assented, if we could have suspected it should have been undertaken before we heard it was
in action; and therefore we do wonder how it can be answered,
seeing your attempt is not in the capital traitor's county, that you
have increased our list.   But it is true, and we have often said,
that we were ever won to expense by little and little, and by
protestation of great resolutions in generalities, till they come to
particular execution, of all which courses whosoever shall examine
any of the arguments used for excuse, shall find your own proceedings beget the difficulties, and that no just causes do breed
the alterations of lack of numbers.   If sickness of the army be
the reason, why was there not the action undertaken when the
army was in better state? if winter's approach, why were the
summer months of July and August lost?   If the spring were
too soon, and the summer that followed otherwise spent, if the
harvest that succeeded were so neglected as nothing hath been
done, then surely we must conclude that none of the four quarters
of the year will be in season for you and that Council to agree

of Tyrone's persecution, for which all our change is intended. Further we require you to consider whether we have not a great cause to think that your purpose is not to end the war, when you yourself have often told us that all the petty undertakings in Leix, Munster and Connaught, are but loss of time, consumption of treasure, and, most of all, our people, until Tyrone himself be first beaten, on whom all the rest depend. Do you not see that if this course be in all parts by his sinister seconding all places where any attempt be offered, who do not see that if this course be continued, that it is like to spend us and our kingdom beyond all moderation, as well as the report of their success in all parts hath blemished our honour, and encouraged others to no small presumption? We know you cannot so much fail in judgement, as not to understand that all the world seeth how time is delayed, though you think that the allowance of that Council.

How often have you told us that others, that preceded you, had no judgement to end the war, who often resolved us [that], until Lough Foyle and Ballyshannon were planted, there could be no hope of doing service upon the capital rebels? We must therefore let you know, as it cannot be ignorance, so it cannot be want of means; for you had our asking, you had choice of times, you had power and authority more ample than ever any had, or ever shall have. It may well be judged with how little contentment we seek this and other errors. But how should that be hid which is so palpable?

And therefore to leave that which is past, and that you may prepare to remedy matters of weight hereafter, rather than to fill your papers with impertinent arguments, being in your general letters savouring still in many points of humours that concern the private of you, our Lord Lieutenant, we do tell you plainly, and you that are of our Council, that we wonder at your indiscretion to subscribe to letters which concern our public service, and directed to our Council take, which is not wont to handle things of so small importance.

To conclude, if you say that our army be in a list nineteen thousand, [and] that you have them not, we answer then to you, our Treasurer, that we are evil served, and that there needs not so frequent demands of full pay. If you will say that the muster master is to blame, we must muse then, why he is not punished. We say to you, our General, if we would *ex jure proprio judicarie* [*sic*], that all defects by musters, yea though in never so remote garrisons, have been affirmed to us to deserve to be imputed to the General. For the small proportion you say you carry with you of 3,500 foot, when lately we augmented you 200 [*sic* : error for 2,000] more, it is past comprehension, except it be that you have left too great numbers in unnecessary garrisons, which do increase our charge, and diminish our army, which we command you to reform, especially since, by your continual report of the state of every province, you describe them to be in worse conditions than ever they were before you put foot in that kingdom. So that whosoever shall write the story of this year's action, must say that we were at too great charge to hazard our kingdom, and you have taken great pains to prepare for many purposes, which perish without undertaking. And therefore because we see now, by your own word, that the hope is spent of this year's service upon Tyrone and O'Donnell, we do command you and our Council to fall jointly into present deliberation of the state which you have brought our kingdom unto, and that by the effect which this journey hath produced, and why these garrisons which you will plant so far within the land, in the Brenny and Monaghan, as others have written shall have the same difficulties. Secondly, we look to hear from you and them jointly, how you think fit that the remain of this year shall be spent and employed, in what kind of war, and whose, and with what numbers : which being done and sent hither in writing with all expedition, you shall then understand our pleasure in all things fit for your service; until which time we command you to be very careful to meet with all inconveniences that may rise in the kingdom, where the evil-affected will grow so insolent upon our evil success, and the good subjects grow desperate, when they see the best of our defending them. We have seen a writing, in manner of a catalogue full of challenges, that are impertinent, and of comparisons, that are needless, such as hath not been before this time presented to a State, except it be done more with a hope to terrify all men from censuring your proceedings. Had it not been enough to send us the testimony of the Council, but that you must call so many of those, that are of so slender judgement and none of our Council, to such a form of subscription? Surely, howsoever you may have warranted them, we doubted not but to let them know what belongs to us, to you, and them. And thus, expecting your answer, we end, at our Manor of Nonsuch, the 14th of September, 1599.

XLV. To Robert Devereux, Earl of Essex

Two days after the dispatch of the previous letter, Captain Lawson came to Court bearing a personal letter from Essex to the Queen. He explained that on the 6th September he had met Tyrone in parley and had agreed to a truce. The Queen immediately sent Captain Lawson back with the following letter, together with a personal letter which has not survived.

Essex, however, did not await the answer to his letter. On the 28th September he suddenly appeared, with many of his officers, at Nonsuch, and went up to speak with the Queen, who was not yet dressed. Contrary to express orders he had left his command with the Earl of Ormonde and the Council and come over to explain his actions in person.

September 17, 1599.

Right trusty and right well beloved Councillor, we greet you well. By the letter and the journal which we have received from you, we see a quick end made of a slow proceeding, for anything which our forces shall undertake in those quarters, which you pretended to visit, and therefore doubt not but that before this time you have ended the charge of the last two thousand which we yielded for other purposes, and of the three hundred more destined only for Ulster service.

It remaineth, therefore, that we return you somewhat of our conceits upon this late accident of your interview with the rebels. We never doubted but that Tyrone, whensoever he saw any force approach either himself or any of his principal partisans, would instantly offer a parley, specially with our supreme general of that kingdom, having often done it with those of subaltern authority; always seeking these cessations with like words, like protestations, and upon such contingents as we gather these will prove, by your advertisement of his purpose to go consult with O'Donnell.

And, therefore, to come to some answer for the present. It appeareth by your journal that you and the traitor spoke half an hour together, without anybody's hearing; wherein, though we that trust you with our kingdom are far from mistrusting you with a traitor, yet both for comeliness, example, and your own discharge, we marvel you would carry it no better; especially having in all things since your arrival been so precise to have good testimony for your actions, as whenever anything was to be done to which our commandment tied you, it seemed sufficient warrant for you if your fellow councillors allowed better of other ways, though your own reason carried you to have pursued our directions against their opinions; to whose conduct, if we had meant that Ireland, after all the calamities in which they have wrapped it, should still have been abandoned, then it was very superfluous to have sent over such a personage as yourself.

You have dealt so sparingly with us in the substance, by advertising us, at first, of the half-hour's conference only, but not what passed on either side by letting us also know you sent commissioners, without showing us what they had in charge, as we cannot tell, but by divination, what to think may be the issue of this proceeding. Only this we are assured of, that you have prospered so ill for us by your warfare, as we cannot but be very jealous lest you should be as well overtaken by the treaty. If this parley shall not produce such a conclusion as this intolerable charge may receive present and large abatement, then hath the management of our forces not only proved dishonourable and wasteful, but that which followeth is like to prove perilous and contemptible. Consider then what is like to be the end, and what will be fit to build on.

To trust this traitor upon oath is to trust a devil upon his religion. To trust him upon pledges is a mere illusory; for what piety is there among them that can tie them to rule of honesty for itself, who are only bound to their own sensualities, and respect only private utility.

And, therefore, whatever order you take with him, yet unless he yield to have garrisons planted in his own country to master him—to deliver O'Neale's sons, whereof the detaining is most dishonourable—and to come over to us personally here, we shall doubt you do but piece up a hollow peace, and so the end prove worse than the beginning. And, therefore, as we do well approve your own voluntary profession, wherein you assure us you will conclude nothing till you have advertised us, and heard our pleasure, so do we absolutely command you to continue and perform that resolution. Pass not your word for his pardon, nor make any absolute contract for his conditions, till you do particularly advertise us by writing, and receive our pleasure hereafter for your further warrant and authority in that behalf.

Given under our signet at Nonsuch, the 17th day of September, 1599, in the forty-first year of our reign.

XLVI. To the Commissioners at Boulogne

In May 1600, an attempt, through the mediation of the French King, was made to conclude the war with Spain. Commissioners from both sides met at Boulogne, but nothing was accomplished, as neither side would yield on the point of precedency and the Spaniards refused a compromise. The treaty was therefore abandoned. Her patience being exhausted after two months' quibbling, the Queen wrote to the Commissioners:

Greenwich, July 19, 1600.

Having seen your letters bearing date the 16th of July, we find it very strange that the Audiencer is not yet returned, and therefore mean no longer to abide the hazard of any dishonour; seeing by your long stay through their delays we may be suspected in the world to be greedy of that which we have been only induced to, with an opinion that their sincerity in those proceedings would not have come short of their protestations. As for the propositions of Richardot, we know his fashion is always to take liberty by speaking as a private man to make advantages of offers and discourses, to which he will be bound no further than to serve his own turn, and therefore we like well of your answers in that kind; for we are not disposed upon any new propositions to post our Commissioners from France to Holland upon so slender grounds, and therefore we have thought good in this sort to direct you. First, whatsoever the Audiencer brings, to stand firm to give them no priority; though in any other kind (as heretofore ye are instructed) we can be content you fall into a course of moderation, so it be not to our prejudice.

Next for a final answer, ye must now deliver to the Commissioners, that having informed us of their proceedings you have received order, that if the Audiencer do not return by the end of this next week with such direction as may reconcile that point of precedency, so as you may return to treaty without any note of dishonour to us; we have directed you to return over hither immediately, and so it is our pleasure that you should do whom we sent over for that purpose. For as it is strange that they would be so senseless as to think that we would yield any superiority; so it is strange that all this time there should not be an answer returned, seeing that which is offered by us standeth with so much reason.

XLVII. To Thomas Butler, Earl of Ormonde

In April 1600, the Earl of Ormonde with the Earl of Thomond and Sir George Carew met Onie McRory, one of the Irish rebels, in a parley. After an hour's inconclusive talk the rebels surrounded the party and pulled Ormonde off his horse. The others escaped, but Ormonde remained a prisoner. On his release, the Queen wrote as follows:

July 21, 1600.

We are sure that there need not many words from us to make you know how great contentment the news of your delivery hath brought us, who were much more deeply wounded to apprehend the peril of your own life, when it depended upon the savage humour of faithless rebels, than for any other particular that concerned ourself, though there could nothing have happened, for many respects, more prejudicial to our service. Concerning the conditions which we have seen, to tell you true, we were so fully pleased with the contentment of your safety as we little troubled ourselves to examine the particulars, making this one ground for all, that nothing hath passed the thought of our faithful Lucas which was unworthy of his constant and loyal profession, howsoever the same might be assailed with lewd and vile temptations.

For the present, therefore, you must take this with you, that it will remain a good while for a quarrel between us and you, whensoever we remember that you, whom long experience had taught so many better rules, would be the cause, through lack of foresight, to give such a wretch the triumph to have the Lieutenant of our army in his mercy. And yet, for all that parenthesis, let Lucas comfort himself that he, which is our *hasta la muerte*, shall never deserve more trust than we will give him, nor desire more happiness than we do wish him and his. For all things else, we require you to impart your purposes from time to time with our Deputy, with whom you may use freedom, as well in regard of his own respect to you as the confidence that we repose in him.

XLVIII. To James the Sixth, King of Scotland

Written on receipt of the news of the Gowrie conspiracy. The official story of this sensational affair was that on 5th August the King whilst out hunting was persuaded to enter the castle of the Earl of Gowrie at St. Johnstone by a strange tale of a mysterious pot of gold. After dinner he was decoyed by himself into a little study where Alexander Ruthven, the Earl's brother, would have murdered him, but his cries for help were overheard by his courtiers who happened to be passing underneath the window. After an exciting battle on the stairs both brothers were slain, and the King rescued. As is not uncommon in conspiracies when there are no survivors of the other party, very different versions were spread abroad. For the rest of his life, King James observed the fifth of August as a day of especial thanksgiving.

August 21, 1600.

At the horrible fame of the execrable fact that was spread abroad of your live's danger, when I remember that a King you are, and one of whom since your cradle I have ever had tender care, I could not refrain to send you this gentleman of purpose in post both to congratulate your happy state as to inform me both how it was, and how you are in health and state, praying God that with His potent hand hath stretched it out for your defence. And though a King I be, yet hath my funeral been prepared (as I hear) long or I suppose their labour shall be needful, and do hear so much of that daily as I may have a good memorial that I am mortal, and with all so be they too that make such preparation before hand, whereat I smile, supposing that such facts may make them readier for it than I. Think not but how wilily soever things be carried, they are so well known that they may do more harm to others than to me. Of this my pen hath run further than at first I meant, when the memory of a Prince's end made me call to mind such usage, which too many countries talks of and I cannot stop mine ears from. If you will needs know what I mean, I have been pleased to impart to this, my faithful servant, some part thereof, to whom I will refer me, and will pray God to give you grace to know what best becomes you.

Your loving sister and cousin,

E.R.

After Essex's failure in Ireland, Charles Blount, Lord Mount-joy, was sent over as Lord Deputy, and from the first he made head against the rebels. By constantly harrying them and destroying their supplies he broke their spirit. His successes continued throughout 1600, but in 1601 a new difficulty arose. In September the Spaniards sent a force to help Tyrone which landed at Kinsale. Mountjoy surrounded Kinsale, but by Christmas he was in a critical position, for Tyrone was coming to the help of the Spaniards, and the English force, weakened by disease, was inferior in numbers to the Spaniards and the Irish. On 24th December Mountjoy utterly routed Tyrone; a few days later the Spaniards in Kinsale surrendered upon honourable terms. In 1602 he continued to stamp out the rebellion, and towards the end of the year Tyrone asked for peace.

XLIX. To CHARLES BLOUNT, LORD MOUNTJOY

Mountjoy, in spite of his successes, felt that he was being ill-supported at home and unjustly criticized at Court. In a letter to the Queen he had bitterly likened himself to a scullion. The Queen thereupon wrote familiarly to assure him that she fully realized his loyalty and efficiency.

December 3, 1600.

MISTRESS KITCHENMAID,

I had thought that precedency had been ever in question but among the higher and greater sort; but now I find good proof that some of more dignity and greater calling may by good desert and faithful care give the upper hand to one of your faculty, that with your frying and other kitchen stuff have brought to their last home more rebels, and passed greater breakneck places, than those promised more and did less. Comfort yourself therefore in this, that neither your careful endeavour, nor dangerous travails, nor heedful regards to our service, without your own by-respects, could ever have been bestowed upon a Prince that more esteems them, considers and regards them than she for whom chiefly I know all this hath been done, and who keeps this verdict ever in store for you; that no vainglory, nor popular fawning can ever advance you forward, but true vow of duty and reverence of Prince, who two afore your life I see you do prefer.

And though you lodge near Papists, and doubt you not for their infection, yet I fear you may fall in an heresy which I hereby do conjure you from; that you suppose you to be back-bited by some to make me think you faulty of many oversights and evil defaults in your government. I would have you know for certain that as there is no man can rule so great a charge without some errors, yet you may assure yourself I have never heard of any had fewer; and such is your good luck that I have not known them, though you were warned of them.

And learn this of me, that you must make difference betwixt admonitions and charges, and like of faithful advices as your most necessariest weapons to save you from blows of Princes' mislike. And so I absolve you *a poena et culpa* if this you observe. And so God bless and prosper you as if ourself were where you are.

Your Sovereign that dearly regards you.

L. To Henry the Fourth, King of France

The expenses of the Irish war were a growing embarrassment to the Queen. She therefore pressed the French King to pay back the money which she had lent him for his wars. Henry, however, always regretted his inability and continually put the Queen off with promises. At the same time he complained through his Ambassador that his subjects received tardy justice in the Court of Admiralty for the wrongs committed by English pirates.

Translated from the French

December 1600.

We have not wished to detain this gentleman here longer lest his absence be contrary to his instructions and for the much closer bringing together of the bond of our friendship as he has begun and faithfully borne himself therein. And as we desire that it may not be otherwise between us than to augment and increase it by all means on all occasions; it is to our great regret that we are constrained to complain in good earnest of the little regard which we apprehend has been borne us by the delays and denials in succouring us in the urgency of our affairs with that wherewith we assisted you in your greater need. Of which the default besides the unthankfulness still increases, as you may realize, our displeasure.

And if these lively reasons in such an extremity cannot effect merely the restitution of one's own, seeing that nothing can be required more reasonable, far from receiving like courtesy, what other effects of friendship may be promised but exceeding great and evident contempt? And as for the desire to pay us with the excuses that your necessities, which for ever overburden you, do not allow you to give us the satisfaction which we desire, we will remember, if it please you, that we were not guarded by such excuses against your need; on the contrary that we did all we could, in spite of the necessity which then pressed us hard, to give you content; and, although this inconvenience still oppresses you somewhat, surely considering the state in which our affairs now are, it is more than reasonable that the need of the owners be the first service of that which can give them ease and belongs to them. But since you know now the reasons for the rightness of our urgency, we pray you very affectionately that without using us with any more postponements, which might be produced endlessly, as each one grows passionate and stiff in his own interests, be willing to make clear to us, what you wish to do, so that we may found upon it our judgement and the ground of what we have to expect, and resolve of ourselves in the same way in our affairs. But seeing that we do not press you upon any feigned urgency, we pray you to dispose yourself to give us better content, and to act that we may be raised up by some charge on the state for this next year, and so consecutively for following years, according as we have charged this gentleman to solicit you on our behalf.

He will also give you account of the care we have taken to give justice to your subjects, as much for the quittance of our honour as to content you; and he will tell you the reasons and the difficulties which have prevented us in some cases from effecting what we desired, begging you to believe that it has not been our fault that they have not received the satisfaction that belongs to them; but it is difficult in the state in which our affairs are to set right all the evils and inconveniences which the license of war can cause; which ought not to give cause to tax our justice, as you yourself can remember often to have pointed out to us in your own defence on like occasion. Our aforesaid Ambassador will also point out to you the complaints of several of our people, to which we pray you give order that the prompt justice may be done.

LI. To Henry the Fourth, King of France

The Queen continued to press for the repayment of the war debt due from the French King.

Translated from the French

January 1601.

The current of your prosperity, victories and good fortunes has flowed so swift that hardly have I received news of one than another follows, insomuch as your Ambassador will be my witness with what cheerfulness I received the good intelligence, returning for it humble thanks to the Lord God, Whom I doubt not you acknowledge the sole means of putting in your head such good and opportune resolutions, and praying Him continue His favours always on your part.

To speak of the tardiness of the arrival of my Ambassador, I promise you that this has been far from my intention, but after his return to me, there were matters which greatly touched his estate, which considering your distant abode from these quarters, made him more bold to prolong the time; but being ready to set out, I commend him to you with such a weighty negotiation as he will communicate to you, and beg you to imagine what it is for a Prince such as I have shown myself in your affairs to receive no other recognition than fair letters and speeches recognizing merit. Words are leaves, the substance consists of deeds, which are the true fruits of a good tree. Yet consider how I cannot be insensible of so many goings and comings, so many procrastinations from one time to another; so that I am ashamed that all the world should see with how little respect I have been used for all the speed that I have shown in hastening my succours to you, so that if they had had ears so deaf, your state would have been fully conscious of it. There is nothing in the world I hate more than to call to remembrance a benefit; but it is not my fault, for had I been better treated, I should have been far from such imputations. And besides to end this, in the Name of God, consider better what touches your honour; do not act that I have just cause to remove my affection from such a Prince as I see prefers before me all other nations of whatever small worth they be. And not to trouble you further I will end this as

Your good Sister,
ELIZABETH R.

LII. TO HENRY THE FOURTH, KING OF FRANCE

On hearing of the news of the failure of Essex's rebellion, which occurred on Sunday, 8th February, the French King sent to congratulate the Queen on her escape. Amongst those implicated was Sir Henry Neville, her Ambassador to the French Court, who was in London at the time and on point of departing for France. Neville took no part in the rising, but he had previous knowledge of it which he had not revealed; he was arrested and sent to the Tower. The Queen had not yet appointed a successor, and entrusted the task of pressing her claim for the repayment of the war debts to Neville's secretary, Ralph Winwood.

Translated from the French

March 20, 1601.

MY VERY DEAR BROTHER,

I blushed yesterday when I received your letter, so full of affectionate honour and amiable recognition of extreme cheerfulness for the Divine Goodness shown on my behalf for my delivery from a treason so close and inward, for I remembered that the delaying of my Ambassador or of some other had retarded my deliberate purpose of congratulating you upon your honourable marriage, together with your happy return to Paris. But I hope that your Ambassador will bear witness with me of the urgent occasion which caused it, and also that everything was ready for his crossing the sea when strange things revealed themselves by the very proceedings which somewhat touched him. I would never wish to send you anyone of whom there was the least suspicion of any fault. And for witness of what was done, I present you with the two letters which were written at the same time, begging you to take them with good liking, until I send you a fitter person as Ambassador. And that it please you in the meanwhile to hear favourably the secretary of the other, whom since his return, you have heard declare the negotiations which greatly affected me, and that I may receive some answer therein.

Not wishing to trouble you further but to pray the Creator to keep you in good life and long,

Your very affectionate Sister,

ELIZABETH R.

LIII. To PEREGRINE, LORD WILLOUGHBY

Lord Willoughby, after distinguished service in the Netherlands, was now Warden of the Scottish Borders. This letter, one of a number on Border problems, illustrates the Queen's conviction, often expressed at the end of her reign, that amongst the younger generation there were no adequate successors to the elder statesmen, of whom few now survived.

Whitehall, March 21, 1601.

Although we have forborn to write unto you since your going down, yet have we from time to time directed both our Council in general and our Secretary in particular to acquaint you with our pleasure, as well as to take notice of some private good services done by you and the Treasurer in apprehending of such as you had so great cause to suspect : wherein we do commend your case to providence. We had likewise thought to have written to you about those differences risen in the Town of

Berwick whereof you are Governor. But forasmuch as we perceive some things grow by misunderstanding between you and some of the Council established, and all the controversies for the most part are for some petty rights and incidents to officers or Councillors in their places : we will leave those things to be answered by our Council and herewith by our own letters will only touch those points which are of more importance.

First we know that you can well consider that in all government nothing giveth greater encouragement for practice nor more weakeneth for defence than when there is either dissensions in deed or opinion of which there is so great notice taken there of late; as we rather wonder that no pernicious effects have ensued, than promise ourselves that it shall not break into peril hereafter except it be timely prevented. Wherein because we will deal as clearly with you as we have done with the Marshal (between whom and you we have heard there hath been some misunderstanding) and because we assure ourselves that we shall find so great an affection to our service in you (of whose discretion in all your employment the world hath taken notice) as you will not for any private [sic] suffer impediment to our service we have both straightly imposed upon the Marshal a charge to respect you as the Governor in all things that appertain unto you, and do mean after some month's respite (for which he hath earnestly sued) to send him down unto you so well informed of our resolution to have all good agreement between you as we do know it shall well appear unto you that he will give you no just cause of unkindness, or sever himself from you in our services, in whom we find a very good desire not only for our service but for your own particular to live in all things comfortably with you as any gentleman can do with a Governor, your respecting him as he deserveth, of which we make no doubt though peradventure some bad instruments shall never want to do ill offices between you. It is true that we do think it very fit to admonish you to give straight order that no excess of resort of Scots be suffered in that garrison, but that (excepting the commerce upon market days and such like for the necessary support of the place) it be used as frontier towns ought to be, in which your experience teacheth you best, that all wise commanders hold those places only well governed where most jealousy[1] is used, which is quite contrary there if it be as is reported by the Scots themselves, who do not stick to say that they may freely come into Berwick by one device or other as into Edinburgh. Next we do require you to see that your government there be not slandered by the error of those who for private gain do make that place a sanctuary for bankrupts and outlaws, rather than a town of war, nor that any person married with the Scots be suffered to have place there. Further, concerning the matter of Musgrave and Selby, we think fit to let you understand that as we have and will plainly make our mislike appear to Musgrave for his factious and lewd petition here exhibited against you. So for things that are in question between you and our Council there established we cannot allow that any council of war shall be made judges either of their authority or of their offences : although we are not unwilling in case of danger or other difficulties in inferior things that you do call unto you according to the article of our establishment such principal persons of discretion to consult withal as the time shall need. But we have now gone further in this particular than we meant to have troubled ourselves, not doubting but that you, that see how much they daily abound in practice,[2] will rather dispense with the errors of private men, who may forget themselves out of some humour of profit, or petty credit in their offices than by making the dissensions so notorious to make that place a subject of scorn, which being ruled by a person of your reputation abroad and at home, ought still to serve for an example and bridle to those that would go about to malign it or our service.

Lastly we pray you to believe that we are very sorry to understand of your indisposition of body, and the rather because we know how apt you are to hurt yourself by overmuch care and labour in our services wherein we would have you spare yourself as much as you may for we would be loath your health should be more overthrown by those occasions, considering how long it is before men of service be bred in this age. And now by the way we will only touch this much of that whereof we are sure an angel of Heaven could hardly have made you a believer; that

[1] The MS. reads ' ialously '.
[2] Sedition.

is [*sic*] appeareth now by one's example more bound than all or any others, how little faith there was in Israel.

LIV. TO JAMES THE SIXTH, KING OF SCOTLAND

On receiving news of Essex's conspiracy and its failure, King James sent the Earl of Mar and the Abbot of Kinloss ostensibly to congratulate the Queen on her escape, and to discuss such matters as were in dispute between the two Courts. Actually the purpose of their mission was to prepare the way for the King's accession, particularly with Sir Robert Cecil. The Queen was not deceived.

April 1601.

MY GOOD BROTHER,

At the first reading of your letter, albeit I wondered much what springs your griefs might have of any of my actions, who knows myself most clear of any just cause to breed you any annoy, yet I was well lightened of my marvel when you dealt so kingly with me, not to let them harbour in your breast, but were contented to send me so well chosen a couple, that might utter and receive what you mean, and what I should relate. And when my greedy will to know did stir me, at first access, to require an ease with speed of such matters, I found by them, that the principal causes were the selfsame in part that the Lord of Kinloss had two years past and more imparted to me, to whom, and to others your ministers, I am sure I have given so good satisfaction in honour and reason as if your other greater matters have not made them forgotten, you yourself will not deny them.

But not willing in my letters to molest you with that which they will not but tell you (as I hope), together with such true and guileless profession of my sincere affection to you as you shall never have just reason to doubt my clearness in your behalf, yet this I must tell you, that as I marvel much to have such a subject that would impart so great a cause to you afore ever making me privy thereof, so doth my affectionate amity to you claim at your hands that my ignorance of subjects' boldness be not augmented by your silence; by whom you may be sure you shall never obtain so much good as my good dealing can afford you.

Let not shades deceive you, which may take away best

substance from you, when they can turn but to dust or smoke. An upright demeanour bears ever more poise than all disguised shows of good can do. Remember, that a bird of the air, if no other instrument, to an honest King shall stand instead of many feigned practices, to utter aught may any wise touch him. And so I leave my scribbles, with my best wishes that you scan what works best become a King, and what in the end will best avail him.

Your most loving sister, that longs to see you deal as kindly as I mean,

ELIZABETH R.

LV. TO CHARLES BLOUNT, LORD MOUNTJOY

On receipt of certain news that the long expected Spanish reinforcement had at last landed in Ireland, the Queen sent a personal letter with the official letter notifying him that reinforcements were on the way.

October 4, 1601.

Since the brainsick humour of unadvised assault hath seized on the hearts of our causeless foes, we doubt not but their gain will be their bane, and glory their shame, that ever they had the thought thereof. And that your humour agrees so rightly with ours, we think it most fortunately happened in your rule, to show the better whose you are, and what you be, as your own hand hath told us of late, and do beseech the Almighty power of the Highest, so to guide your hands that nothing light in vain, but to prosper your heed, that nothing be left behind that might avail your praise, and that yourself in venturing too far make not the foe a prey of you. Tell our army from us, that they make a full account, that every hundred of them will beat a thousand, and every thousand theirs doubled. I am the bolder to pronounce it in His name, that hath ever protected my righteous cause, in which I bless them all. And putting you in the first place, I end, scribbling in haste,

Your loving Sovereign,

E.R.

LVI. TO CHARLES BLOUNT, LORD MOUNTJOY

A personal letter of encouragement denying that Mountjoy's proceedings are being adversely criticized at Court. Cecil enclosed a fair copy ' lest you cannot read it '.

c. 1601.

O what melancholy humour hath exhaled up into your brain from a full fraughted heart that should breed such doubt bred upon no cause given by us at all, never having pronounced any syllable upon which such a work should be framed. There is no louder trump that may sound out your praise, your hazard, your care, your luck, than we have blasted in all our Court and elsewhere in deed.

Well, I will attribute it to God's good Providence for you, that (lest all these glories might elevate you too much) He hath suffered (though not made) such a scruple to keep you under His rod, Who best knows we have more need of bits than spurs. Thus *valeant ista amara; ad Tartaros eat melancholia*

Your Sovereign,

E.R.

LVII. TO CHARLES BLOUNT, LORD MOUNTJOY

Written on receipt of the news of Mountjoy's victory over Tyrone and of the terms of surrender agreed with the Spaniards.

January 12, 1602.

ELIZABETH R.

Right trusty and well-beloved, we greet you well. The report which your letters by Danvers have brought us of the success it hath pleased God to give you against our rebels and the Spaniards combined with them, was received by us with such contentment, as so great and happy an accident could afford. Wherefore although we (as ever we have done in all other happiness which hath befallen us) ascribe the highest praise and thanks to His Divine Majesty: yet forasmuch as we do account that they who are the servants of our State in like actions are made participant (in a second degree) of His favour bestowed on us by their virtue and industry, we cannot but hold them worthy of thanks from us as they have received honour from Him. Among

v

whom, you being there the chief (not only as chiefly put in trust by us but as we plainly perceive in vigilancy, in labour, and in valour in this late action) we could not forbear to let you see how sensible we are of this your merit. It is true that before this good success upon the rebels, we were in daily attention to have heard of some quicker attempt upon the town (than any was made), both in respect that your own letters tended to such sense, and especially because protraction of time brought with it apparent dangers, as well of access of new supplies from our foreign enemies as of defection of a people, so unconstant of disposition, and so rebellious to government as those of that nation ever have been. But we at that time having understood by those journals, which were committed to St. John and Danvers, some reasons which have moved you to the course you have taken rather than to have used speed in attempting, seeing all assaults are accompanied with loss, and every loss, in such a time, multiplied in rumour, and wholly converted by practice, to the prejudice of the cause in question, which is maintained (now as things do stand), by the reputation of your army, we do now conceive that all your works have had their foundation upon such reasons as you thought most advantageous for our service. It remaineth therefore now (and so we desire it may be made known to our army that have served under you, in such manner as you shall think best to express it), that as we do know they have endured many incommodities in this siege (which we would have been glad they could have avoided, having made so good proof of their valour and loyalty, as they have done at this time, so as we rather seek to preserve them, as the best treasure of a Prince, than to suffer them to waste, if otherwise our Kingdom could have been kept from danger of foreign conquest and intestine rebellion), so we expect it at the hands of the better sort of our servitors there that it shall well be infused into the minds of the rest, that whatsoever either our own directions or expending of treasure could do (for prevention of those difficulties which follow all armies, and are inseparable where the war is made in a climate so ill-tempered for a winter's siege) hath been royally and providently afforded them. A matter of much more charge and uncertainty because all our care and direction have attended the wind's and weather's courtesy. To conclude with answer to your demands for further supplies of men. Although we hope that the time is so near of the final conclusion of your happy success against the remnant of the strangers in that poor town, being pressed with so many wants, and with the despair which our late victory will add hereunto, as that hardly any supplies sent from us can come, before it have taken effect; yet because you may perceive how much we attribute to your judgement in anything which for our affairs is there desired, we have (as by our Council hath been signified unto you) given order for four thousand men to be sent thither out of hand, with the full proportion of munition which you desire. In which kind of provisions we find so great consumptions as we must require you to take some better order with them that have the distribution thereof. For if it be observed what quantities have been daily sent over, and yet what daily wants are pretended, the expense will be found insupportable, and so much the rather, because all men know that whatsoever the Irish Companies receive (except now in this action) is continually converted for money to the use of the rebels.

> Given under our Signet at our Palace at Whitehall, the 44th year of our reign, the twelfth of January 1601.

Above the signature at the head of the letter, the Queen wrote in her own hand:

Though for fear of worse end, you did desire (as we confess we once thought to direct) to end this work, before either enemy or rebel could increase the peril of our honour, yet we hope that no such adventure shall be more made, but that their confusion be ere now lighted on their own heads. And let Clanrickard and Thomond know, that we do most thankfully accept their endeavours. For yourself, we can but acknowledge your diligence, and dangerous adventure, and cherish and judge of you as your careful Sovereign.

LVIII. TO JAMES THE SIXTH, KING OF SCOTLAND

Written in answer to an offer of assistance in Ireland. The 'evil accident' to the Queen's arm was an attack of rheumatism, which considerably upset her temper, and may partly account for the sarcastic thanks for the King's good wishes.

February 3, 1602.

MY VERY GOOD BROTHER,

Though matter I have long to lengthen my letter, yet you must bear with few lines, driven thereto by an evil accident of my arm, and yet my memory shall never be short to keep in mind your ready kindness, which the offer of your subjects' service made me know, together with the care and speech that [you showed] therein, as also the good warning you gave me of a supposed army from Spain for England; which though I nothing fear though they came, as nothing doubting but their speed should be as shameful to them as the precedent hath been; yet my thanks for your care, together with your good counsel, not to neglect such a malice, binding me to conceive that you would be loath that any disaster should arrive to her that yet (God be praised) never tasted of any. And thus I end to trouble you longer, with mind to bide

Your affectionate sister,

ELIZABETH R.

LIX. TO CHARLES BLOUNT, LORD MOUNTJOY

The reduction of the rebels' strongholds continued throughout the year 1602, Mountjoy being adequately supported from home.

July 15, 1602.

Right trusty and well-beloved, we greet you well. Although we have heard nothing from you directly since our last dispatch, yet we impute it to no neglect of yours, having so great cause to judge the best of your actions, when every dispatch from other parts of our Kingdom reports of great honour in the success of our army under you, a matter specially appearing by those letters which we have seen directed to our Treasurer of Wars in Ireland, containing the discourse of your marches, and abiding in the heart of Tyrone, and the recovery of that island, and that ordnance of ours, which had been foully lost before. In which respect we value the same so much the more acceptably. We have also thought good at this time to add this further, that we are glad to find that you are joined with Dockwra and Chichester, because that is the thing which hath been long wished, often attempted, but never before effected (being indeed the true consequence of our plantation, with great expense both at Lough Foyle and in the other parts of Ulster). So as when we perceive that now the time is come when you may make an universal prosecution, and when we find that your own words give such hope that this ungrateful traitor shall never be able to hold up his head again, if the Spaniard do not arrive, we thought it fit to touch these two things following. First to assure you that we have sent a fleet to the coast of Spain, notwithstanding that our former fleet returned with the carrack, there to attend his coast, and all such fleets as shall be prepared to annoy us. Next we do require you, even whilst the iron is hot, so to strike, as this may not only prove a good summer's journey but may deserve the title of that action, which is the war's conclusion. For furtherance whereof we have spared no charge, even now again to send a magazine of victual and other necessaries to those places by which you may best maintain those garrisons with which you resolve to bridle those rebels.

We have heard likewise from Carew, our President of Munster, that he hath taken the Castle that was held by the rebels at Bearhaven, and defended with the Spanish ordnance. In that Province we find by him that there is a constant expectation of Spanish succours, for which reason, and considering what promises the King of Spain doth make them, and with what importunity they beg it at his hands, beside one other craft they use, to hide from him all fear, which might divert him from that enterprise, agreeing amongst themselves, how great soever their miseries be, to conceal the same from him and his ministers, as appeareth well by a letter of O'Donnell's own hand intercepted of late, by which he writes to a rebel called O'Connor Kerry, desiring him to advertise him of the state of Ireland, but in no sort to deliver any bad report of their losses, because he would be loath that the Spaniard should know it.

We do require you very earnestly to be very wary in taking the submissions of these rebels, who ever make profit of their coming in. Some let slip of purpose by the arch traitor, others when they have compounded for their own peace, are notoriously known to fill their countries with more cattle than ever they had in seven years before, which is a matter that most notoriously discovereth that the great bordering traitors (whose countries are sought to be laid waste) do find a safe protection for their goods under them. A matter whereof we speak in no other sort than by way of caution, knowing that no rule is so general, either to leave or take, which may not change in respect of circumstances.

Given under our Signet. At our Manor of Greenwich the fifteenth day of July, in the four and fortieth of our reign.

To this letter, in the margin, the Queen added in her own hand:

We con you many lauds for having so nearly approached the villainous rebel and see no reason why so great forces should not end his days, whose wickedness hath cut off so many, and should judge myself mad, if we should not change your authority for his life, and so we do by this. Since neither Spaniard, nor other accident, is like to alter this mind, as she that should blush to receive such indignity after so royal prosecution. We have forgotten to praise your humility, that after having been a Queen's kitchenmaid, you have not disdained to be a traitor's scullion. God bless you with perseverance.

Your Sovereign, E.R.

lx. To Charles Blount, Lord Mountjoy

Written on learning that Mountjoy had captured the Castle of Dunboy.

August 1602.

Your Sovereign, E.R.

My faithful George, how joyed we are that so good event hath followed so troublesome endeavours, laborious cares, and heedful travels, you may guess, but we best can witness, and do protest that your safety hath equalled the most thereof. And so God ever bless you in all your actions.

LXI. To James the Sixth, King of Scotland

January 6, 1603.

MY VERY GOOD BROTHER,

It pleaseth me not a little that my true intents without glosses or guiles are by you so gratefully taken, for I am nothing of the vile disposition of such as while their neighbour's house is likely to be afire, will not only not help but not afford them water to quench the same. If any such you have heard of toward me, God grant He remember it not too well for them. For the Archduke, alas, poor man he wisheth everybody like himself except his bonds, which, without his brother's help, he will soon repent his signory.

I suppose that considering whose apert enemy the King of Spain is, you will not neglect so much your own honour to the world (though you had no particular love to me) as to permit his Ambassador in your land that so causelessly persecutes such a Princess as never harmed him. Yea, such a one as, if his deceased father had been rightly informed, did better merit at his hand than any Prince on earth did ever to other. For where hath there been an example that any one King hath ever denied so fair a present as the whole seventeen provinces of the Low Countries? Yea, who not only would have denied them, but sent a dozen gentlemen to warn him of their sliding from him, with offer of keeping them from the near neighbours' hands, and sent treasure to pay the shaking towns from lapse. Deserved I such a recompense as many a complot both for my life and kingdom? Ought I not to defend and bereave him of such a weapon as might invay myself? He will say, I help Zealand and Holland from his hands. No. If either his father or himself would observe such oath as the Emperor Charles obliged himself, and so in sequel his son, I would not [have] dealt with others' territories. But they hold those by such covenants, as not observing, by their own grants, they are no longer bound unto them. But though all this were not unknown to me, yet I cast such right reasons over my shoulder, and regarded their good, and have never defended them in a wicked quarrel. And had he not mixed that government, contrary to his own laws, with the rule of the Spaniards, all this had not needed.

Now for the warning the French sent you of Veson's ambassade to you. Methinks the King, your good brother, hath given you a good *caveat* that, being a King, he supposeth by that measure that you would deny such offers; and, since needs you will have my counsel, I can hardly believe that, being warned, your own subjects shall be suffered to come into your Realm from such a place to such intent. Such a prelate, if he came, should be taught a better lesson than play so presumptuous and bold a part afore he knew your good liking thereof, which, as I hope, is far from your intent; so will his coming verify to much good Mr. Simple's asseverations at Rome, of which you have ere now been warned enough. Thus you see how to fulfil your trust imposed in me (which to infringe I never mind), I have sincerely made patent my sincerity, and, though not fraught with much wisdom, yet stuffed with great goodwill. I hope you will bear with my molesting you too long with my scratching hand, as proceeding from a heart that shall be ever filled with the sure affection of

Your loving and friendly sister,

ELIZABETH R.

LXII. TO CHARLES BLOUNT, LORD MOUNTJOY

At the end of 1602 Tyrone offered to submit on terms, but the Queen refused. Tyrone then wrote to Mountjoy that he would submit, simply and absolutely, to her mercy. When his letter was forwarded to the Queen, her ministers, realizing that the long war was ruining the country, begged her to accept his submission. She was very unwilling, but at last yielded and sent the following letter.

Richmond, February 16, 1603.

We have seen the submission made by Tyrone which you have sent us, and perceive the course which you have taken thereupon, which hath been to give no such credit to his words, either in deed or appearance, as upon those fair pretexts to give over any other good means of his prosecution; which if you should have done upon this overture, the same effect might follow which hath done before, when in the instant of his submission he hath been deepest in practice; in which respects we acknowledge that you have proceeded very discreetly.

And now to speak of the course he holdeth. We conceive the world hath seen sufficiently how dear the conservation of that Kingdom and people hath been unto us, and how precious we have been of our honour, that have of late rejected so many of those offers of his, only because we were sorry to make a precedent of facility to show grace or favour to him that hath been the author of so much misery to our loving subjects. Nevertheless because it seemeth that this is a general conceit that this reduction may prove profitable to the State by sparing the effusion of Christian blood (the preventing whereof Christian piety teacheth us), and because the manner of the submission maketh the best amends that penitency can yield to offences against sovereignty (if amends there can be after so horrible treasons), we are content to lay aside anything that may [be] herein contrary [to] our own private affections, and will consider that clemency hath as eminent a place in supreme authority as justice and severity. And, therefore, to the intent that either effect may fall out which is expected by his submission, or the ingrafted falsehood and corruption of his nature may declare itself, we are content, and so we give you authority hereby, to assign him a day with all expedition to make his personal repair to you; when we require you to be careful to preserve our dignity in all circumstances, assuring him, that seeing he referreth all absolutely to our grace and mercy, where we would never have yielded that if he had kept his former courses of presumption to indent with us beforehand, we are now contented that you do let him know he shall have his life, and receive, upon his coming in, such other conditions as shall be honourable and reasonable for us to grant him. And thus much for that which he shall need to know before his coming in; which if he do accept without any other particular promise procured from you beforehand, then could we like it very well that you should make stay of him in safe custody until you hear our further pleasure; whose meaning is, not to break our word in the point of his life, for which it is only given, but only to suspend his liberty till we see whether any conditions which shall leave him free again to return as he came, can make us in better state than we are now, when we shall have nothing to trust to but the ordinary assurances which can be had from traitors. And these our letters shall be your sufficient warrant and discharge in this behalf.

LXIII. To Charles Blount, Lord Mountjoy

The day after writing the previous letter, the Queen again wrote to Mountjoy, giving him more precise conditions for Tyrone's surrender.

Richmond, February 17, 1603.

Forasmuch as we (in our former letter) have made you see that we do not retain so deep an impression of the heinous offences committed by Tyrone (for which he hath made himself unworthy to live), but that we can be content to yield him a life to save so many of our subjects : and although we would take it for an acceptable service, if he might be taken in so, by the words of his late submission, as we might have him in our power without violating of public faith; yet rather than we would, for our own satisfaction, let go any such opportunity as his personal submission (whereof universality of opinions concur that good use might be made), we can be content, if he shall come in upon such humble terms as are formally contained in his submission, that you shall not only receive him as is expressed in the other letter; but forasmuch as it may be, when the time comes to perform what he hath promised, he may particularly stand upon assurance of liberty also, as well as life, before he will come to you, we are then contented that you do in that case give him your word for his coming and going safe, though you should in other things not agree. And for your better judgement and knowledge how in such case we mean to dispose, we do give you warrant hereby to pass him our pardon upon these conditions.

First, our pleasure is, upon no consideration to give him our pardon except he do come personally where you shall assign him to receive it.

Secondly, that, in point of religion, he presume not to indent;

seeing it savours but of presumption, when he knows so little fear of prosecution.

Thirdly, he shall publicly abjure all manner of dependency upon Spain and other potentates, and shall promise to you to reveal all he knows of our enemy's purposes, and refuse the name of O'Neill.

Fourthly, he shall not presume to treat for any but himself and his own natural followers of Tyrone; but shall leave all others (over whom he unjustly usurps, either as vriaths, or as dependents, and over whom he can challenge no superiority but as a chosen head of rebellion), and absolutely to make their own suits for themselves.

He shall yield to such places for garrisons, and such portions of lands, and composition besides to be reserved as you shall think fit for our service; with this condition, to banish all strangers from him, and call home his followers that do maintain the rebellion in any other Province, together with such a subjection to sheriffs, and execution of justice, as you shall think fit for our service and the present time.

And, as heretofore, he offered to send over his eldest son, if you can get it, to be disposed at our pleasure, either in Ireland or in England. All which being done, we leave the rest of your proceedings to your own best judgement, so to dispose of him in one kind or other as shall be fittest for our service. This being our end in the writing of both these letters: first, to let you see what we wish to be done, if it may be, in the first kind, as is contained in our other letter; next, to let it appear to you and the world, that seeing there is so general a conceit that good may happen thereby, that we will not leave any course untried which can be expected of any Prince to take in commiseration of her distressed and loving subjects of both her Realms, whose conservation she preferreth before any other worldly thing.

Lastly, because we do consider that his being nearer with you for some time (if it could be procured) would be a good security from those practices, which may be doubted he may fall into when he returneth (seeing how common it is to them to neglect either faith or pledges when the breach of any condition may serve their turn), we do only recommend unto you, that the longer he doth remain under your wing the better : but because we do confess that we remain assured of your affection to use all things to the best for us, and see that you have extraordinary foresight and judgement in the government of that Realm, we do attribute so much to you in the handling of this matter, as we leave it and the rest of the particular conditions (mentioned in the former letter, or in this) to your discretion, who may see cause to vary in some circumstances, which are not worthy the sending to us to know our pleasure in, but to be altered as you shall see cause. Only in these two letters we show you two things : in the first of 16th of February, our desire appears to have him stayed if he would come in without asking any more than he doth; and in this other, our resolution (rather than he should not come at all) to give you authority to secure him both of life and liberty, and coming in upon those terms, both to maintain your word really (as it is given in our behalf and which shall never be violated) and rather than to send him back unpardoned to be a head still of rebellion, to afford him these above mentioned, or other reasonable conditions, considering the long work you find it to extirpate him, and the difficulty our estate findeth to maintain that action which must finish it.

For the rest, concerning some enlargement of your authority, in case you see occasion to increase [the Council] at any time [by] some members; we minded not to tie you to such strictness in petty things, having committed so much trust to you in greater: and therefore we have given order to our Council to direct our letters to the Treasurer for the same, and hereby do give you authority to do it, and to use the advice of as many or as few of the Council in this as you shall think fit to do in this service; requiring you, above all things, to drive him to some issue presently,[1] because contrariety of successes there, or change of accidents in other parts, may turn very much to our disadvantage. For which we are still apt to believe that he lieth in advantage, and will spin out all things further than were requisite, with delays and shifts, if you do not abridge him.

[1] i.e. immediately.

After the two letters had been signed and closed, the next day the Queen sent a further instruction by Cecil, which he conveyed in a private letter to Mountjoy that very clearly reveals the loneliness and uncertain temper of the old Queen in her last days, and the difficulties of her ministers. Cecil urged Mountjoy to make a show of obedience, and, having detailed the additional terms which the Queen would exact from Tyrone, he wrote:

'*Now, Sir, know I pray you hereby, that this is her own, and neither our propositions nor conceit; but rather suffered* pro tempore *than we would lose the former warrant, by contesting too long against that which will die as soon as she is satisfied from you that we have obeyed her, and that you find the impossibility of these things which she would be glad of, but so as not to prevent the rest; and, therefore, now I have done all and said all, I know in these last I have said nothing, and yet in obeying I have done much. And so hoping, by your next dispatch, you will write that which is fit to be showed to her Majesty, and that which is fit for me to know* (a parte), *in which kinds all honest servants must strain a little when they will serve Princes, I end.'* To this Cecil added a postscript: '*You see that though I know what your answer will be for these things, yet that I adventure to write my conceit, how you should satisfy, by writing that " you would have done it if it would not have hurt the whole". I would not do this to two men living, and under my hand to no man; if otherwise it should be. If, therefore, you will, for accidents unlooked for, return this my letter, I will thank you; your warrants for that which you must do, or can do, remaining under her own hand.*'

The peace with Tyrone was the last public event in the reign.

In the second week in March Queen Elizabeth fell ill, suffering from sleeplessness and a quinsy in the throat. She seemed to recover and on the 19th received Sir Robert Carey, but she grew rapidly worse, and in the early hours of the 24th she died, leaving her kingdom to King James of Scotland.

APPENDICES

APPENDIX I.—GENEALOGICAL TABLE

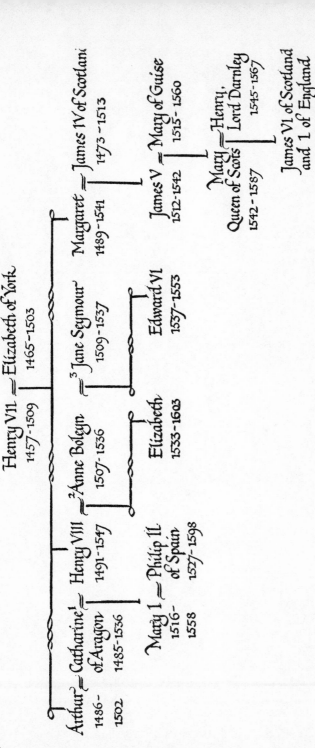

W

APPENDIX II

LIST OF AUTHORITIES

1. *Manuscript Collections*

(a) In the British Museum: Additional, Cotton, Harleian, Lansdowne.

(b) In the Public Record Office: State Papers of various categories (Domestic, Scotland, Foreign, etc.).

(c) In the Bodleian Library: Ashmole, Smith, Tanner.

(d) At Hatfield House: Manuscripts of the Marquis of Salisbury. References are to the volume and page of the Calendar.

2. *Printed Sources*

(1) BRUCE. *Letters of Queen Elizabeth and King James VI of Scotland.* Edited by John Bruce. Camden Society. 1849.

(2) DEVEREUX. *Lives and Letters of the Devereux, Earl of Essex.* By the Hon. Walter Bourchier Devereux. 2 vols. 1853.

(3) DIGGES. *The Compleat Ambassador.* Edited by Sir Dudley Digges. 1665.

(4) ELLIS. *Original Letters, Illustrative of English History.* Edited by Sir Henry Ellis. Three series of 3, 4, and 4 vols. 1834-1848.

(5) FORBES. *A Full View of the Public Transactions in the Reign of Queen Elizabeth.* Edited by Patrick Forbes. 2 vols. 1740-1.

(6) GREEN. *Letters of Royal and Illustrious Ladies.* Edited by Mrs. M. E. Green. 3 vols. 1846.

(7) HAYNES. *A Collection of State Papers, From Letters and Memorials left by William Cecil, Lord Burghley.* Vol. i by S. Haynes. 1740. Vol. ii by W. Murdin. 1759.

(8) LODGE. *Illustrations of British History.* Edited by Edmund Lodge. 3 vols. 1838.

(9) MORYSON. *An Itinerary Containing His Twelve Years' Travel....* Written by Fynes Moryson, Gent. 1617. References to the Maclehose edition, 1907.

(10) MURDIN. See HAYNES.

(11) STRICKLAND. *Lives of the Queens of England.* By Agnes Strickland. 1854.

(12) UNTON. *Correspondence of Sir Henry Unton.* Edited by the Rev. Joseph Stevenson. Roxburgh Club. 1847.

(13) WINWOOD. *Memorials of Affairs of State. . . . Collected chiefly from the Original Papers of Sir Ralph Winwood.* By Edmund Sawyer. 3 vols. 1725.

Abbreviations

HOL: Holograph in the Queen's handwriting throughout.

L.S.: Original letter signed by the Queen.

Pr.: Printed in.

Tr.: Translated in.

CHAPTER I

   I. Cotton MSS., Otho, cx, f. 235. HOL. Italian. Pr. and Tr. Green, iii, 176.

   II. Smith MSS., 68:51. Copy. Pr. Green, iii, 177.

  III. S.P. Dom. Edward VI, ii, 25. HOL. Pr. Strickland, iv, 25.

  IV. Pr. Strickland, iv, 26, from Hearne's *Sylloge.*

   V. Pr. Strickland, iii, 275, from Hearne's *Sylloge.*

  VI. Hatfield MSS., i, 64. Pr. Haynes, p. 89.

 VII. Ashmole MSS. 1729, art. 6. Pr. Green, iii, 219.

VIII. Lansdowne MSS. 1236, f. 33. HOL. Pr. Ellis, II, ii, 155.

  IX. Lansdowne MSS. 1236, f. 35. HOL. Pr. Ellis, I, ii, 153.

   X. Cotton MSS., Vespasian, Fiii, f. 48. HOL. Pr. Ellis, I, ii, 146.

  XI. Harleian MSS. 6986, f. 23. HOL. Pr. Ellis, II, ii, 145.

 XII. Lansdowne MSS. 1236, f. 39. HOL. Pr. Ellis, I, ii, 163.

XIII. Cotton MSS., Vespasian, Fxiii, f. 173. Pr. Ellis, II, ii, 210.

XIV. Lansdowne MSS. 94, f. 21. Copy, probably HOL., endorsed by Burghley, ' Copy of a lre wrytt by ye lady Elizab. Grace to ye Lady Knolles.' Pr. Green, iii, 279.

 XV. S.P. Dom. 1554, iv, 2. HOL. Pr. Ellis, II, ii, 254.

XVI. Harleian MSS. 39, f. 14. Pr. Green, iii, 296.

XVII. Lansdowne MSS. 1236, f. 37.

CHAPTER II

   I. Pr. Strype, *Annals of the Reformation*, Chap. XI.

  II. S.P. Foreign 1560, No. 766. Copy.

 III. MS. Baker; Harleian 7037, f. 265. Pr. Ellis, II, ii, 263.

 IV. S.P. Scotland, vol. i, 1006. Burghley's Draft, much corrected.

  V. Hatfield MSS., i, 261. Pr. Haynes, p. 369.

 VI. S.P. Foreign 1562, No. 682. Pr. Forbes, ii, 53.

VII. S.P. Foreign 1563, No. 82. Burghley's Draft. Pr. Forbes, ii, 278.

VIII. Pr. (French) Forbes, ii, 314. Tr. Additional MSS. 35831, f. 123.

 IX. S.P. Foreign 1563, No. 262. Burghley's Draft. Pr. Forbes, ii, 328.

  X. S.P. Foreign 1563, No. 811. Draft. Pr. Forbes, ii, 428.

 XI. Pr. *Archæologia*, xiii, 201.

 XII. S.P. Scotland, vol. ii, No. 95. HOL. Tr. in Calendar.

XIII. Pr. *Sidney Papers*, i, 7. The original, formerly at Penshurst, is now lost.

XIV. S.P. Foreign 1566, No. 614. Burghley's Draft. The original is apparently missing.

xv. S.P. Scotland, vol. ii, No. 477. Tr. in Calendar.
xvi. S.P. Scotland, vol. ii, No. 529. Burghley's Draft, much corrected.
xvii. Pr. and Tr. Strickland, iv, 268, from French MS. formerly at St. Petersburg (Leningrad).
xviii. S.P. Scotland, vol. ii, 722. Tr. in Calendar. ' Copy of the Q.'s majesties letter to the Scottish Q. written with her own hand.'
xix. Cotton MSS., Caligula, Ci, f. 367. Original L.S. endorsed, ' This lre was sent to the Scotts Q. by the Bish: of Ross.' S.P. Scotland, vol. ii, No. 930. Burghley's Draft.
xx. Pr. and Tr. Strickland, iv, 286.
xxi. Hatfield MSS., i, 423. Burghley's Draft. Pr. Haynes, p. 529.
xxii. Hatfield MSS., i, 425. Burghley's Draft. Pr. Haynes, p. 533.
xxiii. Hatfield MSS., i, 442. Draft. Pr. Haynes, p. 555.
xxiv. Hatfield MSS., i, 455. Burghley's Draft. Pr. Haynes, p. 572.
xxv. Cotton MSS., Caligula, Ci, f. 517. Draft corrected by Burghley.
xxvi. Additional MSS. 30156, f. 30. Copy. Pr. Digges, p. 9.
xxvii. S.P. Dom. Addenda 1566-79, vol. XVII, 113.
xxviii. Cotton MSS., Caligula, Cii, f. 214. L.S.
xxix. Cotton MSS., Caligula, Cii, f. 251. L.S.
xxx. Cotton MSS., Caligula, Cii, f. 334. L.S.
xxxi. Hatfield MSS., i, 479. Burghley's Draft. Pr. Haynes, p. 601.
xxxii. Cotton MSS., Caligula, Cii, f. 368. L.S.
xxxiii. Cotton MSS., Caligula, Cii, f. 410. L.S.

CHAPTER III

i. Additional MSS. 30156, f. 152B. Copy. Pr. Digges, p. 106.
ii. Additional MSS. 30156, f. 185B. Copy. Pr. Digges, p. 129.
iii. S.P. Scotland, vol. iv, 125; Cotton MSS., Caligula, Ciii, f. 144. Burghley's Drafts.
iv. Ashmolean MSS. in the Bodleian. HOL. Pr. Ellis, I, ii, 263.
v. Additional MSS. 30156, f. 326B. Copy. Pr. Digges, p. 226.
vi. Additional MSS. 30156, f. 329B. Copy. Pr. Digges, p. 228.

VII. Additional MSS. 30156, f. 380. Copy. Pr. Digges, p. 259.

VIII. Talbot Papers, vol. F, 41. Original. S.P. Dom. 89:39. Copy. Pr. Lodge, ii, 79.

IX. Additional MSS. 30156, f. 437. Copy. Pr. Digges, p. 297.

X. Additional MSS. 15891, f. 25. Copy.

XI. Pr. Strickland, iv, 314. I do not know the original of this famous letter.

XII. S.P. Foreign 1574, No. 1309-12. Pr. *Archæologia*, XXVIII, 397.

XIII. Pr. *Nugæ Antiquæ* (1804), edited by T. Park, vol. i, 127.

XIV. S.P. Ireland 51:39. Pr. Devereux, i, 104.

XV. Pr. Devereux, i, 119.

XVI. S.P. Scotland, vol. v, 253.

XVII. Cotton MSS., Galba, Cvi, ii, f. 66. L.S.

XVIII. S.P. Foreign 1579, No. 566. Tr. in Calendar.

XIX. S.P. Foreign 1579, No. 662. Copy. Tr. in Calendar.

XX. Additional MSS. 15891, f. 6. Copy. A French copy in S.P. Foreign 1579, No. 674. Pr. Nicholas, p. 106.

XXI. Hatfield MSS., ii, 298. Draft.

XXII. Hatfield MSS., ii, 305. Draft.

XXIII. Additional MSS 15891, f. 15. Copy. Pr. Strickland, iv, 453.

XXIV. Hatfield MSS., ii, 366. HOL.

XXV. Hatfield MSS., ii, 281. HOL. Dated ' [1579] ' in Calendar, but as Simier's disgrace was in 1580, I have inserted the letter here.

XXVI. Hatfield MSS., ii, 380. HOL.

XXVII. Hatfield MSS., ii, 479. HOL.

XXVIII. Hatfield MSS., ii, 459. Draft.

XXIX. Hatfield MSS., ii, 460. Draft on same sheet as above, endorsed in the Queen's hand, 'To Monsieur, my letters.'

XXX. Hatfield MSS., ii, 430. Copy.

XXXI. S.P. Foreign 1581, No. 416. HOL. unsigned.

XXXII. S.P. Foreign 1582, No. 570. HOL. Draft. Tr. in Calendar.

XXXIII. Hatfield MSS., ii, 502. Copy.

XXXIV. Hatfield MSS., ii, 504. Copy.

XXXV. Additional MSS. 15891, f. 92B.

XXXVI. S.P. Foreign 1583, No. 217. HOL. Originally folded as a three-cornered note, fastened with yellow silk and sealed.

XXXVII. Harleian MSS. 787, f. 66. Pr. Strickland, iv, 470.

XXXVIII. Cotton MSS., Julius, Fvi, 30. Copy. Pr. Ellis, I, ii, 294.

XXXIX. Hatfield MSS., iii, 10. Copy.

XL. Cotton MSS., Galba, Evi, f. 244. HOL. Draft.
XLI. Pr. Bruce, p. 16, from Ryder MSS., Eliz., No. 2. HOL.
XLII. Pr. Bruce, p. 19, from Ryder MSS., Eliz., No. 22. HOL..
XLIII. Pr. Bruce, p. 22, from Ryder MSS., Eliz., No. 20. HOL.

CHAPTER IV

I. Cotton MSS., Galba, Cviii, f. 22. Copy.
II. Cotton MSS., Galba, Cviii, f. 27. HOL. Draft.
III. S.P. Ireland 123:34. HOL. Postscript.
IV. Cotton MSS., Galba, Cix, f. 200. ' Copy of her Majesty's letter written with her own hand.'
V. S.P. Holland and Flanders. Tr. in Calendar.
VI. S.P. Holland and Flanders 1586.
VII. S.P. Scotland, vol. viii, No. 738. Other copies in Lansdowne MSS. 1236, f. 44; Cotton MSS., Caligula, Cix, f. 606. Pr. Strickland, iv, 509. There are differing versions of this famous letter.
VIII. Pr. Strickland, iv, 511.
IX. Pr. Bruce, p. 39, from Ryder MSS., Eliz., No. 5. HOL.
X. Pr. Strickland, iv, 531.
XI. Pr. Bruce, p. 41, from Ryder MSS., Eliz., No. 6. HOL.
XII. Pr. Bruce, p. 43, from Ryder MSS., Eliz., No. 7. HOL.
XIII. Cotton MSS., Caligula, Cix, f. 201. Minute. Pr. Ellis, I, iii, 22.
XIV. Cotton MSS., Galba, Di, f. 283. Copy.
XV. Pr. Bruce, p. 47, from Ryder MSS., Eliz., No. 8.
XVI. Pr. Bruce, p. 52, from Ryder MSS., Eliz., No. 10. HOL.
XVII. Pr. Devereux, i, 205.
XVIII. Cotton MSS., Galba, Div, f. 200. L.S.
XIX. Pr. Devereux, i, 201.
XX. Pr. Bruce, p. 55, from Ryder MSS., Eliz., No. 24. HOL.
XXI. Pr. Strickland, iv, 429.
XXII. Sloan MS. 4160. Copy. Pr. Strickland, iv, 429, ' original at Hagley '.
XXIII. Pr. Bruce, p. 57, from Ryder MSS., No. 27. HOL.
XXIV. Pr. Bruce, p. 63, from Ryder MSS., No. 29. HOL.

CHAPTER V

I. Pr. Strype, *Annals of the Reformation*, vol. iv, No. liv.
II. Pr. and Tr. Strickland, iv, 616.
III. Pr. Unton Correspondence, p. 43.
IV. Pr. Unton Correspondence, p. 55. Burghley's Draft.
V. Pr. Unton Correspondence, p. 94. Burghley's Draft.
VI. Hatfield MSS., iv, 143. Pr. Murdin, p. 644.

VII. Pr. and partly Tr. Strickland, iv, 618, from Keralio, v, 459.

VIII. Pr. Devereux, i, 267.

IX. Pr. Bruce, p. 75, from Thompson MSS., p. 88. Copy.

X. Pr. Bruce, p. 71, from Ryder MSS., No. 13. HOL.

XI. Hatfield MSS., iv, 343. Minute. Cotton MSS., Titus, Cvii, f. 161.

XII. Pr. Bruce, p. 90, from Ryder MSS., Eliz., No. 16. HOL. Checked (and some minor alterations made from) Hatfield MSS., iv, 382. Endorsed by Burghley, 'Copy of her Majesty's letter, written with her own hand, to the King of Scots'.

XIII. Pr. Bruce, p. 103, from Ryder MSS., Eliz., No. 18. HOL. Hatfield MSS., iv, 541. HOL. Draft.

XIV. Hatfield MSS., v, 13.

XV. Pr. and Tr. Strickland, iv, 641, from MS. formerly in the Imperial Collection at St. Petersburg (Leningrad).

XVI. Hatfield MSS., v, 105.

XVII. Hatfield MSS., v, 297.

XVIII. Hatfield MSS., v, 324.

XIX. Pr. and Tr. Strickland, iv, 644. Original formerly in the Imperial Collection of autographs at St. Petersburg (Leningrad).

XX. S.P. Dom. 254:54.

XXI. Pr. Bruce, p. 112, from Ryder MSS., Eliz., No. 17. HOL.

XXII. Hatfield MSS., vi, 32.

XXIII. Hatfield MSS., vi, 129.

XXIV. S.P. Dom. 257:24.

XXV. S.P. Dom. 257:32. 'Copy of her Majesty's letter, with her own hand, to the Earl of Essex.'

XXVI. Pr. Devereux, i, 345.

XXVII. Hatfield MSS., vi, 368. Copy.

XXVIII. Hatfield MSS., vi, 376. Draft in Essex's hand.

XXIX. S.P. Scotland, Border Papers, vol. ii, No. 651. Copy.

XXX. Hatfield MSS., vii, 314. Copy. S.P. Dom. 264:54. Copy in Burghley's hand.

XXXI. Pr. Devereux, i, 445.

XXXII. S.P. Dom. 264:118, 119. Copies.

XXXIII. Hatfield MSS., vii, 433. Draft corrected by Burghley.

XXXIV. Hatfield MSS., vii, 449. Burghley's Draft.

XXXV. Pr. Hakluyt's *Voyages*, Everyman Library Edition, v, 77.

XXXVI. S.P. Ireland 201:123.

XXXVII. Pr. Bruce, p. 121, from Thompson MSS., p. 106. Copy.

XXXVIII. Pr. Bruce, p. 125, from Thompson MSS., p. 128. Copy.

XXXIX. Hatfield MSS., viii, 550. HOL.

XL. S.P. Ireland 202, pt. iii, 64.

XLI. S.P. Ireland 205:113.

XLII. S.P. Dom. 272:106. Burghley's Draft.

XLIII. Additional MSS. 34224, f. 30. Copy.
XLIV. S.P. Ireland 205:170.
XLV. Pr. Devereux, ii, 73.
XLVI. Pr. Winwood's *Memorials*, i, 219.
XLVII. S.P. Ireland 207, pt. iv, 36.
XLVIII. Hatfield MSS., x, 288. Copy.
XLIX. Pr. Calendar of Carew MSS., No. 494. Copy.
L. Hatfield MSS., x, 435. Copy.
LI. Pr. Winwood's *Memorials*, i, 307.
LII. Pr. Winwood's *Memorials*, ii, 308.
LIII. S.P. Scotland. Border Papers, vol. ii, 1343. Copy.
LIV. Pr. Bruce, p. 134, from Thompson MSS., p. 110. Copy.
LV. Pr. Moryson, iii, 22.
LVI. Tanner MSS., lxxvi, 17.
LVII. Pr. Moryson, iii, 122.
LVIII. Pr. Bruce, p. 142, from Thompson MSS., p. 119. Copy.
LIX. Pr. Moryson, iii, 187.
LX. Pr. Moryson, iii, 287.
LXI. Pr. Bruce, p. 154, from Thompson MSS., p. 120. Copy.
LXII. Tanner MSS., lxxvi, 280. L.S.
LXIII. Tanner MSS., lxxvi, 285. L.S.

INDEX